HOLLYWOOD'S OTHERS

HOLLYWOOD'S OTHERS

LOVE AND LIMITATION IN THE STAR SYSTEM

KATHERINE FUSCO

Columbia University Press
New York

Columbia University Press
Publishers Since 1893
New York   Chichester, West Sussex

Copyright © 2025 Columbia University Press
All rights reserved

Library of Congress Cataloging-in-Publication Data
Names: Fusco, Katherine author
Title: Hollywood's others : love and limitation in the star system / Katherine Fusco.
Description: New York : Columbia University Press, 2025. | Includes bibliographical references and index.
Identifiers: LCCN 2025008636 (print) | LCCN 2025008637 (ebook) | ISBN 9780231220910 hardback | ISBN 9780231220927 trade paperback | ISBN 9780231563451 ebook
Subjects: LCSH: Motion picture industry—United States—History—20th century | Motion picture actors and actresses—United States | Fame—Social aspects—United States | Other (Philosophy) | Hollywood (Los Angeles, Calif.)—History—20th century
Classification: LCC PN1993.5.U65 F87 2025 (print) | LCC PN1993.5.U65 (ebook) | DDC 384.80979494—dc23/eng/20250425

Cover design: Elliott S. Cairns
Cover image: Lon Chaney in *The Phantom of the Opera*, from *Wid's Weekly*, February 1925.

GPSR Authorized Representative: Easy Access System Europe, Mustamäe tee 50, 10621 Tallinn, Estonia, gpsr.requests@easproject.com

CONTENTS

Acknowledgments vii

INTRODUCTION
1

PART I. THE BABIES

1 SEXING FARINA: *OUR GANG*'S "LITTLE FELLOW"
AND OTHER FANTASIES OF BLACK CHILDHOOD
21

2 FORGETTING SHIRLEY TEMPLE:
AMNESIA, TECHNOLOGY, AND THE ABSTRACTED CHILD
47

PART II. THE NOBODIES

3 "FEAST YOUR EYES, GLUT YOUR SOUL":
FEELING WITH LON CHANEY
79

4 UNREAL REMEMBRANCE:
BLACK STARS AND THEIR WHITE AUDIENCES
104

PART III. THE UNHAPPY

5 UNHAPPY VICTIMS:
THE UNREADABILITY OF STAR SUICIDES
139

CONCLUSION
167

Notes *175*
Selected Bibliography *199*
Index *207*

ACKNOWLEDGMENTS

This book was a labor of love that at times I thought would never be completed. The period in which this book was researched, written, and revised included the first Trump presidency and a global pandemic. My state university faced budget crises and the departure of valuable colleagues whose positions were eliminated; more personally, struggles with infertility and encounters with the kind of terrible men who lurk in institutional spaces proved disruptive, to say the least. I start with this somewhat grouchy litany because these are the conditions under which many a woman has written or is currently writing her book. I'm with you, friends—this book is for you.

This period also included some very good things that are nonetheless not conducive to the writing of books: the birth of my second child and the early years of both my daughters' lives. Without the support of the many people and institutions I will mention here, it would not have been possible to complete *Hollywood's Others*.

Finding the sometimes delightful, sometimes awful, and always amazing materials that form this book's evidence required archival support, and I was lucky to work with wonderful physical and digital archives. Archives I visited includes the W. E. B. Du Bois collection at UMass Amherst, special collections at Cornell, and the George Eastman House in my hometown of Rochester, NY. I spent a wonderful week as a very pregnant researcher at the Black Film Center/Archive (BFC/A) at the University of Indiana, where I was assisted and energized by contact with then-director Terri Francis and archivist Ronda Sewald. Two very different archives are worth special mention. I have made multiple sojourns to the lovely Herrick Library in Beverly Hills, CA, where Louise Hilton was an invaluable help and Phil Garcia made me feel most welcome. This book would not have been possible without the Lantern Media History website. As a scholar with small children who was researching and writing through the early years of the pandemic, the Lantern Site kept me from losing all hope—enormous gratitude to Eric Hoyt and his team for keeping this book alive.

These archival trips were made possible by a number of funding sources: a Modernist Studies Association research grant, a research fellowship from the BFC/A, and a series of Scholarly and Creative Activity Grants from the University of Nevada, Reno. Although not an official funding source, my cousin Nicole Wegman lent out her apartment, helping to defray the costs of research on trips to New York.

My editor Philip Leventhal deserves an enormous bouquet of thanks. He has stayed with this project over many years and has engaged in deep and productive conversation about how best to manage the feedback the developing manuscript received. What a joy to be edited! Thanks as well to assistant editor Emily Simon, who helped me bring the completed manuscript over the finish line.

This book has received tremendously helpful and sometimes tough feedback, especially in the early stages. I am so grateful to the anonymous readers who gave generously of their time to make this book better. I love my "reader number two"! Additionally, a version of chapter 1 originally appeared in *PMLA* 133, no. 3 (May 2018), published by the Modern Language Association of America, and a version of chapter 3 originally appeared in *Cinema Journal* 57, no. 4 (Summer 2018), now the *Journal of Cinema and Media Studies*. I owe many thanks to the peer reviewers for those journals as well.

At the University of Nevada, Reno, I was lucky to develop this book under the leadership of three department chairs who championed faculty research: Eric Rasmussen, Ashley Marshall, and Lynda Olman. I also received help from student research assistants including Karthik Kotrech, Kahlia Nassaino, and Scott Shumaker.

My wonderful colleagues in the department of English have also been generous with their time and encouragement. I have written alongside both Nasia Anam and Elisabeth Miller. I have received feedback at various points from Ann Keniston, Jen Hill, and Michael Branch, as well as general encouragement from Chris Coake and Justin Gifford. I want to especially highlight the thoughtful generosity of Dan Morse—the best colleague a person could have. Dan, thanks for making it all better.

Other colleagues and friends have also contributed to the life of this project and my well-being during the long slog of bookmaking: Mikaela Rogozen-Soltar, who has been a writing buddy; Stephanie Lauer, who has been a running buddy; and the women of my book group, who ensure a measure of joy and camaraderie at least every other month. David Rondel and Stephanie Gibson—my god, what we have lived through together. Thank you for your seemingly boundless hospitality, the good company, and being go-to companions over the past decade-plus. And then there is a forever coconspirator, Nicole Seymour, a model of scholarly and personal vivacity without whom I cannot imagine navigating this profession.

A number of colleagues in modernist and film studies have also supported this book. Justus Nieland, Erich Nunn, Brooks Hefner, and Sarah Gleeson-White have all written letters of support at various moments over the past several years. A rose to Debra Rae Cohen, whose leadership at *Modernism/Modernity* has helped young scholars feel encouraged and valued. Alix Beeston, Jordan Brower, Pardis Dabashi, and Maggie Hennefeld have all encouraged this project; I stand in awe of these scholars and their fearful creative energies. The work has also been developed through conversation and contact with Sunny Stalter-Pace, Julie Grossman, Donna Campbell, and Julia Stern, whom I see as scholarly kindred spirits. Will Scheibel has been a particular friend to me and to the project, reading a messy chapter at a messy time. Will, I am so delighted to have come up alongside you in this profession. And I must thank Sarah again for her reading, for her wonderful company, for the weekly emails, for being such a dear friend. The members of my Friday

Zoom writing room are also due thanks for being steady companions in the weekly development of this manuscript over the past several years.

Others have played roles in the development of the book, perhaps without knowing it. Naomi Greyser, thank you for organizing such a fabulous conference on affect theory, way back when. Two scholars whom I did not know personally or well nonetheless had tremendous intellectual influence on this book's development and passed during the time I was finishing a draft: thank you to both Richard Dyer and Lauren Berlant for your brilliance. The organizers of Le Giornate del Cinema Muto, including Jay Weissberg, are responsible for the chapter at the heart of this book. It was during one of the festival's children's screenings that I first fell for Farina. Thanks as well to Michael Phillips of the *Chicago Tribune* for giving me the opportunity to talk film to nonacademic audiences.

Less directly, I owe thanks to Rochester's The Little and Nashville's The Belcourt movie theaters for my film education—what a lucky break to have lived the first decades of my life in great movie theater towns. I also wish to thank the stars who populate this text. In my first book, I spent a lot of time with authors and filmmakers whom I ultimately came to dislike. Not so with *Hollywood's Others*. Like audiences in the 1920s and 1930s, I love these stars, and I found strange, even therapeutic connections to these companions, even as I attempted a distanced look at what they offered fans of their own era.

I blame my father for an odd taste in film and film stars. Matthew Fusco introduced his daughter to the Marx Brothers and also *Allegro non Troppo* at a formative age. Thank you to all the Fuscos: Matt, Peggy, and Emily, for your love and your encouragement.

Finally, to Blake and the girls, what can I say? Girls, you both inspired and impeded the work, as is your right and duty. Blake, thank you for sticking with me as I stuck with the book, for your reads, and for being my best champion. I love you more than I can say.

HOLLYWOOD'S OTHERS

INTRODUCTION

To begin: a bad bit of beauty advice.

In 1934, Bette Davis's star was rising, due in part to her willingness to take on difficult roles. Davis's roles were difficult in at least two ways: first, they required technical skill, and second, these were unpleasant women.

Davis signed on for roles turned down by other actors who worried they would damage their star personas by playing such nasty parts. By the time *Photoplay Magazine* ran a column featuring beauty advice for Davis, the actress had appeared as Arlene Bradford in *Fog Over Frisco* (Dieterle, 1934), a spoiled little rich girl who takes up with gangsters, and Mildred Rogers, a promiscuous, gold-digging waitress in *Of Human Bondage* (Cromwell, 1934)—a role for which she received a best actress Oscar nomination, the first of eleven such nominations she would receive over the course of her career.

At the time, Davis was under contract to Warner Brothers, which was hesitant to lend her to RKO—the studio making *Bondage*. Davis would later recollect that Warner's could not comprehend "any actress" . . . "want[ing] to play such a part."[1] To understand why Warner Brothers would be reluctant to lend its rising star for such a picture, as well as why other actresses turned down the part, it is useful to understand stardom as it was developing in the first decades of the twentieth century.

Early in the silent period, studios withheld information about their players, letting company names like Mutual or Famous Players–Lasky signal a picture's quality. Gradually, as audiences began to recognize featured actors across a variety of performances, the industry began promoting what Richard deCordova has referred to as the picture personality—an earlier version of what we would today call the star—which drew primarily from the character types performed and limited information about the actor's off-screen life. Over the later 1910s, the picture personality transitioned into stardom as we now know it, as curated information about the off-screen lives of performers became, as deCordova puts it, "a site of knowledge and truth."[2] By the time film transitioned into the talkies and the Depression hit, the star was a major part of the movie-going experience.

While audiences today value the performance of authenticity in their stars—we expect to see social media revelations of celebrities' "private thoughts" and stars posting selfies without makeup—this was not the case in the studio era that dominated from the late 1920s to the early 1960s. During this period, many of Hollywood's most significant stars were under contract to a particular studio and thus appeared in whatever films that studio assigned them.[3] They could take work with another company only if the home studio lent them out. As a result, studios had a vested interest in their stars, and we should think of stardom as a kind of property that could be damaged by roles that might shift public perceptions of a star. This was especially the case following the highly publicized star scandals of the 1920s, which contributed to the film industry's adoption of the Motion Picture Production Code (also known as the Hays Code or just "the Code"). As will be discussed later, Lon Chaney's portrayals of disabled underworld figures were countered by a push in the press to distance him from any sense of deviancy from the norm, whether criminal or physical. With one notable exception—producer Paul Bern, who was married to actress Jean Harlow—the figures discussed in this book are all stars, meaning they had both on-screen roles and interesting off-screen lives that combined to form their personae. This is in contrast to celebrities, who may be famous without having an on-screen personality type with which their biographies interacted. However, the ratio of information between on-screen type and off-screen life could vary significantly depending on the star's background. Thus, the stars discussed within *Hollywood's Others* include both some who look very much like fictional characters or the previous decade's "picture personalities," as in the case of a Black actor from *Our Gang*, and some who transcended their roles in press materials, as in the aforementioned case of Chaney.

During the 1920s and 1930s, the relationship between the studios and the fan magazines was still in flux. While the fan magazines have been popularly understood as a mere extension of studio outreach, this was not always the case. Eric Hoyt describes the 1910s to early 1930s as being the "most heterogeneous and tumultuous" era in the adjacent film trade magazines, and as Mary Desjardins has established in her important research on the Studio Publicity Directors Committee of the AMPP (Association of Motion Picture Producers), the relationship between studios and fan magazines was unruly and, from the perspective of the studios, problematic in the period leading up to the 1934 enforcement of the Code.[4]

While narratives about the Code focus on stars such as Mae West falling from favor or tales of sex snipped from risqué films, movie magazines played a significant but less discussed role in the industry's self-censorship. The Code was a system of self-regulation by the film industry, developing throughout the 1920s and then widely adopted from the 1930s through the 1960s to avoid government censorship. Although the Code has become most closely associated with Will Hays, the film trade magazine publisher and editor Martin Quigley played a significant role. In the trade magazines that targeted distributors (as opposed to fan magazines), looming government censorship was a common topic of discussion; additionally, Quigley was a conservative Catholic who supported a more moral cinema.[5] In 1929 and 1930, during his time as editor of *Exhibitors Herald World* (previously *Exhibitors Herald and Moving Picture World*, a merger between the two trade publications), Quigley was recruited by Hays to revise an earlier cautionary list of "Don'ts and Be Carefuls" into a preliminary version of the Production Code, which would be enforced to varying degrees until its more robust enforcement in 1934 under the Production Code Administration.[6] The Production Code was accompanied by another guideline, an advertising code that was to rule copy published about the film industry, including in fan magazines. Justifying the avoidance of salacious but effective press release writing, which often made its way into both trade and fan magazine ads and features, Quigley wrote, in an editorial in *Exhibitors Herald World*: "Any and every effort of the industry to display a respectable mien to the public cannot possibly succeed if the advertising and publicity published by motion picture companies is of a character which leads the public to believe the worst it may hear about the industry, its pictures and its people."[7] Film magazines, stars, and the Code were thus entangled from the start.

In contrast to trade publications such as *Exhibitors Herald World*, which served an intermediary function between studios and exhibitors, both concerned with protecting the industry from government overreach, the fan magazines served an audience that may have appreciated the very material Hays and Quigley were seeking to suppress: spicy stories about "the industry, its pictures and its people." Fan magazines that emphasized scandalous stars or the bad behavior of ostensibly clean stars threatened the industry's argument that it could keep its house in order. For example, coverage of Harlow, one of the stars discussed in this book, precipitated a crisis that "resulted in studio publicity directors resolving to advise studio advertising offices to not place ads in fan magazines that did not cooperate with the new policy of requiring all writers to gain studio approval of their story ideas before interviewing contract players."[8] Reporters who did not behave risked being blacklisted by studios. As opposed to the more star- and studio-friendly decades that followed the Code's widespread application, what Anthony Slide calls the "studio mouthpiece" era, the 1920s and 1930s represent a brief period when star images in the magazines were as contested as star performances on screen: morality, profits, and potentially subversive appeals to a moviegoing nation were at stake.[9]

It is in the context of Hollywood's coalescing star system and battle to control star images in the magazines that the bad beauty advice for Davis appears. In the 1930s, Sylvia Ulback, fitness guru to the stars, was a regular contributor to the popular fan magazine *Photoplay*. In her column, Ulback answered readers' beauty queries, offered diet tips, suggested exercises for ankle slimming, and proffered unsolicited advice to the leading actresses of the day. In her November 1934 article "Beauty and Personality Are Inseparable," the columnist advises Davis that her many unpleasant roles may ruin her beauty.[10] The article, in the form of a letter to the actress, cautions:

> Your mental attitude shows on your face, Bette Davis. The mental attitude of every woman shows on her face and makes her beautiful or homely, appealing or hard. If you're going to continue to play unsympathetic rôles (and I must say I admire your courage in taking the rôle of *Mildred* and making it sit up and beg), you've got to show me—and the rest of the world—that you're not like that in real life. That you're not actually hard and bitter and cynical. And you must pepper your career with a few sympathetic parts.

The column is brutal in its assessment of Davis's appearance. In a stunning three-sentence sequence, Ulback tells Davis: "Darling, your neck has its faults. Your eyes are too staring. Your jaw line is too prominent." However, the columnist also acknowledges with surprising frankness the difficult world Davis navigates as a woman in Hollywood: "I want you to heed my advice. And I want every girl in the world who has, in the struggle for existence, grown cynical, to learn how to turn that bitterness into lovely, feminine appeal." While there's an acknowledgment of how working women are judged, Ulback's beauty advice merges aesthetic and affective management, warning women of the type Davis played that the visual management of their emotions was key to garnering the world's sympathy.

In her warning to Davis that she will make herself unlikable by playing unattractive characters, Ulback produces a series of conflations resonant with the era's discussions of star personae: a blurring of performance, outer appearance, inner character, and audience attachments. Although Davis was a white woman who would come to wield tremendous power across the decade as the "fourth Warner brother," her selection of roles often associated her with marginalized groups whose claim on national affection was far more tenuous.

In *Hollywood's Others*, I examine the shifting relationships among likability, personality, and performance in 1920s and 1930s star culture. I take up the question of how fan magazines and films managed the promotion of social groups that generated antipathy or indifference for majority-culture Americans off-screen during the tumultuous decades that followed World War I, from the Red Summer of 1919 to the Great Depression. These groups included, among others, Black children, white working children, the disabled, and the poor. In particular, I am interested in how magazines, studios, fans, and stars themselves shaped the discourse that promoted both intense audience interest in and attachment to stars who were seen, in one way or another, as nonnormative. I then examine how this same discourse established and policed the boundaries of such connections. For example, writing about the all-Black-cast musical *Hallelujah* (Vidor, 1929), Dorothy Manners describes the shift in a "public that has not heretofore been too tolerant of the talents of the black man."[11] However, at the same time as she chastises her fellow whites for their previous provincialism and prejudice and applauds a new interest in Negro art, she also limits the degree of kinship that should be seen between rising Black stars and their white counterparts, referring to Nina Mae McKinney as a "vivid black edition of Clara Bow, with great red clusters of cherries dangling from her hat."[12] The charismatic McKinney is rendered as a race-specific copy of the white actress, and one with a humorously gaudy style. She, like the posited white reader, is also aspiring after Bow's original. As Anthony Slide has argued, the fan magazine was "fundamentally a film- and entertainment-related periodical aimed at a general fan, an average member of the moviegoing public who more often than not was female."[13] My interest here is in how magazines and movies defined that "average" American filmgoer in the context of the exceptional, the challenging, the appealingly different, and how they established and maintained a white, middle-class, able-bodied, heterosexually oriented norm. The Manners article is one instance among many of the aperture-like affective management projects taking place in fan magazines: opening and closing invitations for audiences to temporarily connect with stars different from themselves. In what follows, I will argue that stardom, as constructed on screen and in fan magazines, managed such affinities by simultaneously promoting moments of intense cross-group attachment and defining limits on empathy and identification.

STARDOM AS LIMITED INVITATION

While Ulback warned Davis that her tough, cynical persona risked losing the affections of the female fans who were the presumed readers of *Photoplay*'s beauty column, a now-famous instance of identification with Davis came from the Black writer and civil rights activist James Baldwin, who found meaning in the fact that an ugly white woman with "too staring eyes"—he calls them "pop-eyes"—could be rich and powerful.[14] Baldwin's connection to Davis is striking but not unprecedented, as decades earlier mainstream fan magazines encouraged cross-group identifications with stars, albeit in limited fashion. However, rather than focusing on the glamorous white women who have come to represent stardom—although they will appear here as well—*Hollywood's Others* is more interested in the way other stars with less social capital were promoted on-screen and in magazines like *Photoplay*. For example, what did it mean for a white entertainment columnist to claim identification with Black children? Or for little boys to be encouraged to worship a star who played at disability?

This limited invitation to identify across groups happened through a discourse of "universality," rather than the type of commodified particularity that has largely defined film celebrity since Richard Dyer's important work in *Heavenly Bodies*.[15] The call to universality and its erasing of particulars allowed fan magazines to promote Black actors and characters and also posed a "solution" to the anxieties raised by the white stars whose appeal was in their fascinating difference from many audience members, as in the case of Lon Chaney's performances.

Recognizing how fan magazines managed and policed readers' attachments pushes back against certain more optimistic tendencies found where film studies and affect theory (as well as popular accounts of both) meet. For some affect theorists, retraining the human sensorium offers an opportunity for utopian projects, ones capable of making a better world by bridging human differences through redemptive affects. Carl Plantinga's foundational work on film and emotion, for example, has identified the creation of empathy as among film's most important effects. He draws on Béla Balázs's work to "argue that a central way the *visual* aspect of film is significant is in the use of the human face in the *scene of empathy*."[16] More problematic to my mind are accounts such as Ben Highmore's, which posits that an initial, perhaps hardwired, disgust response has transformed our modern sense of aesthetics and that affective pedagogies (e.g., the eating of different foods over time) may retrain the sensorium and allow for the transcendence of cultural misunderstandings.[17] This exposure model for retraining affects is now common, whether in the clichéd haranguing about the dulling consequences of violent media or in equally clichéd "it's a small world, after all" hope for a global community. *Hollywood's Others* is resistant to such easy invocations of empathy; it was largely written over a period in which the #MeToo movement and a predator celebrity president lived side-by-side in the United States and then completed as white Americans turned from Black lives mattering to hysteria over critical race theory and the Supreme Court's overturning of affirmative action. Against the commonplace notion of film as an empathy-producing machine, *Hollywood's Others* proposes a conception of stardom as a technology for policing connection.

To consider the way stardom allowed an audience posited as normative to consume other subjectivities, I draw on work in feminist, queer, and critical race theory that engages matters of feeling more skeptically, as well as the work of scholars of race in the United States who have traced a long history of white attachments to Black performance. These thinkers, including Saidiya Hartman, bell hooks, Sianne Ngai, and Lauren Berlant, among others, clarify the violence at stake in framing sites of identification, however limited. In particular, hooks's conception of "eating the Other" offers an important framework for understanding the limits of the cinema's redemptive work to bridge difference. In her landmark essay, she specifies that the encounter with the Other "does not require that one relinquish forever one's mainstream positionality.... It is by eating the Other... that one asserts power and privilege."[18] The work of hooks and other feminist scholars on the limits of political feeling are thus, to my mind, a crucial counter to work focused on the cinema's redemptive affects.

By examining star discourse's oscillation between promoting and policing audience attachments to fascinating but variously threatening figures, I also build on the work of star and audience studies scholars who have sought to understand the complexity of fan identification—for example, Dyer's work on queer identification with Judy Garland, or Sharon Marcus's work on Sarah Bernhardt.[19] However, stars who belonged to groups that held less social and cultural significance than these actresses also appealed to fans. While not a study of fans and their identifications, *Hollywood's Others* considers the way a nervous industry during the Code's early years wrangled with the question of cross-group connection: How far should star publicity allow for wide-ranging and divergent appeals, and to what degree should they be reined in and funneled into prescribed forms of identification? I thus treat the fan magazines not so much as a source of biographical star information as a school for fandom in a nervous age.

The stars in this book represent a number of groups whose status and claims on rights, care, and visibility were being hotly contested in the 1920s and 1930s, whether that was the child as laborer, Blacks during Jim Crow, or Americans with disabilities. At the same time that legislatures, local censorship boards, and public opinion were weighing in on how these groups should be treated, administrators of the Hollywood Code considered whether they should be seen at all. At times, when celebrities with cultural capital fell out with social norms, as in the case of the white depressives discussed in the final chapter, an additional management strategy put forth by Hollywood was a narrative of disidentification through appeal to a universal norm, as in reactions to the suicide of Paul Bern. Bern was both a producer and husband to Jean Harlow. His depression was framed first as a rebuke of the happiness *any* man would have enjoyed in his enviable position as a wealthy Hollywood insider married to a gorgeous blonde starlet and then as evidence of an intellectual, maudlin sensibility attributed to his Jewish ethnicity. Additionally, films from this period offered metacommentaries on empathic connection or served as instruction for how stars and publics should act, much as fan magazines instructed actors and fans alike on the limits of acceptable behavior. The very quantity of filmic and textual production belies the film industry's awareness and anxiety about the unpredictable nature of fandoms and the various appeals stars offered.

ORGANIZING AFFECTIONS IN THE MAGAZINES

Hollywood's Others traces what we might think of as the industry's uneasy business of affective administration. While perhaps more prescriptive than sociologically descriptive, the fan magazines that proliferated in these decades are a treasure trove of instructions for how a fan should orient toward the era's various stars. Magazines addressed specifically to fans, as opposed to trade periodicals, appeared in the 1910s with the advent of *Motion Picture Story Magazine* and *Photoplay*. The popularity of the magazines grew rapidly throughout the 1920s and 1930s, as measured by the number of different magazines on the market as well as circulation numbers, which Sarah Polley has meticulously tracked. Despite occasional dips attributable to low moments in the Great Depression, the trajectory of the fan magazine grew throughout the twenties and early thirties with an estimated 12,301,005 readers in 1931.[20] As Polley notes, the circulation numbers of publications such as *Photoplay* and *Motion Picture Magazine* (the later title of *Motion Picture Story Magazine*) were such that they cannot be accounted for by a readership consisting solely of the stereotypical "movie-struck girl"; these magazines were part of many Americans' media diet.

Even these estimated numbers are likely modest, as issues circulated among members of a household or among friends. While individual fan magazines came and went, and mergers took place throughout the period, at any given time a devoted fan had a choice of reading materials. The leading magazine shifted across the decades, with *Photoplay* dominating the 1920s and *Modern Screen* coming to prominence in the 1930s. However, to a certain extent, these magazines were interchangeable. Film fans often read on the basis of stars, rather than loyalty to a particular magazine. Fans sought favorite stars *across* the magazines and likely consumed multiple issues in any given month.

While the magazines often functioned as an organ of studios eager to promote their stars in certain ways—wholesome, glamorous, etc.—fans consumed and wrote in to the magazines in idiosyncratic ways. Lies Lanckman has pinned down the identity of letter writers to the magazines, disproving previous assumptions that the letters and queries were fabricated. As Tamar Jeffers McDonald and Lanckman note, "the magazines encouraged interactive readership" from the beginning, with contests, puzzles, and publication of both opinion and query letters.[21] As Jeffers McDonald and Lanckman write of the interactive fan-periodical relationship, the magazines can be seen as "conduits of historical assumptions: assumptions about appropriate gender roles, goals, behavior, desires, and appearance, via the stars and movies whose promotion formed the center of every issue."[22]

In reading for the magazines' pedagogical function, sometimes heeded and sometimes not, *Hollywood's Others* joins the good company of other scholars who have turned to the fan and trade magazines as an important source for tracking the industry's efforts to manage its reputation. For example, as Anthony Slide has argued, the *Photoplay* editor James R. Quirk saw it as his role in the 1920s to police movie morality, acting as a second Hays and using his magazine to offer instruction to Hollywood figures and, one presumes, their fans as well.[23] Vexed or controversial cultural matters were worked through, if not out, in front of fans, as when the magazines reported Bern's suicide or when the stars in question represented a group denied equal footing in the public sphere, as in the case of *Hallelujah*'s all-Black cast.

Promoting and policing star attachments was messy work, and the fan magazines occasionally slipped out of step with fans. In his account of the relationship among ideas of masculinity, stardom, and the Code, Mark Lynn Anderson notes that "reformers became increasingly concerned about the influence that individual performers might have on their audience, and they began to take an interest, just as the fans did, in the on—and off—screen lives of screen stars."[24] As a result, the 1920s and 1930s offer a particularly heightened instance of what Marcus has described as the "drama of celebrity" in which "three equally powerful groups: media producers, members of the public, and celebrities themselves . . . compete *and* cooperate to assign value and meaning to celebrities and to those who take an interest in them."[25] In *Hollywood's Others*, I focus particularly on the media production side of the equation, including films and fan magazines, as well as the involvement, in the case of Shirley Temple's mother, of interested parties in producing magazine copy. However, even in the pages of the relatively industry-propagandizing fan magazines and studio pictures, both stars and their fans can be seen jockeying for position and throwing out challenges to attempts to create clean star narratives.

The digitization performed by the University of Wisconsin's *Lantern* project has made newly accessible the trade publications targeted at and, to a degree, produced by local theater owners, revealing the way a given star's appeal was measured through on-the-ground ticket sales. While this book's focus is primarily on the fan magazines, I occasionally consider the trade publications in order to assess on-the-ground responses of exhibitors featured in columns such as "What the Pictures Did for Me," which offer fascinating moments of star interpretation, as when the theater owners around the nation began complaining about Temple's declining appeal and suggested new career paths for the young star. The trade magazines' suggestions for promotions, or "tie-ins," often reveal a good deal about how local exhibition contexts shaped star discourse.

INDIVIDUALIZING STARS, REAL AND FICTIONAL

By reading films and fan magazines, it becomes possible to see the way some actors in the 1920s and 1930s received treatment that was more associated with the silent-era picture personality—which associated performers primarily with screen roles rather than off-screen life—than the modern star. For Black actors, the distinction between star and role was largely collapsed in fan magazines. Articles describing Hattie McDaniel's speech and cooking, for instance, conflate these potentially distinguishing aspects of the actress's persona with those of her character Aunt Dilsey in *Judge Priest* (Ford, 1934). What deCordova has described as the picture personality's "tautological loop" lingered in the magazines' treatment of Black stars, as well as child stars, as a way to manage cultural anxieties.[26] On the other hand, white adult stars fit the more modern models of "individualizing" stardom described by deCordova.[27] However, these stars risked losing their appeal through the wrong kind of individuation, specifically through their associations with melancholy and mental illness, as in the case of Paul Bern.

Most of the actors and characters who populate these chapters were not widely promoted as glamorous or aspirational. They are also not the recognized sites of countercultural identification that have been important to studies such as Dyer's account of Garland's appeal to gay men. *Hollywood's Others* is interested in the way stars located outside the cultural center, who were neither aspirational goddesses nor iconoclastic icons, nonetheless operated as important sites for working through and containing social anxieties in ways that were foreclosed in the off-screen world of the United States in the 1920s and 1930s.

In its consideration of a diverse set of stardoms, *Hollywood's Others* participates in a tradition of scholarship concerned with differentiating stars, audiences, journalists, and exhibition practices and challenging tendencies to posit a normative, white star as well as an easily manipulated feminine audience. This includes both Shelley Stamp's and Miriam Hansen's foundational work to complicate facile notions of the "movie-struck girl," as well as more recent scholarship that tells the history of Black audiences and film criticism, including but not limited to Miriam Petty's *Stealing the Show,* Anna Everett's account of Black film criticism *Returning the Gaze,* Carrie Teresa's study of Black celebrity journalism *Looking at the Stars,* and new research by Agata Frymus and Pardis Dabashi on Black audiences and exhibition histories.[28] Although assessing audience responses is notoriously difficult, some aspects of journalistic history and circulation data are clear. For example, Black newspapers in the twenties began to feature regular celebrity columns with dedicated gossip beats and entertainment reporters. By reading against the grain, one can also get a sense of what audience behaviors and modes of identification and disidentification these papers were correcting for. As Carrie Teresa writes of one journalist's scolding of Black audiences who laughed along with racist on-screen jokes, "Consumption practices became an important mode of representation to Black journalists. Black journalists took to task fans themselves."[29] *Hollywood's Others* takes inspiration from such efforts to differentiate fandoms in early Hollywood in its consideration of the way a white audience was hailed and instructed by mainstream fan magazines and Hollywood films to view racial difference.

While this book focuses primarily on fan magazines addressed to white readers, the Black press was also interested in mainstream Hollywood movies and engaged in a robust film criticism focused on a different set of social concerns. As Anna Everett recounts, film criticism in Black newspapers, as opposed to the more high-brow or radical magazines, retained in the 1930s what Everett describes as an accommodationist attitude "marked by an integrationist strategy to increase Black participation in the Hollywood mainstream."[30] However, even within this form of economic boosterism, critics would challenge on-screen representations. For example, in its coverage of *Judge Priest*, which featured Black performers in stereotyped roles, the *Chicago Defender* discusses McDaniel as an established show biz figure with a background in radio and vaudeville and describes a potential professional rivalry with Stepin Fetchit (Lincoln Perry): "As is natural with all actors when thrown to work with a new player whose inexperience or poor performance might hurt their own showing, Stepin-Fetchit was a little cool at

INTRODUCTION 15

first, but no sooner did they start rehearsal than he recognized the actress in her and expressed himself as highly pleased. His pleasure was increased when he learned of her long stage, radio and victrola record experience."[31] The article primarily discusses McDaniel's capitalization on new opportunities and the respect she commanded on set: "Hattie was tendered a nice fat contract, the role of Aunt Dilsey being given her with plenty of dialogue and three songs included."[32] In contrast to the white fan magazines, this coverage emphasizes the gap between the actors and the characters they played and firmly establishes McDaniel and Perry as professionals at work.

The difference between coverage of McDaniel in the Black press and in white fan magazines illustrates both the treatment of Black performers in mainstream periodicals and the larger challenge for writing about stardom in this period. Over the course of five chapters, *Hollywood's Others* will discuss a celebrity who was treated as something of a character in the drama that played out after his suicide (Bern is even labeled a character type, "father confessor"); a young actor who is referred to almost exclusively by his character name (Allen Hoskins, better known as Farina); and stars whose personalities receive consistent and highly articulated sculpting across profiles and interviews (Shirley Temple, Lon Chaney). As a result, what constituted a "star" in this period is a slippery thing, including, as I have just argued, modern actors who were still treated very much like picture personalities, studio executives about whom the press created elaborate stories and characterizations, and actors whose star personae integrated aspects of their biography with their screen role. *Hollywood's Others* treats this variety under the sign of the "star," in part to show just how messy and variable stardom and efforts to regulate it could be.

FROM ADORATION TO ANTIPATHY

Hollywood's Others traces a roughly but not strictly chronological path through three sections, beginning with "The Babies," stars who were promoted as lovable and beloved; moving to "The Nobodies," performers about whom little was shared but onto whom much was projected; and ending with "The Unhappy," who were censured and scolded for failing to perform enthusiasm. Despite this relatively straightforward trajectory of a fall from likability, none of the responses these stars drew from the press were simple. Instead, even in the case of the lovable "babies," stardom as worked out through performance and publicity entailed a great deal of boundary drawing, whether promoting Allen Hoskins/Farina as long as he appeared suspended in childhood or encouraging Shirley Temple fans to maintain an amnesiac relationship to her famous mother and early filmography.

"The Babies" consists of two chapters: the first considers Allen Hoskins, better known as *Our Gang*'s Farina, while the second takes on the most famous star in this book, Shirley Temple. In the fan magazines and the *Our Gang* episodes in which he appeared, Farina's gender was treated as changeable, creating a mystery around the child star that was part of the performer's star appeal. Building on the work of scholars of Black childhood such as Robin Bernstein and Kyla Wazana Tompkins, this chapter asks how it was that for a time in Jim Crow America a Black child star with a changing gender was promoted as the nation's most beloved celebrity. A decade later, during the Great Depression, another child was taken to the national bosom. Chapter 2 examines the mechanisms by which an actress with a famous stage mother came to be seen as the ultimate adoptable child. While Temple films' spectacular treatment of their star encouraged audiences to imagine they might have the little actress for their own, as Michael Rogin notes, writing in the very different context of 1980s action films, "spectacle is about forgetting."[33] Temple's spectacular cuteness and its amnesiac effects worked hand-in-hand with magazine stories and film reviews that encouraged audiences to forget her biography, her training, the mediocrity of her plots, and all manner of labor—from the star's, to her mother's, to her Black choreographers', to the matter of child labor more broadly.

"The Nobodies" considers two very different cases that both involved concealing biographical aspects of performers' off-screen lives. Chapter 3 takes up Lon Chaney, an actor famous for his performances of characters with disabilities and disfigurements, alongside the most notorious film of his longtime collaborator Tod Browning, 1932's *Freaks*. The chapter considers the way Chaney's stardom indexed anxieties around the limits of sympathy and empathy when it came to disabled Americans at a time when the nascent Code was also making suggestions about who could appear on-screen and what acts and conditions were and were not deserving of empathy. Films with Black actors also presented test cases for the limits of industry promotion, and the 1920s and 1930s offered many iconic Black performances, particularly in *Hallelujah* and *Imitation of Life* (Stahl, 1934). Chapter 4 considers these two films alongside the John Ford film *Judge Priest* to trace the way Black supporting players were made to authenticate white nostalgia for an imagined South in the press and on-screen, particularly through moments of song. Drawing from the work of Alice Maurice, Desirée Garcia, and others to examine the way Black singing was established as a sign of the real in Black-cast musicals as film transitioned to sound, the chapter traces Black singing's movement from starring attraction to nostalgic "atmosphere."

Finally, in "The Unhappy," the problem of dissatisfied glamorous, white, and normative celebrities comes into view in the form of famous suicides. The kinds of pleasurable identification or self-projection the press promoted to audiences came under threat in the cases of these unhappy stars. Chapter 5 takes up actress Thelma Todd and film producer Paul Bern to ask what it means that celebrity suicides (or rumored suicides) should be so productive of conspiracy theories. Against the backdrop of the Great Depression and highly publicized suicide rates in Los Angeles newspapers, famous cases of suicide (or mysterious deaths) generated elaborate conspiracy theories that cast these deaths as murders. A part of this conspiratorial thinking involved interpretive claims that either the dead were happy or, if they were not, that they should have been. This was particularly so in the case of Bern, who was married to Jean Harlow at the time of his death. In contrast to coverage of Bern, whom magazines framed as indulgently and ethnically morbid, coverage of Harlow portrayed the actress as appropriately managing her grief by not inflicting it on others.

Any book is a project of selection. There are other performers from the era who also had vexed and interesting stardoms. The glamorous Chinese American film star Anna May Wong, for example, had a career that spanned the silent and sound eras and had her stardom shaped by the Code's caution against depictions of interracial love. However, Wong's stardom was highly individuated, if still limited by the era's anti-Asian racism. As I have suggested, the stars gathered here reveal the pervasive treatment of childhood, of Blackness, and of disability as available for audience members' projections as signs of universal suffering or love. This was both a lucrative aspect of their stardom and a threat that needed to be managed. In contrast, normative white celebrities could threaten aspirational identification by stepping out of line through too much individuation. By way of conclusion, I consider the final issues of *Photoplay*, which appeared in 1980 but featured much discussion of 1930s stars in its coverage of two powerful white female stars on the rise, Meryl Streep and Bette Midler. Once again, discourse that might seem belated or like a hangover from an earlier period served to discipline stars: fall in line or we'll fall out of love, the magazine warns.

I
THE BABIES

1

SEXING FARINA

Our Gang's "Little Fellow"
and Other Fantasies of Black Childhood

Amid a string of gossipy witticisms about celebrity divorces and marriages, Herbert Howe spared a paragraph of his July 1925 *Photoplay* humor column "Close-Ups and Long-Shots" to offer this convoluted joke about a child actor: "Little Farina, known in private life as Hot Dog Hoskins, sent an indignant note in hot Ethiopian declaring she was a respectable single man though colored."[1] Full of racial jabs about respectability, language, gender instability, and an exchange of one food-based name for another, Howe's joke distills broader trends that had been swirling since this particular member of *Our Gang* appeared in 1922. By the time Farina made his way into Howe's column, the actor portraying the character—Allen Hoskins—was among the most popular film stars working, appearing sometimes as a little girl and at others as a little boy. For example, in 1923's *Dogs of War*, Farina is a little girl, as she is in *Sunday Calm*, another film from the same year. In *Sunshine Ltd.* (1924) Farina is a little boy; in 1923's *A Pleasant Journey*, Farina's gender is unspecified, as is the case in 1924's *High Society*. As Hoskins aged, Farina's gender stabilized, but his early career entailed him playing a character who might be a little girl at one moment and a little boy at the next, even within the same film, as in the case of 1924's *Seein' Things*.

Exhibitors, trade periodicals, and competing studios were quick to realize *Our Gang*'s significance and the profits to be earned by exploiting the American public's interest in a ragtag gang of kids. In addition to professional rivals to Hal Roach's series such as *Baby Burlesks* (featuring baby Shirley Temple) and Larry Darmour's *Mickey McGuire* series, the 1920s and 1930s saw a veritable pandemic of imitation *Our Gangs*. These knockoffs included both amateur film series and the widespread look-alike contests that produced their casts. In 1926, for example, the children of Salmon, Idaho "drove parents, teachers, and Rex [theater] officials crazy, asking how many freckles the star kid had, how old Farina was, did the fat boy have to wear pants, and a steady stream of like questions."[2] Among this particular group of would-be Gang members, a little girl "made up wonderfully" won first prize for her Farina costume. Film periodicals also document the public's lively participatory relationship to the series. A *Motion Picture News* article from 1928 advertises a nationwide talent contest to be sponsored by eighty-nine theaters across twenty-five cities, promising that a new cast member will be selected from "all the young embryo stars."[3] And the *Exhibitor's Trade Review* article "Start an 'Our Gang' Day" advises theaters to create a themed day to increase "goodwill and a well-satisfied patronage."[4] The article proposes enlisting local Boy Scout troops, sponsoring father and son games, and including athletic programs and picnics. If audience members could not win their way into the series via a triumphant talent contest performance, the magazine articles suggest, they might nonetheless transform their communities to better mirror it.

While costume contests may reveal that young children participated in a rather simple form of identification with members of the Gang, the reputation of the series as part of civil rights history suggests its position as a more complexly aspirational piece of U.S. popular culture. As Julia Lee documents, race leaders tied hopes to *Our Gang* as well: W. E. B. Du Bois was an early fan, featuring Sunshine Sammy in the NAACP's short-lived children's publication *The Brownies' Book*.[5] Such idealistic accounts of the integrated series positioned *Our Gang* as pursuing an aim similar to the *Brownies' Book*'s goal of teaching "Universal Love and Brotherhood for all little folk—black and brown and yellow and white."[6]

As late as 1940, African American film critic Lawrence Reddick described the series as "the first welcome break from the usual Black stereotypical constructs."[7] Though one assumes Reddick's and Du Bois's aspirational views of the series' political import were not identical with the more quotidian concerns of white theater owners or fans, African American civil rights leaders and mainstream white publications alike positioned the integrated *Our Gang* comedies as an ideal model of small-town American life.

Despite its tremendous influence, *Our Gang* has received little scholarly attention, the exception being Lee's excellent study *Our Gang: A Racial History of the Little Rascals*, which takes *Our Gang* research in a promising new direction, complicating earlier notions of the series as either racially progressive or damningly mired in Black stereotypes.[8] Rejecting dichotomous views of *Our Gang*, Lee positions the series' promise of a society that "included women as well as men, Black people as well as white" in relation to its "enemy," "the world of Jim Crow."[9] For Lee, *Our Gang* is thus simultaneously ambitious and dishonest, as the series held out a utopian possibility premised on ignoring the on-the-ground realities of American racial violence. She explains: "By 1922, the year of *Our Gang*'s debut, America was eager for the reassuring myths and comforts of childhood."[10] A review of publicity for the series supports Lee's account of *Our Gang* as a barometer for America's worst and best selves. Further, I will argue, the two prevailing views of the series—*Our Gang* as integrationist and *Our Gang* as racist—are not exclusive but mutually constitutive, as revealed through the series' most popular star: Farina, a Black child whose gender fluctuated. I argue that Farina's peculiar characterization, drawn from a long history of racist tropes, allowed for a very specific kind of promotion of a Black star in the 1920s.[11]

Why should an ambiguously gendered Black child become a popular series' breakout star? The question is particularly vexing given the acutely hostile race relations that characterized the years Farina delighted American audiences. During Farina's tenure in *Our Gang*, Du Bois edited *The Crisis*, organ of the NAACP, in which he published cultural commentary, accounts of lynching, and evidence of racial achievement. The pages of Du Bois's magazine document that the era of the child star, including Black child stars, was also one of particular animus toward Black men. For example, during *Our Gang*'s first year, Du Bois ran stories covering voter suppression in Kentucky and Virginia (January 1922), attempts at but ultimate failure to pass the Dyer Anti-Lynching Bill (April and August 1922), and segregation in higher education (August 1922). It was during this period of heightened racial terror, the second era of the Ku Klux Klan, that Du Bois hoped to produce social change through his magazine's two-pronged focus on exposing racial atrocity and promoting images of Black bourgeois life.

Discussing possibilities for bringing the magazine to a white audience, a series of letters between Du Bois and a white *Crisis* reader offers anecdotal evidence for the difference between white views of Black children and white views of Black men. The reader, William C. Lee, proposes putting "little boys at work selling the paper on the street." However, he offers this caution: "If colored boys of 15 were to sell it, antagonism might be aroused; but little fellows of 8 and 10 could do it without being suspected of any improper ambitions or aims, and the appeal of their childishness would lead to many sales."[12] The disjuncture between the loving embrace with which Lee imagines white America folding the Black boy to the national bosom and his concern about the "colored boy of 15" exemplifies a pattern of thought in the way white Americans conceived of Black adolescents—or, rather, the way white Americans could not conceive of Black adolescence at all. As most lay consumers of *Our Gang* know, aging threatened all cast members, but, as the strange case of Farina demonstrates, it was a special problem for the *Gang*'s Black actors. As this chapter will document, in the 1920s, the Black child star powerfully performed what Robin Bernstein has described as "racial innocence": "the performance of not-noticing, a performed claim of slipping beyond social categories."[13] By attending to the fact that the series' integration happened via Black children, and through a "little fellow" with shifting gender in particular, we can see *Our Gang*'s episodic treatment of Farina as a formal response to broader national anxieties about Black masculinity and racialized sexuality that allowed white fans to partake in a fandom characterized by pleasurable racial innocence.

SELLING FARINA'S SEX

Starting his career at the age of one and performing from 1922 to 1931, Hoskins appeared in more than one hundred of the Hal Roach *Our Gang* films, more than any other member of the gang.[14] Farina's stardom quickly eclipsed that of the series' original Black child Sunshine Sammy (Ernie Morrison), whose sibling he regularly played. As Paula Massood has documented, Morrison was to have been the anchoring star of another series, an idea that never came to fruition because of anxieties about the market for a property so centered on a little Black boy.[15] Although his "brother" was denied top billing in a series of his own, Farina became *Our Gang*'s clear favorite. Being the favorite did not, however, mean gentle treatment: compared to the rest of the gang, Hoskins's character suffered a tremendous amount of on-screen violence. Whether exploded, tarred and feathered, run over by a train, stuck with quills, or, less spectacularly, as introduced by a title card in "The Cobbler," spanked "so often she can hardly find time to sit down," Farina endured all manner of bodily tortures.[16] As both the contest-winning little girl in Idaho and "The Cobbler's" introduction to Farina indicate, the child's beloved and suffering body was otherwise spectacular, too: from installment to installment, Farina's gender changed.

This flexibility around the gendering of Hoskins's character was no accident—a matter of neither sloppy movie watching nor bad reporting and ad copy. As baby Farina gained public notice, audiences became fascinated with whether the child was a boy or a girl, often writing to periodicals' Q&A columns to ask about both the character's and the actor's gender. The two categories were frequently conflated, as in the Howe joke, "she was a respectable single man though colored." Creator Roach deliberately encouraged confusion around Farina's sex to bring attention to his star and his series.[17] Traces of Roach's strategy appear in the dubious description of life on set from a 1924 *Photoplay* article: "Next came *Farina*, the small colored person who is usually referred to on the lot as 'It.'"[18]

While the instability around Farina's gender might be attributed to a general sense of young children as presexual, Farina's treatment is different from that of the white characters. Jean Darling, who began acting in *Our Gang* comedies around age three, for example, did not receive this treatment and was instead teasingly dubbed a "career vamp" ("Youthful Futurists"). And gender ambiguity followed only briefly the gang's other baby sibling, Jackie Condon, whom periodicals described primarily in terms of boyish messiness, calling him "the kid who combs his hair with an egg beater" and rendering phonetic depictions of rough-and-tumble speech such as his proclamation that he "don't wann be p'lite."[19] Moreover, while the white members of the gang such as Jean and Jackie retained the names of the actors who played them, this trend did not extend to the Black rascals, who were dubbed with non-gender-specific, food-like designations: Farina, Buckwheat, Mango, and so on.[20]

Though by 1924 some periodicals reflect the knowledge that the actor playing Farina was a boy, this was hardly standard practice. Within a single July 1925 issue of *Exhibitor's Trade Review*, for example, both male and female pronouns are used to refer to Farina over a number of pages concerned with marketing tie-ins. The article "Use Your Local Papers," explaining the importance of exploiting newspaper ads to promote the films, offers a brief film summary: "Farina, the little colored member of the gang, not being tall enough to take a good smack at the cop, proceeds to bite him for all he's worth."[21] An article on the facing page suggests a promotional gimmick: theaters might mail women "little envelopes . . . containing a black face powder, with a card announcing that Farina, Queen of Our Gang uses this powder to keep beautiful."[22] Strangely, the film to be promoted with the powder is *The Love Bug* (1925), one in which Farina is clearly a boy. Even when the plot specified Farina's gender, then, popular discourse played fast and loose with the character's gender. Other magazines treated Farina and Hoskins as neither female nor male, instead using ungendered racial epithets, including references to Farina as a "black dot," a "chocolate drop," and "pick." Tavia Nyong'o groups such references among dehumanizing racial kitsch items including lawn jockeys and pepper shakers, explaining that while such items are meant to be good-natured "harmless fun," they nonetheless express something quite significant about the racial views of the consuming white public.[23] Extrapolating from Nyong'o's formulation, we might ask: If Roach and periodicals attempted to create banal "fun" around their Black star, what is the meaning that lurks beneath the kitschy performance of a Black child with a variable gender?

OUR GANG'S STRATEGIES OF CONTAINMENT

Approaching the question of why Farina was so popular, we might begin by considering *how*. Here *Our Gang*'s formal organization offers some answers. Roach had a formula and a format that worked: the property spans film shorts, television series, and a number of feature films. *Our Gang*'s neighborhood kids getting into funny scrapes endure in part because they played out their days within the bounds of an episodic series. Lack of continuity between installments enabled Roach to replace aging stars and introduce new characters with little disruption. Because the episodes did not develop an ongoing narrative, recastings and rehashings could take place without disturbing the overall story world. Beyond the implications for casting, the serial and the episodic have different implications for narrative appeal: seriality excites desires for narrative closure and pleasurably frustrates those desires, while the episodic fulfills desires for repetition.[24] But these differences also have character effects worth attending to. In addition to their varying exploitations of audience memory and forgetting, the serial and the episode impinge differently upon character subjectivity over time. For example, an episodic series maintains coherent character tropes (a freckled child, a fat child, a rich child, etc.) much more than it develops characters.

The episode's and the serial's relationships to subjectivity become especially clear in the silent era's film serials and episodic films, which exploited their varied possibilities to comment on gender anxieties. Maggie Hennefeld's work on episodic series featuring early film comediennes, for example, identifies the episode's capacity to unleash and then contain social unrest: While characters may "raze public institutions like police stations and film theaters and throw bourgeois gender norms into crisis . . . no matter how much havoc is wrought in one episode, everything can be reset to normal by the onset of the next."[25] While the episode's containment strategy offered one response to changing gender norms, silent film serials offered a different strategy for managing gender. Though serial queens and kings alike were subject to the potential violence of the cliffhanger ending, Ben Singer demonstrates the serial's association with the new woman in particular: "The genre as a whole is thus animated by an oscillation between contradictory extremes of female prowess and distress, empowerment and imperilment . . . a wish-fulfillment fantasy of power betraying how tentative and incomplete that social emancipation actually was."[26] As a 1920s series, *Our Gang* exploited audience knowledge of both traditions, alternately hearkening back to the anarchic vaudeville-inflected gags of early film comedies and riffing on the popularity of the serialized melodrama when it suited to indulge its own play with gender and race.

FIGURE 1.1 Male Farina as serial queen.

The 1924 film *The Sundown Limited* illustrates many of these formal distinctions as well as their implications for intersections between gender and race in *Our Gang*. Early in the film, another Black child, "Powder Puff," wants to hop aboard the train on which the Gang is playing, but according to an intertitle that serves to introduce Farina, the "quota" has already been met. Equally a descriptor of the series' casting, the language of quotas emphasizes that Blackness in the series functions as an adaptable form into which many different bodies might be slotted. In his own explanation for not including Powder Puff, Farina establishes his gender for this film, rolling up his sleeves and taunting, "Why you always following us men?"

Though the film positions Farina as a little boy, around five minutes in, Farina becomes involved in one of the series' more violent gags, one typically associated with the serial queen. Failing to heed the engineer's warning not to play with the train in his absence, Joe and Mickey start driving and lose control, sending the locomotive chugging swiftly forward as the others chase behind. The gag about technology out of control quickly turns violent as the train reverses and Farina finds himself trapped on the tracks by one of his clownish shoes. As the train bears down, the others scatter, abandoning their friend. The film cuts to Farina, braids standing on end; next, a point-of-view shot gives the audience a view of the child being run over (a gag retained from the cinema's early days). The train barrels on, and Farina recovers, though still stuck. The gag repeats as Joe and Mickey struggle to control the train. In total, the train runs over Farina four times before an engineer saves the day, extracting Farina from the tracks. An episode that repeatedly runs over Farina, a popular Black child actor occupying the typical narrative space of a white woman, *The Sundown Limited* raises racial and gender anxieties and then diffuses them through violent jokes that can only be made funny by the series' episodic structure. When Farina appears as a damsel in distress trapped on the railroad track—that stock-in-trade of the serial melodrama—the film teases both the episode's amnesiac quality, which allows a character to pop up whole after being crushed in the prior episode, and the serial's dependence on selective remembering. As the film makes clear, even when an episode specifies

Farina's gender, the character's flexible sexing across the series haunts any particular performance.

Moreover, through its episodic form, *Our Gang* inoculates itself against the integrationist threats with which it flirts. In her account of the sitcom, Jane Feuer distinguishes between the episodic and the serial in terms helpful for unpacking *Our Gang*'s appeals and limitations: "The self-replication of the episodic series depends upon a continual reintegration of the family; that of the continuing serial depends upon the continual disintegration of the family."[27] Feuer defines family expansively, a stretching of the category's boundary apparent in *Our Gang*'s episodes, in which parents are either absent or disruptive to the group's unity. However, this utopian fantasy has a limit, also tied to the series' episodic form. In most episodes, Farina and Sammy appear to be arriving from somewhere off-screen. Whereas the white children are already at play or engaged in an activity at the opening, *Our Gang* features a recurring gag in which the two Black children show up late to the action in a rickety mule-drawn cart, suggesting some different origin point to which they will return. At the end of each episode, upon the gang's reunification, audiences are not called upon to imagine a next time in which the white and Black children grow up together, working or living in an integrated adult world. Instead, each time, they start from scratch.[28]

The racial neatness of the episode's boundaries balances the series' unruly experiments with identity, which appear as early as the eponymously named 1922 episode *Our Gang*. Here, the white character Flora begins the episode attracted to rough-and-tumble Jimmy (another white child), but finds her attention pulled by "model boy" Patrick Melrose (also white) until the gang swaps the latter's fancy clothes for rags. Within the episode, integration risks confusion, as the potential of Blacks and whites switching places is played for laughs. The boy who takes Patrick Melrose's fancy clothes is Sunshine Sammy. When Patrick's mother searches for her son, she spies a familiar figure in fancy jacket and trousers with its back to her; when the figure turns, revealing a Black child, she recoils in horror. This joke on the results of miscegenation—the idea that white children might, surprisingly, turn out to be Black—is of a piece with an overall pattern of disguises and mistaken identities that appears throughout the *Our Gang* comedies.

Across the films, Roach exploits a tension between images of integrationist possibility and the structural limits of a narrative form that reflected a larger segregationist structure. In another 1922 episode, *Young Sherlocks*, Sammy again appears in a narrative position that might traditionally belong to a white boy, only to be firmly returned to his station by the end. When Mary Jane (a white girl) is kidnapped, Sammy (here appearing with the actor's name Ernie) and Jackie (a white boy) act as her rescuing heroes. Once the rescue is achieved, the episode concludes with a brief fantasy sequence, meant to illustrate Ernie's tall-tale recounting of events. Ernie recollects he "took all the [reward] money, an' Ah bought a city—a whole city." The city he imagines is "Free Town," a riff on Garveyism and a magical place where he is mayor, appearing in a suit and top hat. However, this fantasy of an interracial paradise ruled by a benevolent Black mayor is interrupted by the arrival of Ernie's mother, who brings him back to reality, scolds him for neglecting Farina, and rushes her children home—a finale that affirms the separation between races by plucking the Black children from their surrogate family and reasserting their place in a Black one. Time and again, *Our Gang* flirts with ideas of integration, and even race mixing, only to set things back to racial order.[29]

SEX AND SLAPSTICK

While all the members of *Our Gang* were contained by the series' episodic structure, the within-storyworld impossibility of arriving at sexual maturity distinguishes Farina's treatment from that of his white pals, suggesting something about the particular version of Black subjectivity the series and the publicity around it offered. The white rascals, though contained by the same episodic temporality as Farina, might be described as *leaning toward* sexual development, thus occupying a different kind of childhood innocence than the Black children. That is, the white children enact courtship rituals we believe they will perform with greater seriousness as they grow older: audiences can easily imagine a future when their behavior will be no longer precocious, but appropriate. Playful anticipation of adult sex games appears in courtship plots centered around Mary, who is described in 1923's *The Champeen* as "the innocent cause of many a black eye" and in 1923's *Lodge Night* as "not yet a vamp—but give her time," and Jean Darling, who appears as a "vamp" in the promotional story "Youthful Futurists." Through such proleptic joking, the series' presentation of the white rascals instructs audiences in heterosexual puberty's ideal temporality, teleology, and narrative form, in which the goal of human development is the successful completion of an arc that passes from infancy through childhood and puberty to adulthood and reproduction.[30] By these lights, even though episodic, we can understand the white characters' forward lean toward adolescence as an indicator of their participation in the larger narrative structure of human development, whereas Farina's bouncing back and forth counts as a way of never making such progress, an indicator of the character's status as less than fully human.

In contrast to *Our Gang*'s white children, who contain futures of adult gender and sexual identity, the Black children are firmly denizens of the episode, a temporal space with its own implications for subjectivity. An amnesiac relationship to subjectivity and gender and sex stability appears with special regularity in another form of episodic children's entertainment notable for its violence—cartoons that take disruptions to a subject's coherence to preposterous extremes. For example, describing Hanna-Barbera's famous cat and mouse series, Paul Wells emphasizes the cartoon's disruption of coherent identities: "When Tom becomes an object he is rendered both genderless and without identity. . . . This is achieved by violating the consistence of Tom as a *character* through relocating him as an infinitely flexible two-dimensional *form*."[31] Implicit in Wells's provocative reading of Tom's transformations is a sense that there is a male cat Tom that endures across the episodes of the series, even as its body is subjected to myriad violent transformations, including transformations of sex, within an episode. Earlier cartoons, including "Steamboat Willie" and the Krazy Kat comic strip and shorts, also

FIGURE 1.2 "Youthful Futurists": puberty's teleology on display.

experimented with radical transformations of different characters, with Willie treating various animals aboard his boat as musical instruments and Krazy appearing as a he or a she at various times throughout the George Herriman series. With a disproportionate exposure to violence compared to the other children, and with variable sexing, Farina thus participates in the tradition of animated characters. Extrapolating from Wells, then, we might say that *Our Gang*'s violent treatment of Farina and its episodic transformations of his sex both participate in episodic slapstick violence's violation of the subject's identity coherence. The implications of this pleasurable disruption to Farina's character through a transformation of his *form* are particularly sinister in the context of the era's anti-Black violence.

That a Black child should partake in the traditions of animation's violent metamorphoses should not surprise us, nor should the centrality of gender instability to these shifts. Both habits of representation raise questions about humanity's borders, and, as a number of thinkers have shown, such lines of demarcation were frequently drawn through race and gender at once.[32] As Mel Chen puts it, the genitals are "a tremendously loaded 'organ,'" linked to "geopolitical and social orders which are vastly more complex and intersectional than to systems of gender alone."[33] In the context of Jim Crow Black-white relations, this was particularly the case. Without stable gender and spectacularly tortured, Farina testifies to the series' positioning of the Black child just outside the human, a location that justified all manner of violence against the character at the same time that it was promoted as a source of incredible fascination.

Farina's many bodily transformations participate in the *Our Gang*'s larger pattern of treating the child as an animated *thing*. For example, 1923's *No Noise* introduces Farina with a title card that specifies Farina as female but not quite human: "Little Farina is gifted. She will eat anything—Pins, needles and wire nails preferred." Following this note, Farina appears in an ensemble of large men's boots, raggedy dress, short pants, and multicolored beanie hat, a patchwork costume assembled of garments male and female, child and adult in origin. She then proceeds to eat the gang's treasures, a collection that entails a corkscrew, hammer,

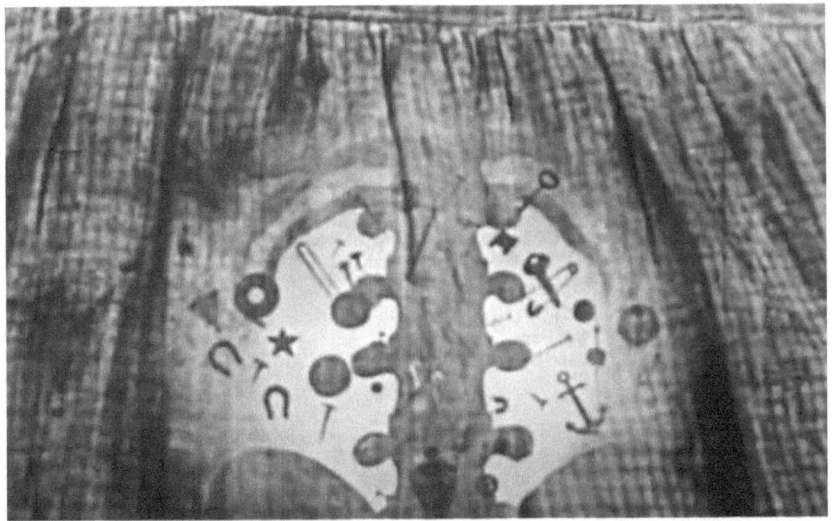

FIGURE 1.3 What Farina is made of.

knife, nails, and marbles. Through costuming, the description of her eccentric repast, and the character's connection to machine parts, *Our Gang*'s *mise-en-scène* positions Farina as a special case. If little girls are made of sugar and spice, and little boys consist of snips and snails, Farina is neither—instead, an ambiguously gendered Black child made of very strange stuff indeed. A slapstick figure, Farina incorporates dangerous material to no consequence.

Beyond the violence that accompanies episodic comedy, Farina's diet of metal findings aligns her with the world of objects, an association enforced when the gang goes to the hospital to visit Mickey, who is suffering from tonsillitis. At the hospital, Farina enters an X-ray machine and we see her insides, a composition that includes bones, but also metal parts. Such treatment appears in an earlier episode as well, when an ambiguously gendered Farina appears connected to a machine in *Young Sherlocks'* fantasy of plentitude. Brother Ernie's utopian "free town" includes a Goldbergian milk machine that links a cow's udder to his baby sibling's mouth via a complex system of tubes, updating the ongoing jokes about Farina's perpetual hunger through the creation of a cow/

machine/baby chimera. Across these episodes Farina's flexible gendering and status as a human *thing* bear out Wells's supposition that changes in *form* entail violation of character, here removing the Black child from the identity category occupied by white playmates.

Farina's fall out of progressive, narrative, human time is also literalized in the series' slow-motion treatments of the character, which create a within-episode reinforcement of the child's special temporality. *No Noise*, for example, features a chloroformed Farina running through the hospital, shoes flopping. Farina bounces slowly down an unadorned hallway with white walls. Against this blank background, the child is strikingly decontextualized. Moreover, the scene appears to have been shot twice, the two perspectives edited together to extend the joke, one supposes. Whereas Farina runs from the left side of the screen to the right in the first shot, following the cut, Farina runs from right to left. Whether accidental or not, the strange editing and directional shift, along with the wall's blankness, buttress the feeling produced by the slow motion as Farina floats round and round like a zoetrope's horse, never arriving at a destination. Farina's runs, here and in 1924's *Seein' Things*, participate in a larger cultural pattern of Black children suspended in time, and thereby removed from the time of biological reproduction and evolutionary advancement. A scaled-down embodiment of beliefs in whiteness as historically progressive and Blackness as primitive or backward, Farina's status as a strange sibling within the *Our Gang* family contributes to a larger story of white supremacist narrative of the "family of man."[34] In popular entertainments, these views manifested in stereotypical depictions of Black adults as childlike, as well as the pickaninny type, characterized as the playful recipient of cartoonish violence and as having an innocent relationship to sexuality.[35] These portrayals appear in popular fictions, including the most famous tales of plantation life, *Uncle Tom's Cabin* and *Gone with the Wind*, in which Topsy's claim about her origins and Prissy's insistence on the total mystery of childbirth separate Black babies from human reproduction, thus maintaining the open secret of plantation rapes, denying the significance of Black familial relations, and foreclosing the idea of Black sexuality.[36]

With its foreclosure of coherent sex, let alone sexuality, for its Black star, the episodic form of the *Our Gang* comedies revises nineteenth-century inspirations for Farina, specifically *Uncle Tom's Cabin*'s Topsy, who gave rise to both the pickaninny type that populated vaudeville stages and to what Bernstein refers to as the "libel" against Black children, the idea of their insensitivity to pain.[37] Whereas in Stowe's novel, Topsy undergoes a character change over the course of the narrative, redeemed from the wild pickaninny type through her Christian conversion, the popular "Tom shows" and minstrel routines that followed retained only the Topsy of *Uncle Tom's Cabin*'s first half—in other words, suspending her movement toward maturity and adulthood, cutting off her narrative. The trope of the "pickaninny out of time" offers a very particular aesthetic enjoyment of Black childhood. Participating in a decades-long lineage of fantastical nonaging Black children, Farina's slow-motion runs offer more than a simple visual joke about his/her badly fitting clothes: these moments in which a lone Farina floats by, isolated in the frame, emphasize the character's place outside of progressive temporality. Instead, the child appears to defy both gravity and time, suspended in the air, an image of Black childhood that might never arrive at its destination. While the series forecasts puberty and adult sexuality for white children, its depictions of Black children posit a separate, episodic temporality.

Transforming the child's body by erasing previous identities, the series also adds another data point to Jacqueline Goldsby's study of lynching and representation, which positions "anti-Black mob murders as a networked, systemic phenomenon indicative of trends in national culture," part and parcel of American modernity's technologies.[38] Though she uses "serial" to describe lynching's nationwide creep, Goldsby's account of national memory resonates against *Our Gang*'s episodic narrative structure.[39] Reading lynching against print media and visual culture, Goldsby argues "'the business of money-making' urged white Americans to be 'thrilled' with horror at the news of lynching in one moment, only to 'forget' the murders in the next."[40] In *Our Gang*, the amnesiac structure of racial atrocity is doubled: repetitively enduring violence and coming into new genders, Farina cannot remember what traumas have previously taken place; so too the audience "forgets" they have seen the character before and takes pleasure in repetitions of violence and erasure of gender.[41] As a result, through the "healing" nature of episodic form, the series renders fascination with anti-Black violence innocent, as the cartoonishly resilient Black child's body promises to return unscathed for more punishment in the next film.

Our Gang's episodic treatment of Farina appears in its most spectacular form in 1924's *Seein' Things*, which incorporates a number of characteristic tropes—Farina's hunger, pickaninny iconography, a shocking amount of violence—as well as a within-episode gender shift.[42] The film opens with the gang barbecuing a stolen chicken, a feast to which they have not invited baby Farina. After a much-pantomimed demonstration of hunger, Farina jumps into a mud puddle and splashes the picnickers with muck. Farina is then established as a little girl when one of the other children threatens: "I betcha we'll strangle her for this." As she runs away, Farina happens upon a grocery deliveryman, who accidentally drops food off the back of his truck. Farina tucks into the surprise feast, and an intertitle jokes, "three more chicken would have filled Farina to capacity." The gag includes a comedic potbelly, a visual joke enhanced further by the typical slow-motion scene that follows, in which Farina runs, belly bouncing, huge shoes flopping.

From here, *Seein' Things* takes the fantasy of a Black child out of time to hyperbolic extremes with a midstory shift in gender. When big-bellied Farina arrives home, her mother scolds her "eating meat—now you'll have a nighthorse [nightmare]." Once Farina is put to bed, the film world shifts to Farina's dream, in which the character undergoes a costume change and appears as a little boy, in a tuxedo with tails, complete with cane and spats. The boy Farina flirts with a little Black girl (a rare appearance in the *Our Gang* comedies), kissing her behind his hat and later dropping to one knee to swear his love. No comment or mention of the change occurs, but the rest of the film keeps Farina in this masculine attire as the nightmare develops with increasingly cartoonish violence: a series of scenes unfolds in which the little boy is hunted by the other rascals, who have grown huge; runs away by jumping into the ocean; and is blown through the air by construction dynamite, finally falling from the top of a building and smashing into the sidewalk stories below. Upon awakening, Farina delivers the episode's closing gag line: "ah eat mush from now on." Of course, this final punch line can only be a lie. Audiences know Farina will return in the next episode to be hungry another day.

AGING OUT OF FAVOR

If one way to understand adolescence is via a narrative in which puberty acts as the climactic gateway or "pivot" between childhood and adulthood, then the episodic form of the *Our Gang* comedies becomes very important indeed, with actors aging out of the cast at the moment they enter puberty, and early episodes featuring a beloved character whose very gender begins anew with each new episode.[43] Such ambiguous gendering allows the series to flirt with integrationist ideas and to center a Black child star while simultaneously foreclosing the threat of miscegenation. Put slightly differently, we might say that the series' most progressive attitudes require its most regressive characterizations.

The stereotypical ideas about Black childhood that sentenced Farina to violent outrages episode after episode also formed the core of the promotional materials that helped make Hoskins the series' most important star. Broadly acknowledged as the audience favorite, Farina received more screen time, generated more press, and more frequently graced *Our Gang*–related tchotchkes than his compatriots. For example, in 1925, *Moving Picture World* magazine reported that "Little brown and fuzzy Farina at last has reached his goal in filmdom . . . Hal Roach lets him get before the camera eye more than any of the rest of 'Our Gang.'"[44] In a short *Film Daily* article detailing merchandise including "Our Gang Kiddie Jewelry," "Our Gang Art Needlework," "Our Gang Toffee Candies," and "Our Gang Umbrellas," only one character is mentioned by name amid the catalog of goodies otherwise more generically related to the series. The article notes that the music lover may purchase sheet music for the new song, "Little Farina, Everybody Loves You," a novelty promoted by one New York store with "a display of phonographic instruments, on one of which was seated a life-size doll representing Farina."[45]

And love Farina everyone did, at least according to magazine publicity. Reports of Hoskins's retirement take a markedly different tone from accounts of departing white actors. The retirement of one of Farina's colleagues is put simply, "Mickey Daniels, the boy with the freckles, is getting big and leaving for vaudeville"; similarly, *Modern Screen* reported that Johnny Downs is "the living example of what an 'Our Gang' child actor can grow up to be," for he has "clipped his curls and toured in vaudeville."[46] A notice about RKO's *Are These Our Children* posits, "If you love youth and who doesn't, you'll have the time of your life watching the youngsters in RKO's dramatic picture," including "little Mary Kornman, who used to be the *Sweetheart* of Our Gang outfit."[47] Positioning *Our Gang* as a kind of showbiz finishing school, these articles treat white children's aging as natural and healthy, the necessary next step following their well-documented childhoods.

The necessary opposite of admiring tales of *Our Gang* members graduating to more mature roles were hostile accounts of aging stars clinging to the cherubic roles of their youths. Apparently exhausted by the child actor fad, journalist and critic Huntly Carter cautions that when it comes to young people on-screen, "a little of them goes a long way." Carter continues: "Hundreds of people also sighed with relief when Baby Peggy retired from the screen at the age of eight or so, and others are delighted that Jackie Coogan—who was rather unconvincing when he went on trying to look six after he was ten—has now had a manly haircut and will in future play big boys' parts."[48] Indeed, the matter of Coogan's hair, made famous in Chaplin's *The Kid* (1921) appears to have distressed many, with one fan complaining to *Photoplay* magazine: "An American boy of his age with a bang! It is inconceivable. The boy has had all childhood directed out of him! A few runs with 'Our Gang' would much benefit the child; right down to little *Farina* with the 'twelve pound' look of shoes could give Jackie valuable pointers."[49] While Carter found relief in Baby Peggy's departure, and the critic as well as more casual fans found Coogan's fringed haircut inappropriately youthful, accounts of Farina's retirement register a real loss. In England, *Boy's Cinema*

FIGURE 1.4 "Too big to be cute anymore."

magazine described Farina's special hold on audiences: "The departure of Farina is certain to be regretted by millions of picturegoers. For though the other 'Our Gang' youngsters were all favorites, it was the little Black boy who could roll his eyes so comically that really engaged our interest most. Some of you may remember that when Farina first appeared in films he was always dressed as a girl."[50]

With Farina defined by a shifting gender and violent misadventures, for no member of the cast was aging as problematic as for Hoskins. Evidence of aging's especially problematic status for Hoskins appears in a *Photoplay* article that stages its own time-lapse effect. Three images of Farina illustrate the top half of the first page of "Retired at Eleven," documenting Hoskins's career with *Our Gang* from 1922 until his retirement in 1931. Describing the end of the photographic sequence, the copy reads "almost eleven and too big to be cute anymore."[51] The author, Leonard Hall, begins by deploying both predictable racial stereotypes and the neuter pronoun "it" in relaying Farina's origin story: "Nine years ago a tiny black dot was tossed to the mercies of that gang of young hellions known as 'Our Gang.' There was practically nothing to this dot but huge, rolling eyes and a mass of kinky woolen hair. It was christened *Farina*, dressed in rags and immediately hit in the face with a cocoanut custard pie."[52] Despite, or perhaps because of, this dehumanizing view of Farina, Hall is able to make a remarkable claim about the way white audiences responded to the character: "Farina fascinated us because he (it was *she* at the time) was the perfect incarnation of poor, witless Man's struggles against inscrutable, and very rough and dirty, Fate." Further into the article, Hall puts it slightly differently: "And we loved Farina—because Farina, a three-year-old fragment of ebony, was ourselves."[53] Here, Farina's ability to stand for the suffering of everyman appears predicated on the character's ability to be described through multiple and conflicting referents. In the first instance, Hall manages to pack the masculine, feminine, and neuter pronouns into the subject position of the sentence, using the ontic hinge of the verb *to be* to balance a Farina that is simultaneously he, she, and it—"he (it was *she* at the time)"—against "Man" writ large. Portraying an infinitely elastic character, the description again emphasizes Farina's flexible, slapstick body.

In this article, Farina's double distance from the author as a comedic Black child opens him up to serve metaphorically as a vehicle for the experience of adult white existential pain. A more explicit account of an ungendered Farina as the one who appeals appears in the second example, in which Farina's status as an object, a fragment of ebony, allows the author's identification. Over the course of this article—which mourns Hoskins's aging as much as it does his disappearance from the series—Hall's identification and affection are pegged to the Black child's triumvirate qualities of cuteness, youth, and, importantly, gender ambiguity.

Not so the actor who played Farina as he approached adolescence. Measuring Hall's appreciative account of baby Farina against his description of the pubescent Hoskins reveals that identification with the child is important identification with a *thing*, as Hall puts it, a "black dot" with "practically nothing to" it. The nothingness, which might be interpreted as an account of Farina's diminutive stature, might also suggest a different pleasure offered by the Black child, a particularly racialized sense of Locke's infant *tabula rasa*.

If all child stars are to some degree blanks, this sense of the child as empty container for adult projections is only heightened by the white habit of imagining Black children as ungendered things. Entrance into puberty, then, affiliates the child star too much with adult subjectivity, a realm characterized by white disidentification with Black fellow citizens in the age of Jim Crow. The severing of adult white–Black child affinity appears in Hall's descriptions of the aging actor. In addition to the middle picture's description of the pubescent Hoskins as "almost eleven and too big to be cute anymore," the text represents Hoskins as "a spindly colored boy of eleven." The article implies that no one wants to see a Black child age. Instead, Hall frames Farina's adolescent future as distasteful and alienating. For Hall, becoming a Black man—transitioning from "it" to "he"—means Hoskins cannot be an everyman.

Returning to William Lee's letter to Du Bois, Farina improved upon Lee's appealing "little fellows" by potentially not being a fellow at all, just little. But perhaps more troubling than this foreclosure of Farina's manhood is its appearance in tandem with the strong investment in Farina's mysterious sex that *Our Gang* and its promotional materials encouraged. Stoking a fascination with Farina's sex, Roach's series resonates with white violence focused on Black genitalia. Farina's shifting gender shows the way *Our Gang*'s narratives could pleasurably enact the forbidden desires of a white supremacist nation, thus slightly revising the psychic balm Robyn Wiegman argues the lynched body offered the mob: "limp and hanging bodies function as the specular assurance that the racial threat has not simply been averted, but rendered incapable of return."[54] A slapstick riff on the lynch victim, Farina does return, constantly resurrected by the series' episodic structure. Indeed, Farina's friends are as likely to appear in the role of lynch mob as they are to act as a makeshift family. In addition to the extralegal violence implied by *Seein' Things*'s "I betcha we'll strangle her for this," the episode *Lodge Night* features a riff on the KKK in the form of the Cluck Cluck Clams, and in the episode

High Society, Farina appears in the guise of a mob victim, tarred and feathered. Nevertheless, cartoon-resilient Farina remains unharmed, starting each new episode just as cute as before.

But this is a resurrection that entails its own violence, as the character's and the child actor's gender must be repetitively erased in order for the "fun" of an ambiguous Farina to remain on-screen. While Farina's resurrections heal the episodic violence of explosions and suppers of nails and screws, the series' episodic forgetting of Farina's gender entails the repetitive erasure of his/her sex. In the context of Hoskins's well-documented dislike of being made to wear a dress when playing Farina, we see the painful way in which the series again and again denies Farina's statement in *Sundown Limited* that he is one of "us men," a disavowal shared by the press materials that mourned Hoskins's maturation.[55]

The declaration of manhood was precisely what the lynch mob denied, both figuratively and literally, as it responded to a rising Black middle class's assertion of economic and political participation in U.S. daily life with accusations of sexual misconduct followed by murder and genital mutilation. Less violent, but kindred in spirit, jokes about Hoskins's impending manhood offer an emphatic refusal of such claims by rendering them preposterous. The *Exhibitor's Trade Review*, for example, reported: "Farina, the unbleached American child who is a 'she' in those delightful Our Gang Comedies, has arrived at the age where he wishes to claim his manhood. He (for that's just what Farina is) doesn't want to bother about 'keeping that schoolgirl complexion' but does want to acquire pants and suspenders an' everything."[56] The joke's logic situates Black manhood as a type of nonsense. With its tortured pronoun use, the article pokes fun at Farina's hopes to "claim his manhood," a wish made to seem as ridiculous in the reader's mind as the child's applying creams to maintain girlishly soft skin. It is precisely the relationship between absent adult Black masculinity and the series' playfully inclusive world that explains the disgust at an aging Farina we find in Hall's article. If manhood has historically been linked with citizenship, it's no surprise that only an ambiguously sexed baby Farina offers a comforting working through of American multiculturalism. While a star who leaned toward Black manhood would have threatened real political consequence, the ungendered or ambiguously gendered Black child could be treated comfortably as a cute thing, making no claims on a political future.

FARINA'S ENDINGS

The promotion of child stars generally and Black child stars particularly as empty vessels for adult projections meant the individual child who happened to occupy that slot at any given moment was imminently replaceable. So, when the actor playing Farina reached age eleven, the character did not enter puberty's narrative arc, but ceased. Though Farina disappeared from *Our Gang*'s story world, his type lived on in Buckwheat—who, in addition to making the transition to sound, also received episodic sexing and was played first by a little girl, Willie Mae Taylor, and then by a little boy, Billie Thomas. Because of *Our Gang*'s episodic structure, the young child Farina, sometimes a girl, sometimes a boy, sometimes gender ambiguous, went on to the immortality that is television syndication. However, the hypothetical adolescent Farina that could have been never was. Instead, as puberty impended, this person, the hypothetical Black youth, disappeared from the small-town alleyways, sidewalks, and dirt lots in which *Our Gang*'s never-aging children played.

Though we might see *Our Gang*'s investment in Farina's prepubescent gender ambiguity as part of the series' larger anarchic pleasure, or as part of a carnivalesque rule breaking that takes place among the children more broadly, such joys are mitigated by the fact that it is the Black child, specifically the Black male actor, who is the site of gender play. Most cynically, if Farina's seeming ability to forever postpone adolescence is what allows the integrationist pleasures and partial identifications we see in film periodicals, then the temporality of such progressive dreaming comes up for question. If a Black child's participation in the series requires that he never grow up to be a Black man, the goal of integration is as stalled as Farina's slow-motion jogs. For Farina to be the delightful "chocolate drop," the character must fall out of the temporality in which white boys and girls participate. Running through the thick time of slow motion, celebrated in neuter pronouns in periodicals, or restarting stories newly sexed, Farina is the ultimate episodic body: never nourished, always enjoyably punishable, and never threateningly growing or grown. Thus, while a film such as *Seein' Things*, in which Sammy pals with the white boys and Farina features in her own adventure, may seem exemplary of the utopian racial impulses with which scholars and critics alike credit the series, the narrative hinge that is Farina's midpoint gender transition reminds us of the important impossibility built into utopia's etymology. The happy integrated town is not just nowhere in space, but nowhere in time as well.

2

FORGETTING SHIRLEY TEMPLE

Amnesia, Technology, and the Abstracted Child

A ble to contain paradox in one tiny, appealing package, Shirley Temple was the ideal star for the 1930s. Embodying Richard Dyer's claim that "stars frequently speak to dominant contradictions in social life," Temple was a pro and an innocent; an orphan with a stage mother; a wealthy celebrity and an urchin.[1] Most importantly for the film industry, though, Temple was an adorable mechanism for recasting all relationships as personal.

An example of the personal and possessive feelings Temple inspired appears in a series of letters routed through an earlier era's emblem of girlhood: Mary Pickford. In a note to Pickford, Arthur Loew, the grandson of film magnate Adolph Zukor, requests his "Aunt" Mary's intervention in a matter of the heart:

> It seems that I am in difficulties pertaining to one Shirley Temple. The summer before last Adolph, Warner, and I went out to her house twice in the afternoon and had a very gay time. Then I left L.A. to return to Tucson for the winter. When I got home I decided to write Shirley a letter. I received an answer from her not long after that was very nice, and sounded like she wanted to keep up the correspondence. Therefore, I wrote back, and at the same time asked for a picture. Ever since there has been a dead silence.[2]

After responding to the "lovelorn" Arthur, Pickford intervened on his behalf by writing directly to the object of his affection:

> Arthur says he met you the summer before last and he is very desirous of having a photograph of you autographed to him. If you could spare a little time to drop him a note I know he would greatly appreciate it and so would I. I believe he wrote you and received a reply but has written since and not heard from you so he is wondering if his second letter ever reached you. Knowing so well how a personal letter can become mixed up with fan mail I thought I would ask.[3]

Addressing Temple in an insistent and not a little scolding tone, the older star's letter attempts to draw a distinction between relationship types, further blurring the line in the process. Offering Temple a preemptory excuse for her lack of reply, Pickford makes a bridge of shared experience: "knowing so well how a personal letter can be mixed up with fan mail." But despite this understanding gambit, young Arthur's request for an autographed photo, a common fan item, makes Pickford's letter seem disingenuous. At the very least, the distinctions between fan mail and personal mail appear muddy: if stoking affection is personal, it is not clear what differentiates such a solicitation of feeling from a professional's relationship to her fans.

As with the *Our Gang* kids discussed in the previous chapter, star discourse encouraged intense affective attachment to Temple. Temple's adorable picture personality, like Farina's, had its basis in a strange temporality. But whereas Farina appealed by foreclosing the future, Temple's stardom erased the past and transcended narrative temporality. With her shining curls, easily digestible films of good cheer, and broad-based appeal, Temple has been read by scholars as an exemplar of Hollywood's Lethean capacity to relieve beleaguered Depression-era audiences as they whiled away a spare hour or two. Certainly, Temple brought great joy to 1930s audiences. But forgetting was not just an effect of Temple's frothy film plots; forgetting was central to Temple's star persona and the 1930s film industry for which she served as emissary.

Three particular modes of forgetting appear in Temple's films and the magazine discourse surrounding her stardom. First, seeing Temple as precocious often entailed forgetting her early career, so that she appeared as a talented newcomer in her Fox Studio films. As Lori Merish's work on Temple and Tom Thumb suggests, precocity is itself a violation of normative temporality—a mode that weds age and youth via spectacular performance and invites audiences to ignore the labor of professionalism on behalf of personality's naturalness.[4] Second, the recycling of orphan-themed plots in Temple's films allowed audiences to momentarily forget her biographical history, including Gertrude Temple's activity as a stage mother, and imagine the star as adoptable. Third, displays of Temple's cuteness, often paired with technologically advanced film techniques, created moments of nonnarrative spectacle that simultaneously allowed fans and critics to ignore less-than-stellar plots and stoked fantasies about the star's availability. An industry figure closely aligned with the concept of entertainment itself, Temple's amnesia-inducing stardom made it possible to enjoy the idea of her movies even if you did not like a particular one. When Temple's star eventually faded, then, it was not just because she aged into adolescence, but because her loss of childhood innocence entailed an accompanying fall out of spectacle into narrative time. As this chapter argues, all three forms of forgetting promoted a star-fan relationship that was intensely personal while also being intensely abstracted, a mode of relating that was crucial for the motion picture industry at a time when the government threatened its own interventions on behalf of the American child. The Temple personality, which bridged the personal and the professional, and was simultaneously precocious and in need of care, offered a model for both employee-employer and individual-state relationships.

PRECOCITY AND PERPETUAL YOUTH

Following Temple's breakout performance in 1934's *Stand Up and Cheer* (MacFadden), audiences and critics alike wanted to know more about "the little girl with dancing feet and a captivating smile."[5] Fox and the magazines that promoted the film obliged with a tale of fresh talent plucked from obscurity. *Photoplay* reporter Barbara Shaw, for example, wrote: "One day she was just Mr. and Mrs. George Temple's little girl, Shirley. The next day she was star material Shirley Temple—in electric lights." Shaw insists upon Temple's difference from other child stars: "She is pure gaiety and love of life, and miraculous unself-consciousness. She is as natural as a puppy, in a world where children are quickly turned into affected imitations."[6] Two related modes of forgetting appear here: the larger national forgetting that took place in relation to child actors' labor and the more local forgetting that applied to Temple's labor in particular. Emphasizing Temple's unselfconsciousness, her puppylike naturalness, Shaw rehearses arguments for treating acting as a special category of child labor while simultaneously positioning childhood as a precious category vulnerable to modern sophistication and corruption.[7]

Popular conversations about what made a child star successful and legislation around child labor contributed to the sense that the best child stars were in fact not performing, not working. Instead, such children forget themselves in their work and merely play. Shirley Temple's naturalness would both lend credence to child performers' exemptions from FDR's 1938 Fair Labor Standard Act and be an important component of her star persona. Despite Shaw's claim that "One day [Shirley] was just Mr. and Mrs. George Temple's little girl," both Shirley and Gertrude Temple had been hard at work before Temple's supposed overnight success. Tremendous labor went into the young star's creation, beginning even before her birth. Gertrude Temple was a stage mother from the time Shirley was in the womb, coaching the fetus Temple by consuming improving music and important literature.[8] And for two years prior to *Stand Up and Cheer*, Gertrude had already been peroxiding and curling Shirley's famous fifty-six ringlets. Perhaps most importantly, by the time of Shirley's overnight success, she had already appeared in a number of films—eight comedy shorts for the *Baby Burlesks* series and four for the *Frolics of Youth*. At age five, Shirley Temple was no novice.

What does it mean, then, to "forget" this early career? And what is in the *Baby Burlesks* that might be worth forgetting? Whereas the emergent star Shirley Temple appeared in 1934 neatly cleaved from any past, the series *Baby Burlesks,* produced by Educational Film Exchanges, Inc., stands at a messy transitional moment in film history. The eight *Burlesks* appeared between 1932 and 1933, as the Code was coming into focus but not yet rigorously enforced and before the matter of young actors' labor was settled. Reflecting on the series in a 1988 interview, Temple is clear that although she did not mind working, what she did as an infant was work: "If I had to do it all over again, I wouldn't change anything. I probably would have paid for the pleasure of working. . . . I did!"[9] Despite this positive account of child labor, Temple's description of the training practices on set reveals how little like play child acting could be. When the *Baby Burlesks* stars misbehaved, for example, their punishment could include being locked in a black sound box with a piece of ice to sit on, a penalty to which Temple credits her youthful professionalism: "Being in that black box with a cake of ice taught me very quickly that Time is Money. It's work, not play, and you learn to be obedient or something bad happens to you. By the time I got to the Fox studio for my first major film, I knew how to hit a mark. I knew how to memorize lines. I knew how to pay attention."[10]

In contrast to her wholesome roles for Fox, Temple's roles in the *Burlesks* are resolutely pre-Code. The conceit of the *Baby Burlesks,* from which it occasionally wavered into broader vamping, was the repopulation of film plots with infant performers. For example, the scenario *Runt Page* imitates 1931's *Front Page* (Milestone), *Pie Covered Wagon* riffs on the 1923 silent *The Covered Wagon* (Cruze), and *War Babies* parodies 1926's *What Price Glory?* (Walsh). Other films in the series are looser parodies, as in the boxing picture *The Kid's Last Fight,* which replaces the name Jack Dempsey with Diaper Dampsy, or *Kiddin' Hollywood,* which offers a broad Hollywood satire by rebranding industry notables as Frightwig von Stumblebum, Freta Snobo, and Morelegs Sweetrick, this last played by Temple. In this role, Temple's appearance echoes that of Marlene Dietrich's costume in *Blonde Venus*'s (von Sternberg, 1932) "Hot Voodoo" number. In the film, Dietrich enters a nightclub as the captive gorilla of a group of Black dancers, performs a violent striptease that involves removing the gorilla's head and hands, and then reaches for a blonde Afro wig with a decorative arrow through it before singing: "Tom-tom's put me under a sort of voodoo / And the whole night long I don't know the right from wrong." Though Temple sings the more innocent, "We just couldn't say goodbye," she appears to be casting a powerful sexual spell, as indicated by a series of reaction shots of the "men" on set ogling her and a lengthy, passionate kiss from her peewee costar. Between the on-screen cues of *Kiddin' Hollywood* and extra-diegetic information about Dietrich's star persona, the *Baby Burlesks* connect Temple to the scandalous stardoms and films popularly believed to have precipitated implementation of the Code.

Forgetting inconvenient aspects of Temple's past became something of a habit for Fox. As with 1934's *Stand Up and Cheer*, in 1942 forgetting again became a necessary component of promoting a Temple vehicle. *Miss Annie Rooney* (Marin) was a poor girl–rich boy romance, and a remake of a 1925 Pickford film. While Pickford's stardom required audiences to forget that a thirty-three-year-old woman was playing at youthful inexperience, when United Artists marketed *Miss Annie Rooney* as a Temple vehicle, they asked audiences to forget Temple's earlier precocious play at adult sex games. A critical failure, the film remains a notable artifact of film history for showing Temple's "first on-screen kiss," an event wrapped in a cloak of girlish innocence only heightened by her costar (and former *Our Gang* member) Dickie Moore's claim that it was his first kiss on- or off-screen. While Moore's claim may or may not be studio fabrication, the statements about Temple are patently false.

The eight *Baby Burlesks* films document a number of Temple firsts: her first screen appearance (*Runt Page*, 1932), her first on-screen dialogue (*War Babies*, 1932), her first dance (*War Babies*), and her first song, a rendition of "I'm only a Bird in a Gilded Cage" (*Glad Rags to Riches*, 1933), in addition to her first kiss (also in *War Babies*). Across the series Temple bestows and receives a number of kisses, hugs, and lascivious glances, whether playing Morelegs Sweetrick, a night club chanteuse named La Belle Diaperina, or the titular character in *Polly Tix in Washington* (1933), who warns the senator she's corrupting "I'm expensive" and, when denounced by the senator's daughter as "not a good woman," responds by pointing to the jewelry roping her body and saying, "You're crazy, you've got to be good to get stuff like this in these hard times."

If *Kiddin' Hollywood* connected Temple to a scandalous star persona, *War Babies* linked the young actress to an infamous film, Raoul Walsh's 1926 *What Price Glory?*—an early foray into sound for her future studio as well as an example of the sort of production to which the Code reacted. Fox originally released the Dolores del Río vehicle without sound, only to rerelease the film in 1927 with a soundtrack and sound effects. The film focuses on two Marines at war for the affection of del Río's Charmaine de la Cognac. In addition to its place in the history of film sound, *What Price Glory?* was also significant for the scandals it caused: both for routing the serious subject of the war through what the *London Times* called "sensual and farcical themes" and because the actors were very clearly swearing, something noted by lipreading audience members and critics alike. Though *War Babies* contains no toddlers mouthing curses, audiences would no doubt have remembered the famous cursing, and this *Baby Burlesk* does not skimp on its exploitation of the "sensual and farcical" attitudes the *London Times* found so objectionable in the original. Here, Temple reprises del Río's role, this time soliciting the gazes of all the baby soldiers, musicians, and patrons at the inn. Featuring Temple's first extended on-screen dance, the film adds a kiddie veneer to themes of adult sexuality including a visual gag involving a scoop of ice cream dropped down Temple's drawers that causes her to wiggle her bottom vigorously, an exchange of her attentions for the local lollypop currency, and the most shocking kiss of Temple's career: she embraces one soldier while smooching another behind his back—a kiss significantly more scandalous than the one Fox would promote some ten years later with *Miss Annie Rooney*.

Temple's early career and peak stardom unfolded alongside the Code. The plots of her films, in addition to being Code-approved, also frequently follow the Code's logic, emphasizing the importance of managing matters of public well-being within the family, as it were. Not protected by the First Amendment, motion pictures were subject to the regulations of other consumer products; as Richard Maltby notes, the same language of "purity" established by the FDA seeped into discussions of films as well.[11] Additionally, like all industries, the movies suffered during the Depression, with ticket sales falling and major studios, including RKO, Paramount, and Fox—Temple's eventual home—declaring bankruptcy.[12] The industry thus faced a dual crisis: struggling to navigate severe economic losses while also undertaking a public relations battle framed in terms of morality and child welfare, which contained an additional undercurrent of anxiety related to social class and ethnicity.

One response to this uncertainty involved undertaking stronger moves to self-censor. By 1934 the Code was being applied consistently, and the studios and ticket sales had both rebounded, though not to pre-Depression levels. Across the early 1930s, Shirley Temple, like the industry that employed her, would make the move to greater respectability and increased profits, leaving behind the tawdry *Baby Burlesks* for a more lucrative contract with Fox. In the *Baby Burlesks*, Temple appears not just as an object of desire but as a sexually devious and aggressive temptress. Post-Code, Hollywood framed itself, in part through Temple, as a protector of childhood's innocence, whether by putting out press materials emphasizing her healthy diet or suing Graham Greene for his naughty *Wee Willie Winkie* (Ford, 1937) review, in which he referred to the star as a "fancy little piece" and a "complete totsy."[13] The *Baby Burlesks* is an all too explicit indicator of the lie at work in the industry's presentation of itself as a vehicle of uplift and Temple's role as the embodiment of such efforts.

The matter of how to understand Temple as a vehicle for depicting sexual knowingness and innocence has centered much criticism on the star and the construction of white girlhood in the 1930s. Some scholars have taken up the work begun in Greene's review. In such accounts, Temple's attraction is primarily adult and pedophilic, a hypocritically perverse appeal made under the cover of saccharine wholesomeness.[14] In contrast, scholars such as Kristen Hatch, Lori Merish, Gaylyn Studlar, and Pamela Wojcik have used Temple's case to examine the complex cultural and political work carried forth by such superficially transparent terms as *girl* and *child*, *innocence* and *experience*. For example, Merish's work reveals cuteness's ability to connect commodity capitalism to the supposedly priceless realm of familial love. Studlar connects Temple's appeal to specific cultural practices of affection, arguing that, while derived from nineteenth-century "cosseting," her cozy on-screen interactions with adult men "redeemed masculinity" in modernity.[15] More recently, Hatch and Wojcik have suggested that Temple's innocence, in many ways drawn from her nineteenth-century progenitors, was not corrupted by modernity but promised to smooth the path into a new American age.[16] This chapter seeks to add to such discussions an analysis of the *structure* of Temple's appeal. In particular, I consider the formal, technological, and publicity mechanisms that converted all work relationships into care relationships and that made all care relationships personal rather than institutional. As a result, Temple discourse became a way not just of promoting the star as cinematic commodity but of doing so in order to push back on the idea of government as caretaker for the nation's children.

Of course, people knew Temple had appeared in films prior to *Stand Up and Cheer*, but it was more fun to celebrate Shirley's overnight success. Temple's habit of inspiring audience forgetting, despite their knowing very well, was key to the role the star served for the industry. Whether the "spontaneous" childlike performances that allowed fans to forget Temple's training and serious work ethic as child labor laws were being written, or the chaste "first kiss" of *Miss Annie Rooney* and the requisite forgetting of the decidedly unchaste *Baby Burlesks* in a post-Code era, Temple's stardom smoothed the way for the industry she represented and offered up the star for personalized audience attachments.

TEMPLE OUT OF TIME

Reviewing Temple's feature films proved challenging for most writers. This was not just because national papers found themselves having to measure the sophistication of their outlets against films aimed at middlebrow audiences; nor was it simply a matter of deciding whether the audiences for the pictures were adults or children—Temple's appeal was always to both.¹⁷ Whether positive or negative, in fan magazines or urban papers, reviews of Temple's films consistently suggest the star was a spectacle in her own right, transcending her films and resistant to the review genre itself. As Chad Newsom has argued, "reviews of her movies commonly evaluate Temple herself separately from the individual film."¹⁸ For example, *New York Times* reviewers generally agreed upon Temple's excellence, even in very mediocre pictures. In fact, the grudging allowance for her talents becomes part of the drama of a review of *Dimples* (Seiter, 1936). In his take on the film, Frank Nugent opens with an account of the mainstream audience as both feminized and distinctly middlebrow:

> The Shirley Temple-for-President Club reconvened yesterday at the Roxy and displayed flattering attention to their candidate's latest assault upon the nation's maternal instinct. "Dimples" is its apt title, apt because it is just another word for Little Miss Precocity and does not pretend to describe the story material it employs. Why they bother with titles, or with plots either for that matter, is beyond us. The sensible thing would be to announce Shirley Temple in "Shirley Temple" and let it go at that. Or to follow the example of the authors of children's books and call them "Shirley Temple in Dixie," "Shirley Temple at Cape Cod" or "Shirley Temple in Little Old New York."
>
>   This one is the Little Old New York version, the locale more specifically being the bowery.
>
>   It so happens—it always so happens in Shirley's pictures—that the pert little lassie wins the heart of the wealthy old dowager.

The review ends ambivalently: "If we must hand down our verdict, let it be relative. 'Dimples' is not the best Temple, nor the worst. . . . Now leave us alone a while; we want to brood."¹⁹ In the humorously sulky last line, Nugent plays up his role as a highbrow critic forced to encounter a relentlessly cheerful upstart, a character type that would not be out of place in a Temple film. But the review also suggests not just that Temple is the best part of otherwise worthless sentimental claptrap, or even that she transcends it, but rather that there is a critical consensus that when it comes to Temple films, plots are beside the point.

This perplexity when it comes to plots repeats across reviews in the *Times* as well as other outlets. In a review of *Now and Forever* (Hathaway, 1934), for example, a different *Times* critic, Andre Sennwald, begins with a discussion of the film's nonsensical plot: "The honorable profession of second story work comes in for another contemptuous drubbing from the scenarists in "Now and Forever," the new film at the Paramount. So simple are the problems of the craft that the photoplay finds it unnecessary to delve into the kindergarten technique by which its larcenous hero makes a success of his chosen calling."[20] But despite starting with a description of the screenplay's thinness, the review presents Temple as being so cute that she generates a logic of her own: "There is one thing that must definitely be said for this less than striking example of the drama of regeneration. The enormous charm of Shirley Temple is potent enough to make almost any character do almost anything." Like his colleague Nugent, Sennwald too occupies the role of unwilling curmudgeon brought along by Temple, who, in this case, solves the problem of poor screenwriting by providing her own narrative causality. With a description of Temple's charm as a force capable of making any character do anything, Sennwald sets the stage for his broader assessment of the actress and the film: "With Shirley's assistance it becomes, despite its violent assaults upon the spectator's credulity, a pleasant enough entertainment." Because, as reviews note again and again, there is virtually no distinction between star and role, the suspension of causal logic that appears in the film extends to real-world critical encounters as well.

Even as highbrow critics acknowledged their grouchy difference in taste from that of the "maternal" nation, it is not the case that the reviews assumed small-town theatergoers were fools taken in by poorly written scripts. Quite the opposite: reviews repeatedly note Temple's fans' indifference to story, rather than their susceptibility to it, thereby offering an account of a potentially overwhelming fandom that retains its critical capacity. The *Screen Book* magazine review of *Poor Little Rich Girl* (Cummings, 1936), for instance, offers the following rating system: three stars "if Shirley is a favorite" and a single star "if she is not."[21] A *Variety* review of *Dimples* also highlights Temple fans as a distinctive audience: "Narrative for the most part is a feeble little thing, wending its slow and uncertain way from one trite dramatic concept to another.

Regardless of the soggy humor and the straining of human interest the going of Shirley Temple with her fans won't be a bit diminished and they'll still exchange the term 'darling' among them."[22] Both reviews indicate that Temple pictures operate according to a distinctive set of rules, confounding the job of the critic. As a *Movie Classic* review of the film noted, "It is difficult to rate a Shirley Temple picture, and this one, in particular, presents a problem. The story is illogical and unconvincing—but Shirley is at her best. She sings, dances and cavorts so cleverly that her fans will not only overlook the picture's flaws, but acclaim it her best to date."[23] Seeming to give up on the critical enterprise, the review ends, "If you're a Temple fan—and who isn't?—don't miss it." Yet another reviewer agreed with this assessment of the film: "Shirley Temple is becoming embarrassing to the critic—we are constantly having to say that here is her greatest entertainment to date."[24] What seems to be embarrassing to the critic is the wide chasm between Temple's best and the cinema's, one so yawning that the quality of one has nothing to do with the other. In these reviews, Temple appears to be getting better and better even if her films, as they become more and more clichéd, are getting worse and worse.

TECHNOLOGIES OF CUTENESS

As the reviews suggest, something else was at stake in Temple's appeal. This something was her performance as commodity, as Merish has discussed. Because she was so often decontextualized, Temple became an object for audience possession: her stardom conveyed the possibility that in feeling *for* her, audiences might *have* her. In a review of *Poor Little Rich Girl*, the *Chicago Illinois American* puts the idea in rhyming form: "Who cares about a plot when we can have the Temple tot instead?"[25] This desire to *have*, which Temple and her films evoked, is part of her cuteness, which depended on her ability to remain decontextualized despite being famous and was also leveraged as an argument against governmental interventions into the caring economy.[26]

What does it mean to say that history's most popular child star is decontextualized? Certainly, she was everywhere. She appeared on the covers of numerous movie magazines and gave interviews alongside her mother; her first marriage was a major spectacle for fans as well as friends and family; and her eventual divorce and then second marriage were followed closely in the press. Temple was also part of a historical and political imaginary, linked to FDR and national economic recovery through publicity materials that served the star and the president equally, as well as films like *Stand Up and Cheer*, *Just Around the Corner*, and *Dimples*, which dealt with the Depression in more and less direct terms.[27] That audiences and critics could indulge in fantasies that "the Temple tot" could be had indicates the power of one aspect of Temple's star persona that was at odds with the glut of biographical information available. Just as Temple's performances in her films overwhelmed plot—her personality rendering narrative context moot—so too did her film appearances eclipse broader contextual knowledge of the story that was Temple's biographical life.

Throughout her films, Temple receives formal treatment that encourages fantasies of possession. Considering Temple's performances as spectacles directly feeding into such possessive desires helps to clarify why the reviews of her films are so muddled and also why audiences and journalists who were well aware of her parentage nonetheless felt she could be theirs for the having. In its staging of Temple's availability, *Curly Top* (Cummings, 1935) is exemplary, deploying a typical Temple plot and themes and presenting her as adoptable through a series of characteristic formal techniques. The film's credits open onto a series of close-ups introducing its stars, Shirley Temple, Rochelle Hudson, and John Boles. All three top-billed stars receive glamorous treatment, but Temple stands out for both the movement in the image and the implied audience address. Both Hudson and Boles appear with heads attractively angled to give a sense of jawline and cheekbone, gazes slightly off to the side. But before the adult stars appear on-screen, Temple gets top billing. The credit that introduces her opens on a shot of the top of her head, bent forward to give a close-up of the film's titular curls, thereby offering a synecdochical account of the star. Then, rather than the camera moving, Temple tilts her head upward to face the audience directly, then smiles and shakes her curls. This style of fourth-wall-puncturing close-up runs throughout the film.[28] While Boles's and Hudson's images maintain the fiction of a sealed diegetic world, Temple, here and during the narrative that follows, reaches out of the diegesis to establish a more personal relationship with her fans. As Newsom has elaborated, this performance style—created for her daughter and dubbed "dazzle" by Gertrude Temple—was a key aspect of Temple's star appeal and allowed the feeling of her precocity to be maintained even into later performances.[29] Moreover, as she would throughout her career, Temple here stands in for film more broadly, as she replaces the mechanism of the camera by undertaking the tilt via her own star body. Thus, we might begin to track the way cuteness starts to operate not just as commodity but also as technology across Temple's filmography.

The narrative's first half takes place in Lakeside Orphanage, a privately funded institution where Temple's Elizabeth and her adult sister

FIGURE 2.1 Preparing the tilt.

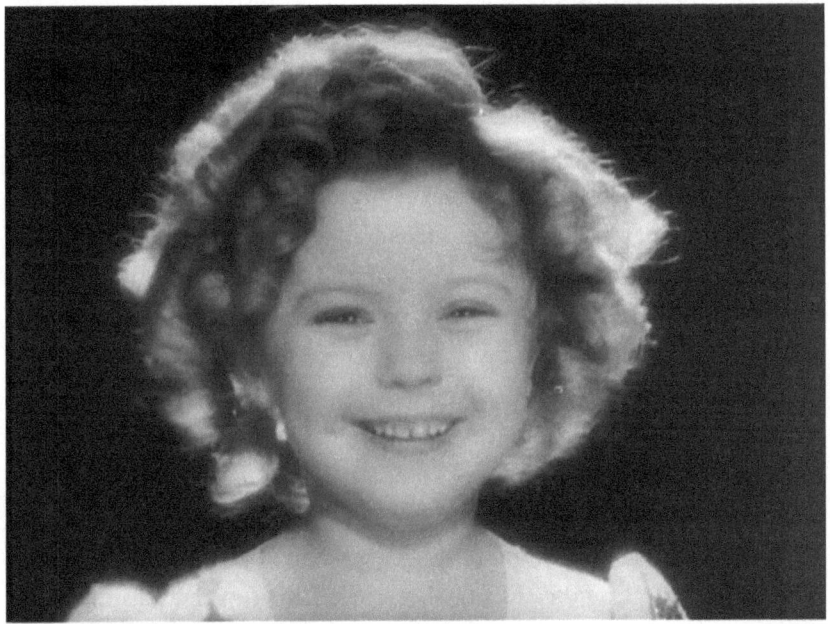

FIGURE 2.2 The big reveal.

Mary (Hudson) reside along with a number of other orphaned girls. The film cuts from an exterior shot of the building to a scene of little girls getting ready for bed and then presents a series of close-ups of girls praying at their bedsides. As the film cuts from one child to the next, Temple is withheld from viewers. Only after the orphanage matrons bid the girls goodnight does the film cut to show a pile of curls on a pillow; then, in an echo of the opening credits, the curls turn over and reveal the star's face. The pattern of withholding, anticipation, and display in these first views of the star is perhaps a residuum of what Tom Gunning describes as the cinema of attractions' willingness "to rupture a self-enclosed fictional world for a chance to solicit the attention of the spectator."[30] Revealing herself not once, but twice, to eager spectators, Temple-as-Hollywood announces through her smile, *here I am, don't I delight you?*

In addition to presenting an orphaned Temple, the film's premise is also familiar in casting Elizabeth as a natural performer: the deceased parents were show people, a convenient excuse for the film's song-and-dance numbers (most famously, "Animal Crackers in My Soup"). The "Animal Crackers" dance scene performs the work of the musical number as suggested by Richard Dyer, offering utopian feelings of energy and connection and solving plot problems through pleasing musical performance.[31] Here, as Temple cavorts through the orphanage's cafeteria, a touring group of trustees happens to catch her impromptu performance, including the grumpy old Mr. Wyckoff and the dashing Edward Morgan. With his distaste for performing children, Wyckoff becomes the negative model for audience and reviewer responses to Temple. In contrast, Morgan responds positively—so positively that he is moved to sponsor Temple's Elizabeth, setting in motion the romance and family consolidation narrative typical of Temple's filmography. Morgan will not only adopt Temple but also marry her older sister by the end of the film, reconstituting the family and pulling the talented young girl out of poverty. After Morgan takes in Elizabeth, the film traverses a number of cute set pieces, including a dinner at which the butler (Arthur Treacher) teaches Elizabeth to use cutlery appropriately, a fantasy montage of the ways Morgan spoils Elizabeth (water skis, a horse and buggy, a hula costume!), and a musical performance to raise money for the orphanage.

But before all of this occurs, a few obstacles to happiness are introduced and the film provides a series of spectacular looks at Temple. After being caught with her horse in the dormitory, for example, Temple appears in the first of a series of shots that follow the formula of the "Temple close-up": the star centered in the frame, eyes wide, looking directly at the camera, and delivering the catchphrase "oh my goodness." This shot and line delivery repeat after the "Animal Crackers" performance, again upon Elizabeth's learning of her wealthy benefactor, and, in the final shot of the film, after discovering her sister and Morgan embracing. With their frontal presentation, direct address, and "branded" image and slogan, these shots share the visual language of advertising. Indeed, so associated was "oh my goodness" with Temple that in 1936's *Poor Little Rich Girl*, Mack Gordon and Harry Revel wrote a song with this title for the star to sing. Such films give credence to Nugent's frustration—"The sensible thing would be to announce Shirley Temple in 'Shirley Temple' and let it go at that"—as Temple vehicles behave as a kind of advertising *mise en abyme*, with Temple films advertising Temple to sell more Temple. And on it goes. Morgan's fantasy montage is a particularly obvious piece of star promotion, with the scenes unfolding like living lobby cards, enumerating a number of possible scenarios for Fox's young celebrity: a bathing beauty film, a period piece, an exotic Hawaiian picture. As Morgan thinks fondly about the various scenes into which he has introduced Elizabeth, the audience also gets a look at Temple in a range of novel settings and perhaps imagines how successful she might be in future films of these types.

In addition to presenting the Temple close-up's direct appeal, *Curly Top* offers several medium close-ups of Temple with arms draped around the neck of caring, potentially adoptive parents. This is the type of "cosseting" behavior Studlar describes, and which appears throughout *The Little Colonel* as well as the teary performance of "What Would I Do Without You?" in *Dimples*. In each instance, Temple's embrace of an older man gives the motivation for that adult character's change of heart and offers a spectacle of care to audiences, thereby establishing Temple as the ultimate love object. Combined, these cinematographic patterns interact in service of Temple's star persona: the close-up creates a feeling of connection across the fourth wall, which, in turn, encourages the viewer to imagine him- or herself as embracing Temple in the manner depicted in her films' cuddly twoshots.

In addition to demonstrating the relationship between consumerism and care in commodity culture, Temple also reveals the importance of synecdoche to the cute, again suggesting the importance of the technology of cuteness to an analysis of Temple. If, as Merish and Sianne Ngai have each argued, the cute is the commodity, the delightful, somewhat anthropomorphized thing, then Temple's ability to be abstracted into parts—a *Curly Top*, *Dimples*, *Bright Eyes*, etc.—is necessarily part of her appeal.[32] As evidenced by both her film titles and the many Temple dolls that circulated, Temple's susceptibility to shorthanding was central to her stardom. From her first feature film onward, Temple appears repeatedly in spectacles of mass production. Indeed, Temple's self-imitation was crucial to her appeal, her proliferation helping audiences to imagine they might have her all while knowing she did not belong to them.

In *Stand Up and Cheer*, for example, Temple appears linked to processes of replication and the kind of bodily fracturing popularized by Busby Berkeley musicals such as *Gold Diggers of 1933*. Temple's character Shirley Dugan and her father James make a special plea against child labor laws, arguing that Shirley "doesn't really work in the act" and "just sort of comes on at the end and she loves it." The film then cuts to the song and dance number "Baby Take a Bow," which illustrates the Dugans' point. Though the song functions to introduce Fox's new child star to audiences, before Shirley appears a bizarre spectacle fills the screen. A row of identically dressed dolls "dance" in a row. As the camera tilts upward, it reveals the dolls to be part of a group of adult dancers' costumes, which include the dolls as the lower portion of pants made to dance by the performers' steps. As the dancers move aside, Temple makes her "debut" through the parting curtain of identical dolls. Singing about his daughter, Shirley's father declares, "I'm presenting her right now," to which the dancers respond, "Who's that bunch of personality?" The scene previews the treatment Temple will receive throughout her career: both the drive to mass-produce her image—whether through dolls or look-alike contests—and her dispersal into parts. Temple's "bunch of personality," while seeming to individualize, suggests the child star is constituted of a cluster of appealing traits. In other words, at this point in her career, she is more bunch than personality.

Curly Top takes this logic further, making Temple's ability to be transformed into a thing the hinge of its adoption plot. As is typical in Temple films, Morgan's decision to become Elizabeth's permanent guardian is solidified through a song—in this case, one that stages a wild synecdochical fantasy that transforms having images of children to having children. Once in love with Elizabeth, Morgan returns to his home's parlor, whose walls are adorned with a number of paintings, including Thomas Gainsborough's *Blue Boy*, Emile Renouf's *A Helping Hand*, and John Everett Millais's *My First Sermon*. After singing "It's All So New to Me" at the piano, Morgan wanders the room, gazing at the artworks on the walls, each of which becomes repopulated with an image of Temple. The close-up insert shots of the paintings are ostensibly from Morgan's point of view, but presented so frontally that this seems impossible. Importantly, each image moves, reenacting in miniature the broader

Temple phenomenon, as the Temple in the painting turns to address her fans directly by smiling, waving, or blowing a kiss. The paintings are suggestive of Temple's ability to build intimacy through a cuteness that cannot be contained by two-dimensional art forms. Whether enclosed by the cinema screen or the gilt picture frame, Temple reaches out and touches viewers directly. The scene is also pedagogical, showing that Temple's direct appeals should be responded to with forms of care. Here, contemplation of the child's image spurs correct action. Coming out of his reverie, Morgan announces to his Aunt Genevieve (Esther Dale) that "the lovely child in the painting" will be coming to live with them. As such, the song is a gloss on stardom generally, and Temple's especially: by gazing upon a spectacular star image, the song suggests, one should be moved to think of the star as one's own. Importantly, the scene also suggests not just that Temple should find a home but that contemplating images of children should spur personal, privatized care reactions.

Because Temple's films are so sentimental, it is easy to overlook their more technological effects.[33] But in both the living paintings of *Curly Top* and another film from the same year, *The Little Colonel* (Butler, 1935), the spectacle that is Temple is joined with the spectacle of film technology, thus directly linking her precocity to that of the medium. Despite its period setting, *The Little Colonel* deploys a distinctly modern film technique. Here, Temple's character, Lloyd Sherman, instigates both familial and national reconciliation by healing the rift between her Confederate colonel grandfather (Lionel Barrymore) and her Yankee-marrying mother, Elizabeth (Evelyn Venable). The film ends with a celebration in little Lloyd's honor, the "pink party" of her dreams, which, following a film otherwise recorded in black and white, is rendered in loving Technicolor. As with *Curly Top*'s paintings, *The Little Colonel*'s magical transition associates Temple with a decorative object, in this case a bouquet of roses that gradually shifts from shades of gray to rosy pinks. Also, as in *Curly Top,* the bouquet appears as an insert shot, after which the film cuts to the garden party, smoothing the transition by first focusing on a rose bush. After her mother inquires about her whereabouts, Lloyd rises up, seemingly from within the bush, wearing a dress and hair ribbons that mirror the color of the flowers. Following the image of the bouquet, the actress's cheery little face appearing among

FIGURE 2.3 Technologies of cuteness.

the leaves looks like nothing so much as a flower waiting to be gathered up and brought inside. Furthering the notion of Temple as a blossom to be plucked, the film ends with the colonel taking Lloyd into his arms, an image that reassuringly emphasizes Temple has been reestablished in a shored-up domestic setting.

PROPER CARE:
MAKING THE PROFESSIONAL PERSONAL

In addition to advertising their star, Temple films function as fairly unsubtle promotional vehicles for the industry itself, emphasizing its family-friendliness and its technological achievements. Temple's example also supported Hollywood's exemption from labor laws codified during the Depression. Her ability to do this work was quite complex.

Hatch and Wojcik have both discussed Temple's precarious position in relation to new valuations of childhood that coincided with child labor laws and redefined the twentieth-century child as "priceless," a status that argued against minors' participation in wage labor.[34] At the same time that the status of the child was sentimentalized, however, children's labor became more important to families during the Depression. And Temple's status as a working minor was particularly tricky because everyone knew how well-paid the young star was. Given the pushmi-pullyu nature of child stars' labor, Fox needed Temple to appear both unexploited—that is, not too associated with work—and unspoiled—that is, as Hatch argues, not too remunerated.[35]

In addition to inflammatory arguments that federal regulation represented a socialist overreach on the part of the federal government, "promoted under direct orders from Moscow," child labor regulation faced opposition in two primary forms: arguments against government intervention in states' rights and arguments against government intervention in the relationship between parents and their children.[36] Attempts to prevent children from wage work raised the problem of children's rights more broadly, as reformers had to assert the more nebulous "right to childhood" against what *Lochner v. New York* had established in 1905 as an individual's "liberty of contract." Particular industries and states where these industries were concentrated had their own interests in fighting regulation and often used the cover of "the family business" as well as arguments about the healthful and educative nature of work to cover economic motivations. Of these industries, agriculture, newspapers dependent on "newsies," and show business represented particularly significant cases.[37]

Temple's films often stage these debates, whether her urchin-like "Dimples" and her ragtag gang of street kids, which might have brought to mind urban child newspaper vendors, or *Stand Up and Cheer*, which contains an explicit conversation about a government that would prevent Shirley from performing in her family stage act. While Jackie Coogan's public rift from his stage parents offered a negative example of acting as an exploitative form of child labor, Gertrude Temple would carefully manage the appearance of both Shirley as laborer and herself as manager. Though not part of her public persona, Gertrude confessed in a private letter that she hoped Shirley's success would solve the family's financial woes.[38] However, in public she "insisted that her daughter's time in the studio was carefree recreation"—although by the 1930s, claims of this type were, as Kasson notes, "a common, even threadbare, defense."[39]

Studio copy and Temple's films combined to frame governmental interventions as damaging to the kind of personal relationships they insisted Temple's professional ones were. Throughout Temple's movies, a dual strategy appears: first, they treat Temple's performances as something she would do for free, even if she is sometimes paid; second, they depict government protection as interfering with natural forms of affection and care. *Curly Top*, for example, illustrates both: first through Temple's performing first spontaneously and then in the more professional context of a fundraiser for the orphanage, and second through its careful delineation of types of care. If being adopted by Morgan is preferable to life in the private orphanage, there's also a worse option on the table in the film. When the old curmudgeon reacts with disgust to the overly indulgent care at the trustee-run private orphanage, he threatens to have it shut down and the children sent to a public one. The governmental intervention here appears as the bad opposite of the interpersonal care Temple solicits from her fans.

The government's status as a potentially damaging meddler in personal affairs is perhaps nowhere as apparent as in *Stand Up and Cheer*, the film that set the stage for Temple films' arguments about appropriate care structures. Titled in the imperative, *Stand Up and Cheer* teaches audiences how to think about its child star's labor as well as their relationship to the government. The film's thin plot involves an FDR-like president appointing a "secretary of amusement" to bring America out of the Depression, explaining, "Any people with a sense of humor can weather depression." The film unfolds as an advertisement for Fox and the movies more generally, arguing that national well-being is dependent on the "discovery" of talent and healthful, good-natured cheer. Shirley Temple's father is one of the secretary's discoveries, and he and Temple put on numbers that save the economy, explained by the film's logic: "Homes are happier because children are happier.... The Depression is over!! There is no unemployment. The people are happy again!"

But despite its presentation of an FDR program as the plot's mechanism, arriving at this happy point depends much more upon personal attitudes and relationships than on the government, as illustrated by the song "I'm Laughing," which features a number of laborers singing lines such as "I'm laughing, and I've got nothing to laugh about / I'm laughing, and brother, so can you" and "I'm laughing, and there's a mortgage around my neck." Moreover, as would be the case throughout Temple's career, governmental care here interferes in the redemptive personal relationships so crucial to her films' plots. Before Temple can perform, Shirley's father, Jimmy Dugan, has to see Cromwell, the secretary of amusement, "about a new rule . . . that a kid under seven can't work in an act," to which Cromwell responds, "we had to make that ruling comply with the laws of the various states." Here, official policy is arbitrary and unfeeling, as opposed to Dugan's knowledge about what is best for his daughter. This moment exemplifies the problem of a state that does not value fatherhood. As Wojcik has argued, "Temple's affiliation with men goes against not only the maternal logic of cuteness but also state and economic logic that links dependent children to mothers, not fathers," as in the case of the Aid to Dependent Children (ADC) portion of the 1935 Social Security Act.[40] Exerting his parental expertise against the state, Dugan explains, "She thrives on it . . . I gotta have her with me." This personalized explanation works on Cromwell, and the scene cuts to the "Baby Take a Bow" number discussed earlier, a scene change indicating that, with government interference disposed of, Shirley and her fans can get what they really want.

In addition to the films' campaign against government care, Gertrude Temple also curated Temple's public image and carefully managed press materials about her daughter, exchanging access to Shirley for editorial approval. In manuscripts at the Margaret Herrick Library, a number of documents feature the sign-off "G. Temple" along with a great deal of redacted material. The changes Gertrude Temple requests often work to normalize the young star's childhood and make Shirley's choices seem natural rather than professional, even if it means correcting what one imagines to have been objective facts. For example, in the draft of a *Motion Picture* article, a description of Temple's appearance—"Enchanting to the eye in a navy blue divided skirt, a blouse of white with navy blue polka dots, her hair in curlers, a white visor shading her eyes"—is corrected by Gertrude to replace the word "curlers" so that the copy reads "her hair tied under a scarf."[41] Elsewhere in the piece, Mrs. Temple corrects the young Temple's slangy speech, "I wouldn't want to be a runt," as well as examples of a perhaps overly involved mother-daughter relationship.[42] She revises a sentence that specified Shirley "accepting, without argument, her mother's dictum that she could not go into the pool with the other children, there being too many colds about" to a more generalized sentence that reads "accepting, without argument, her mother's dictums."[43] And lest she face accusations about putting her daughter on a diet, Gertrude suggests an addition of "Shirley never has liked butter" to follow a sentence that describes the young star ordering her vegetables without the fattening condiment.[44] In one document, Shirley's recollection of her bedtime routine reveals the elaborate process by which her curls are achieved: "And then, after my bath, Mummy puts my hair up in bobby pins, sixty-two curls on thirty-one bobby pins. It makes it easier to fix in the mornings if we do it that way. And while mummy is putting up the curls Daddy reads to me." In place of Shirley's description, Gertrude supplies the following handwritten suggestion: "And then, after my bath, Mummy combs my hair and Daddy reads to me."[45] Throughout, the older Temple's marks and suggestions work to erase the artifice involved in her daughter's appearance and the labor involved in producing the image of cuteness.

Much like the Fox publicity that presented Shirley as an overnight star, Gertrude's edits controlled for aspects of her daughter's star persona that leaned too far into professionalism. In particular, discussions that place Temple in relationship to the industry or a broader craze for child stardom are redacted, as well as too specific references to studio life. For example, in a draft of a story that recounts Temple's thoughts on the Dionne quintuplets, Gertrude subtracts more than she adds. Her deletions include a paragraph in which Shirley tells the reporter that she has one of the quints' pony carts and that "My studio gave it to me. I mean, our studio gave it to me."⁴⁶ Also axed is a philosophical consideration of her similarity to these other child actors: "'Yes,' sighed Shirley comfortably, 'we would have a great deal in common, the quints and I.'"⁴⁷ There are a number of ways to read Gertrude Temple's edits. First, Gertrude preferred Shirley to appear in the context of adults rather than other children, lest she be compared unfavorably to the competition. Second, as Hatch recounts, popular discourse about stage mothers had begun to cast this type as a particularly nasty figure—an unnatural parent profiting off of rather than supporting her young.⁴⁸ Finally, in Shirley's sighed supposition about her connection to the quints, readers might hear it implied that while the actress would share common experience with the famous and extraordinary quintuplets, she would not feel such connection to average American children. Alongside other revisions, this last redaction suggests an attempt to make Shirley seem less Hollywood and more accessible to her wide fan base.

Doing so required recasting Shirley's relationship with the company she worked for as well. Gertrude Temple's edits indicate that she may have believed her daughter's relationship with Fox needed to be put in much more human terms. For example, in a telegram to *Radio Stars* magazine, reporter Gladys Hall writes, "Mrs. Temple would like following changes in my story. . . . change her guard and two men to group of studio friends."⁴⁹ In the notes for a later article for *Modern Screen*, Hall's handwriting on the typed page reads, "Read to Mrs. Temple over telephone 4/1/39 okayed with changes."⁵⁰ The changes included cutting the following paragraph, which, in asserting Temple's normal childhood, describes something very unusual: "Nor does Shirley have a sense of being patrolled. She sleeps entirely alone in her bedroom at home. No guard sits on duty outside her door, as is the practice with many of the children of the stars. Radio beam installations take care of the business of guarding Shirley, efficiently but impersonally, and without her knowledge. The guard who goes on duty at the Temple home at nightfall goes on after Shirley goes to bed and is gone when she rises in the mornings."⁵¹ In addition to recasting professional relationships as friendships and asserting Shirley's normalcy, Gertrude Temple's removal of information about Fox's detectives and guards also keeps her daughter open for fantasies of interpersonal care. This is why the story of her relationship with an adult Black man, the dancer Bill "Bojangles" Robinson, whom Temple referred to as "Uncle Billy," was so popular.[52] The very intimate, nearly familial relationship with Robinson was part of the Temple promotional package, which tended to make all adults around her surrogate caregivers. By contrast, stories of detectives and guards likely made too explicit Temple's status as a financial investment, rather than a child in need of affectionate care.

TEMPLE AGES OUT

As a child, Temple was a star impervious to reviewing. And though her stardom outlasted that of Farina/Allen Hoskins, Shirley Temple's adolescence was similarly accompanied by a fall from popularity. Unlike Hoskins, however, Temple remained in the public eye, both as a celebrity and as an on-screen presence, though her film appearances met with cooler responses as she aged. In her autobiography, *Child Star,* Temple is brutally self-aware of the challenges faced by Zanuck in marketing his aging star: "No longer a cuddly child, I increasingly needed to establish my appeal to adult audiences. Yet the less I remained a child, the less my charm could be sustained for a new generation of children."[53]

Even as Temple's box office appeal waned, however, magazine profiles and human interest stories continued to portray a beloved star growing into a lovely young woman.[54] In fan magazine pieces about Temple marrying, divorcing, or having children, a different version of the Temple precocity narrative is rehearsed. Repeatedly, the articles emphasize her maturity while casting her sensible nature backward through time to remind readers 'twas ever thus with young Shirley. For example, a press release from RKO, the studio that would pair Temple with her first husband, John Agar, in *Fort Apache* (Ford, 1948) and *Adventure in Baltimore* (Wallace, 1949), features an interview with the star on her eighteenth birthday: "Hollywood, May 2—Shirley Temple tossed a spoonful of sugar into her coffee and sighed audibly: 'It's been a long, long time!'

Miss Temple wasn't crooning the jitterbug lullaby of the same name. She had reference to her 16 years as ward of the State of California. This period of regimentation is now over, for Shirley turned 18 last week. Now she's an adult—officially!"[55] Occasioned by Temple's graduation from her minority and titled "Miss Marker Grows Up," the press release implies that while on paper she has been a child, that was only the official line. In contrast, the story presents readers with a coffee-drinking, somewhat world-weary professional married woman, one who has been oppressed by the state's intervention in her personal life, an interference that seems particularly inappropriate given the star's status as a Mrs.: " 'It's been so silly!' said Shirley as we breakfasted in the RKO Studio Cafe. 'Here I am a married woman, yet I've had to attend school four hours a day, take an afternoon nap, and ask permission every time I wanted to do anything other than sleep, eat, or breathe.' "[56] For any long-term fan of Temple, the press release would have felt familiar, a story of a young woman who had found love and made a family, only to face the obstacle of an overly intrusive government. The language "ward of the state" could easily be lifted from *Curly Top* or any number of Temple's early orphan pictures.

But when it came to discussions of her later films and their performance at the box office, trade periodicals and fan magazines took a markedly different turn. Whereas it had been a critical and popular consensus that the child Temple elevated all around her, bringing star power to the weakest of plots, after Fox "retired" their star, her publics held her responsible for a string of mediocre pictures. The *New York Times*, which had granted Temple's excellence even while grumbling over her films' thin plots, turned against the actress as she entered puberty. The paper's review of *Kathleen* (Bucquet, 1941) notes: "MGM, her new sponsors, haven't done right by our Shirley. Out of her indubitable charm they have created a vexatious, pucker-faced little brat full of sugary daydreams to make an audience wince. They have confronted her proven talents with stilted situations that even a Duse couldn't carry off." The review ends somewhat sympathetically toward the actress, albeit without offering any compliments to the film: "In those wistful, winsome close-ups Miss Temple seemed to be trying to say just one thing: 'Get me out of here.' "[57] A year later, Temple bears the brunt of the critic's distaste for *Miss Annie Rooney*, the film publicized as containing the actress's first kiss.[58] If an adolescent Temple playing at babyish pouting was distasteful in *Kathleen*, the *Times* did not find improvement in Temple's portrayal of a teen in what it described as "a very grim little picture." Part of the problem with the film seems to be the age of Temple and her character:

> Gone are the days of the toddling tot, the days of milk-teeth and tonsils. Instead, we now see a Miss Temple in the awkward age between the paper-doll and sweater-girl period, an adolescent phenomenon who talks like a dictionary of jive and combines this somehow with quotations from Shakespeare and Shaw. She even is allowed to register slight comprehension when young Dickie Moore—tchk, tchk!—places a tentative peck on her left cheek. Miss Temple seemed impressed, the folk in the Rivoli balcony just depressed.

The review ends by asking, "Meanwhile, couldn't Miss Temple be kept in school for just a little while?"[59] Looking back, the adult star shared similar views, referring to *Miss Annie Rooney* as a "forgettable" film that nonetheless plagued her as it "continued to glow like some nocturnal fungus."[60] Of *Kathleen*, she offers the offhand remark: "Things were slowly changing. At last, I was only one-half an orphan."[61]

Nowhere, though, was the criticism of Temple as pointed as in the notes from theater owners, doubtless disappointed to see a highly marketable star decline into an uncertain product. *Motion Picture Herald* ran a regular column called "What the Picture Did for Me" that featured letters from theaters around the country reporting on local audiences' responses to the current crop of films. The letters often locate the blame for a given film's failure with Temple herself, and her age in particular. Typical notes from small-town theater owners evidence Temple's core audience abandoning their star in her teen years. One from Columbia City, Indiana had this to say about *Miss Annie Rooney*:

> Shirley should rest on her laurels. "Kathleen" failed and now this one. The first was nothing to shout about and neither is this. We thought that perhaps under a different producer she would come through, which

she did not. She is not as attractive in her adolescence, either, as she appeared to be. What you would call in golf, pressing. So regretfully, we are ringing down the curtain on Shirley.–A.E. Hancock, Columbia Theatre, Columbia City, Ind. Small town patronage.[62]

A letter from Herminie, Pennsylvania, this one about *Blue Bird* (Lang, 1940), also notes the problem of the star's age, speaking directly to the actress: "Yes, Shirley, go to college and when you graduate we will look you over."[63] Other theaters owners reported empty seats, unhappy audiences, and, in the case of a Colorado theater, the need to lower ticket prices, even with a holiday weekend opening.[64] To the former child star no longer young enough to sustain the nonnarrative spectacles of cuteness that had made her so very appealing, theater owners and audiences repeated the message that it was time to disappear from view.

The late films themselves stand as a reminder that Temple's appeal, like Farina's before her, had involved a kind of temporal suspension. In addition to aging, her movement from cute commodity to unappealing adolescent involved a fall into narrative and character. *Young People* (Dwan, 1940), Temple's last film on the Fox contract, showcases a twelve-year-old Temple as an orphan named Wendy who has been adopted and raised by a pair of vaudeville performers, Joe and Kit Ballantine. The first ten minutes of the film rapidly chronicles Wendy's showbiz childhood, including her gradual inclusion in the Ballantines' act. Notably, these early scenes feature footage of Temple from her earlier Fox films, including the hula-dancing set piece from *Curly Top* and "Baby Take a Bow" from *Stand Up and Cheer*. These moments, partially incorporated into the film's narrative but recognizable to the longtime fans who would have constituted *Young People*'s audience, literalize the Temple out-of-time phenomenon as Fox once again presents an adorable baby Shirley to gaze upon. Even in a film that thematized Temple's retirement from the studio and focused quite explicitly on allowing young people to grow up, the spectacle of Temple's perpetual youth constitutes one of the film's most appealing aspects.

In contrast, the twelve-year-old Temple, even as she receives some close-ups, suffers from narrative integration. As critics noted, the film drags. In a speech announcing the Ballantines' retirement from vaudeville to establish a normal life in small-town America—the central plot of the film—Temple tells the diegetic audience it is "hard to say goodbye to an old friend" and exits the stage to strains of "Auld Lang Syne." The film clearly addresses long-term Temple fans with the moment. Nonetheless, with its retirement-based plot and publicity as Temple's last film, *Young People* clearly recognizes that the Temple who will be missed is the spectacularly cute one resurrected by movie magic in the film's early scenes. *Kathleen*, made a year later for MGM, features Temple as a spoiled little rich girl with an absent widowed father. Playing a brat, or at least moody, Temple is clearly acting rather than inhabiting her star persona, and her performance is largely integrated into the film's narrative. With the exception of a dream sequence involving a relatively subdued performance of "Around the Corner," Temple sings and dances very little in the picture. She participates in a round of "Row, Row, Row Your Boat" with her father and his date, but the song occurs as part of the film's ongoing narrative, not a distinct musical number. As in *Young People* before it, Temple's appearance in close-ups and medium shots feature her acting—the "wistful, winsome" closeups—rather than beaming out at her fans across the fourth wall. Theater owners and critics seemed in agreement that this was not the Temple who made box office gold. Shots in which Temple performed a new part while delivering lines projected an inauthentic impression of a character, as opposed to the nonnarrativized star persona audiences so loved.

Perhaps it is not surprising, then, that in 1940, as the actress faced negative reviews and uncertain employment, baby Temple appeared on theater screens once more with the rerelease of her more wholesome, pre-Fox two-reelers, including *Dora's Dunking Donuts* (1933) and *Pardon My Pups* (1934). An ad from the distributor Commonwealth Pictures blasts "At last!," as it promotes "Shirley Temple lovable darling of the screen in a series of delightful two-reel comedies."[65] Truly timeless, this baby darling appears in the ad as the thing audiences have been waiting for, even as they would increasingly reject the aging actress.

II
THE NOBODIES

3

"FEAST YOUR EYES, GLUT YOUR SOUL"

Feeling with Lon Chaney

At 3:00 p.m. on August 28, 1930, all work in Hollywood came to a stop. At every studio in town and every MGM office around the globe, phones ceased ringing, cameras stilled, and business chatter paused as the film industry observed two minutes of silence to memorialize "The Man of a Thousand Faces."

The press surrounding Lon Chaney's death and funeral registered the industry's great love for the actor, but it also painted a much darker picture of his special relationship to film acting. Although complications related to bronchial cancer may have been his killer, popular discourse blamed Chaney's death on the extreme transformations to which he subjected himself over the course of his career. The *New Movie Magazine* made its case in particularly melodramatic terms: "A poet has said that each man kills the thing he loves. It was the thing he loved that killed Lon Chaney."[1] The magazine article then details several of Chaney's most famous and physically grueling performances, explaining: "The real beginning of the end came years ago when Chaney was doing 'The Hunchback of Notre Dame' and 'The Phantom of the Opera' and 'The Penalty.' And the picture with Joan Crawford, in which he played the unknown—an armless and legless man."[2] In addition to demonstrating a remarkably poor understanding of cancer, tragic stories of impending doom added to Chaney's star persona a sense of Chaney as both very close to disability and harmed by that proximity. The Associated Press article covering his funeral, for example, paid special attention to the presence of "numerous deaf-mutes who came to the chapel, Chaney having been an especial hero to them, not only because one or two of his screen characters were thus afflicted but because both of his parents were deaf and dumb."[3] Across postmortem discussions of Chaney as well as publicity during his lifetime, journalists linked the actor to disability, a connection described in ambivalent terms throughout his career.

Two years later, one of Chaney's pallbearers, his friend and frequent collaborator Tod Browning, released a film that relied on performers with disabilities, rather than the impressions of disability that characterized Chaney's work. The 1932 sound film *Freaks* (Browning, 1932) has since become a cult classic—a macabre horror picture that centers on the revenge wrought by circus freaks when a normate woman wrongs one of their own. In the fields of film studies and disability studies, the film has proved a rather difficult interpretive nut to crack. On the one hand, some scholars read *Freaks* as tremendously sympathetic to the actors with microcephaly, quadriplegia, or dwarfism who appear in the film. For these readings, which focus on the moral monstrosity and eventual punishment of the able-bodied "big people," the film portrays the sideshow community as loving, loyal, and normative in various ways—particularly regarding the sanctity of marriage, which the able-bodied big woman betrays by entering falsely into wedlock with the carnival's "midget" Franz.[4] On the other hand, some scholars identify the scene late in the film in which the freaks chase the screaming big woman through a dark and stormy night as retaining the idea of difference as monstrous.[5] This becomes particularly problematic at the film's end, when the big woman's punishment is her transformation, or "enfreakment," into a hybrid bird-woman, a metamorphosis that suggests being visibly disabled is a horrible fate after all. The paradox at the heart of *Freaks*—insisting on the dignity of people with disfigurements and disabilities while also positioning such differences as terrifying punishments—is just the most problematically spectacular instance of a conundrum that silent horror films had been exploring in the decade leading up to sound: where was the line between exploitative display and invitation to sympathy?

The problem with *Freaks*, it would seem, is the film's lack of clarity about how it wants its audiences to *feel*. However, it is this chapter's contention that the affective caginess of pre-Code horror in fact constitutes the genre's ethical contributions, and Chaney's in particular, especially in contrast to film magazine discourse around the star. In partnership with Browning and in collaboration with other directors, Chaney created film meditations on the promises and limits of such seemingly noble affective modes as identification and sympathy—the very feelings that press accounts described Chaney as specially embodying.[6] Against a backdrop of various modes of policing sympathy in the public sphere, Chaney's work explored the gap between ethics and affects, insisting on the nonequivalence between feeling right and doing right, largely by placing roadblocks in the way of the former, an experiment that reached its full expression in *The Phantom of the Opera*. In contrast, what we see in press coverage of Chaney is an attempt to achieve ethical person-to-person relations through the eradication of difference—a finding of similarity beneath foreignness.[7]

In his definitional study *The Philosophy of Horror*, Noël Carroll takes as his central question the matter of why "we subject ourselves to fictions that will horrify us" via a genre he describes as constituted by a "curious admixture of attraction and repulsion."[8] Carroll's classic, if not uncontroversial, account of horror emphasizes not just fear but also disgust, specifically around issues of physical contact and impurity. Although Carroll's reading emphasizes moral horror, the disgust response he describes could as easily be applied to negative reactions toward people with disfigurements. The similarities between Carroll's account of the horrifying and prejudiced reactions toward people with disfigurement should not surprise us, as the horror genre is also the one that most consistently trades in popular fears in its representation of disabled, maimed, or disfigured characters. Or, as that exemplar of film reviewing, the Boy Scouts of America's *Boys' Life*, writes of Chaney's performance in *The Unknown*:

> Lon Chaney is a good example, perhaps the great example of the possibilities in character acting on the screen. We have just been seeing him in a new release, *The Unknown*, and an old one, *Mr. Wu*, both

Metro-Goldwyn-Mayer productions. The make-up and poise in the dual rôles of Mr. Wu, give place in the new picture to remarkable stunt acting as to the armless wonder of a circus. As such he throws knives, eats and drinks entirely with the use of his feet. Outside the circus the arms are released from the body straps. The picture is a startling and weird piece of acting.[9]

The Boy Scouts' reaction to Chaney exemplifies the kind of look at disability that has centered disability studies' skepticism toward the horror genre.[10] If the reviewer does not exactly describe disgust, in calling the film "startling and weird," the writer appears to experience something like what Ato Quayson refers to as "aesthetic nervousness," which is "coextensive with the nervousness regarding the disabled in the real world."[11] The sense that disability's representation and "real" experiences of disability are proximal has guided film scholarship in the area as well.

Published not long after Carroll's treatise, Martin Norden's *The Cinema of Isolation* takes horror films as an especially offensive category for many of the habits of representation articulated by Carroll as the source of horror's fascination. Among the tropes Norden describes is the "obsessive avenger" type, a negative stereotype he credits Browning and Chaney with creating and that he explains created a view of people with disabilities in 1920s cinema as "physically and psychically wounded animals—threats to the patriarchal order that needed punishment."[12] Although he gives no treatment of *The Phantom of the Opera* (Julian, 1925), he offers this take on *Freaks*: "The unsettling film that resulted alternates between cloying sentimentality and outrageous exploitation."[13] Although Norden focuses primarily on the film's creation of negative stereotypes, it is perhaps the audience reaction to horrific presentations of disability that is most concerning: the possibility that faced with "outrageous exploitation," audiences may react with dehumanizing disgust. If Carroll's claims about horror are right, this is significant because, as the cognitive film theorist Brigitte Peucker so succinctly puts it, "Cognitive and phenomenological approaches to perception alike tell us that spectatorial affect is 'real' even when it is film and not reality that produces it. Thus the emotional and bodily response of the spectator can be said to extend textuality into the real world."[14] In other words, while audiences know that the Phantom is fantastical or that bird-woman hybridity is an impossible form of disability, the feelings these characters inspire are nonfictional. But just because feelings matter does not mean they are easily changed—a problem Lon Chaney repeatedly staged, offering a sustained performance of difference in tension with his star discourse.

FILM, SPECTACLE, PUBLICS

The Chaney and Browning horror films of the 1920s and early 1930s foregrounded their presentation of criminality and gruesome visages, offering up spectacles of nonnormativity that flouted regulations seeking to remove visible differences from public view. Earlier, the so-called ugly laws had criminalized the public display of visible disability. Then, in the 1930s, the Code, which forbade gruesomeness as well as violations of the laws of both man and nature, effectively limited the variety of people who might appear in public view. As Susan Schweik details, the ugly laws meant to regulate "unsightly beggars" focused on the supposed violence done by people with disabilities to the visual field.[15] Such laws passed in a number of cities from the late nineteenth to early twentieth century, with Chicago's 1881 law being the most infamous. The Chicago ordinance reads:

> Any person who is diseased, maimed, mutilated or in any way deformed so as to be an unsightly or disgusting object, or an improper person to be allowed in or on the streets, highways, thoroughfares or public places in this city shall not therein or thereon expose himself or herself to public view under penalty of one dollar for each offense. On the conviction of any person for a violation of this section, if it shall seem proper and just, the fine provided for may be suspended, and such person detained at the police station, where he shall be well cared for, until he can be committed to the county poor house.[16]

The ugly laws reveal correspondences among political, ethical, affective, and aesthetic mappings, as judgments of beauty and ugliness became ways of deciding who could be seen and whose appearance deserved punishment. Moreover, the laws turned affective and aesthetic judgments into material practices as the so-called unsightly beggars were forcibly removed from the streets.

Film history offers a corresponding tale of who should occupy the visual field and how, seemingly taking up the policing of disability's display forwarded by the ugly laws. The early horror film's spectacular display of nonnormative faces and disability *might* be attributed to the sense of containment provided by the demonstration space, as opposed to the space of the city street regulated by the ugly laws. Because of the frame's reassuring delimitation of off- and on-screen—essential to Carroll's account of film horror—nondisabled spectators *might* partake freely in looking that would be less acceptable outside the theater. However, both film theory and film history offer reasons to question the idea of the frame as a clean break, quarantining the character with a disability from the normate gazing spectator. For example, Laura Marks argues that films can evoke sensory environments, giving audiences a distinctly embodied experience.[17] And in her work on affect and horror, Peucker reviews the long history of linking the mouth and eye as sensory organs through which one takes the external into the self, thus establishing the relationship between visual and gustatory tastes. Peucker's conception of eye as mouth can help explain both the ugly laws' strange sense of people with disfigurement as somehow violating passersby and Hollywood's regulation of the visual field during the Code years.[18] This sense of the image as feast to be incorporated bodily becomes crucial to Chaney's pre-Code engagement with disfigurement.

Like today's theorists, censors who wrote and applied the Code also knew that film had effects and affects worth attending to. In particular, the Code had implications for the horror genre and, in turn, for filmic treatments of disability. Principle 1 states: "No picture should lower the moral standards of those who see it. This is done when the sympathy of the audience is thrown on the side of crime, wrong-doing, evil, sin." Principle 3 continues in a similar vein: "Law, natural or divine, shall not be belittled, ridiculed, nor must a sentiment be created against it." Other parts of the Code warn against discussions of "impure love," "exposure" of the body, and "vulgarity," which included "disgusting, unpleasant subjects."[19] In her important work on disability and eugenics in early horror, Angela Smith reads the Code's ban on gruesomeness as part of a "eugenic imperative to protect America by identifying the defective body, corralling it, and in extreme instances, disposing it."[20] Some thirty years after the height of the ugly laws, then, Hollywood began undertaking its own campaign, limiting both what could be shown and, importantly, which persons deserved sympathy.[21]

In the wake of the Code, the kind of empathy earlier films showed to disabled figures was foreclosed, and the monsters of the horror genre became less realistic depictions of human difference (in keeping with the taboos on undue exposure and gruesomeness), as witnessed by the explosion of Universal's Mummy, Dracula, and Frankenstein franchises. For example, in Dwight Codr's work on Boris Karloff's influential *Frankenstein* (1931) and polio, he notes, "What surprises is how few films directly confronted the epidemic."[22] But if we take the imaginative leap to see the Code as a latter-day instantiation of the ugly laws, then the simultaneously off-screen and on-scene nature of disability and illness in post-1930 horror should not surprise us at all. American spectators and gatekeepers of decency alike had long had an ambivalent relationship to spectacles of disability. As the Code was enforced, ambiguity around who or what was immoral, gruesome, or, to use the language of the ugly laws, "unsightly or disgusting" evaporated. Pre-Code, Chaney's characters were not so clearly villains, even as they offered bodily difference as a site of horror—thereby holding out the possibility for experiments in sympathy and identification.

SYMPATHETIC FILMMAKERS, CONTAGION HYSTERIA

Known for the depths of their sympathy for people with disabilities, Chaney's and Browning's lives offered romantic and tragic tales linked in biographies to their contact with people with disabilities and their own experiences with disability. However, each also has his own history with the commercial exploitation of disability. Together, Chaney and Browning collaborated on a "circus cycle" of films for MGM that featured not just disability but also the display of disability.[23] As others have noted, Browning's interest in portraying the circus sideshow on-screen is belated, showing the filmmaker's nostalgia for both the cinema's more anarchic beginnings and an earlier moment of more carnivalesque entertainments: the vaudeville review, the freak show, the carnival circuit.[24] Focusing on the circus and sideshow as sites of display, Browning's films foreground experiences of looking. As such, we can understand the director as being at least as invested in exploring the way audiences (both on the screen and off) reacted to disability and disfigurement as he was in disability and disfigurement themselves.

A native Kentuckian, Browning ran away from home to join the circus—the setting of many of his films and the place where he first developed friendships with sideshow performers.[25] Later, Browning would insist on casting people with disabilities in *Freaks,* rather than using actors with makeup, as he had in his earlier collaborations with Chaney. Browning would have to defend this choice to MGM, which received complaints, including from F. Scott Fitzgerald (doing a stint as a screenwriter), about the presence of actors with disabilities on the studio lots. As a historical side note, the disgust Fitzgerald felt at having to share a workplace cafeteria with Browning's cast shows that the modernist author did not experience Browning's transfer of sympathies. Instead, Fitzgerald reported that he had to run out of the cantina to vomit after sharing a lunch table with the conjoined Hilton sisters.[26] In addition to his work with society's outcasts, Browning experienced facial disfigurement firsthand. In 1915, he drove a car into a moving train, killing his passenger and leaving himself with facial injuries, missing teeth, a shattered leg, and (falsely) rumored castration.[27]

For his part, Chaney made a career of playing characters with disabilities or disfigurements, a habit the narratives around his star persona linked to biographical experience. The actor was raised by deaf parents and put himself through physical tortures to create the characters he portrayed—figures who, in their turn, experience extreme suffering in their filmic story worlds. Together, press, biography, and film roles produced an account of Chaney as proximally disabled. For example, a January 1920 *Motion Picture Classic* article credits the actor's talent to his parents, explaining: "Both his parents are deaf and dumb, his mother from birth, his father since he was three. This is, without doubt, the secret of his remarkably expressive face, which mirrors every fleeting thought, for, of necessity, he early mastered the art of pantomime."[28] And in *Photoplay*'s February 1928 issue, Ruth Waterbury locates the source of Chaney's flexible face in his mother's disability: "Lon Chaney was the second of four children born to deaf and dumb parents.... Through the necessity of talking to and understanding his mother he unconsciously learned the art of pantomime."[29] In addition to describing a continuity between Chaney's parentage and his adult career, the press also often reported on the great physical tolls his roles took on Chaney's body, offering a kind of contagion narrative and suggesting the costs of too much of the wrong kind of sympathy that would blur the boundaries between persons with disabilities and those without disabilities.[30] In the *Photoplay* article, Waterbury also reports that "to endure pain for his work brought him a strange joy," an observation that ties Chaney's lived pain to his characters' fictional pain, hinting at a perversity in the performer.[31]

While the idea that physical mimicry should produce emotional identification is not shocking, the publicity around Chaney is so thoroughly committed to the idea of slippage between emotional and bodily likeness that it reverses the causality of physical imitation, casting emotional connection as physical threat. Chaney's stardom thus became a cautionary tale about reacting to the other too much in kind.[32] In the discourse around Chaney's filmography and star persona, too much feeling *for* quickly tips into a dangerously contaminating feeling *with* and feeling *like*, as journalists described the star's interest in portraying the feelings of people with disabilities as threatening to make him join their ranks. The rhetoric that surrounds Chaney's performance as the paraplegic underworld mastermind Blizzard in *The Penalty* (Worsley, 1920) is exemplary.

The film opens with the wrongful maiming of a young child who will grow up to be Chaney's character. Having suffered a traffic accident, the unconscious boy is brought to the operating room of a novice doctor who, rather than performing the correct surgery on a contusion at the base of the boy's head (the cause of the paralysis), mistakes the symptoms for the cause and amputates the boy's legs. As he comes to, the young boy overhears the doctor discussing his mistake, and the seeds for the film's revenge plot are planted. To portray the vengeful Blizzard, Chaney bound his legs tightly behind him and walked on his kneecaps throughout the filming. This immersion in his character was so excruciating that scholars and critics have credited Chaney's physical transformation with both the intensity of his performance—indeed, we often see Chaney's face contorted, gnashing his teeth—and permanently transforming the actor's body, impairing his leg function from then on. A year after the film, a suggestive entry in *Photoplay*'s "Questions and Answers" column responds to a query by answering "*Lon Chaney* is not really a cripple, although he did look it in 'The Penalty,' as the legless man."[33] In such discussions, a too-close sympathy between actor and disabled character raises the specter of contaminating disability as Blizzard's movements become conflated with Chaney's.

The specter of contamination spurred two seemingly contradictory tracks of conversation in Chaney's star discourse. On the one hand, the press emphasized Chaney as a friend to the little guy, to the disfigured, the disabled, and the down-and-out—a sympathy that threatened to overwhelm the performer. For even as the papers lauded Chaney for his ability to identify with those who might be grouped with the ugly laws' "unsightly beggars," they also offered his case as a cautionary tale, noble perhaps, but ultimately tragic. On the other hand, another line of discourse emphasized Chaney's healthful normativity, often by juxtaposing a hyperbolically gruesome appearance that Chaney removes with a wholesome "true" self. In her *Photoplay* article on Chaney, Waterbury looks about for the actor and finds herself startled: "Up against the roof of the stage, some thirty feet high, was a monster bat, waving a friendly hand at me."[34] Here, the excess on both ends—the grotesque appearance of the bat costume and the exaggerated friendliness of the actor—works to distance the actor from the characters he plays and to encourage identification only with the actor. In such accounts, reporters made clear that fan identification with the famous performer need not entail identifying with the characters he portrays on screen.

The problem presented by Chaney's proximity to disability was especially acute because of his status as a particular favorite for children. The *Youth's Companion*, a children's magazine that ran a contest to win an autographed makeup box from Chaney, reveals the ambivalence with which Chaney was marketed to this demographic.[35] Unlike the Boy Scouts magazine, which prudishly found Chaney plain "startling" and "weird," the *Youth's Companion* leaned into the titillating strangeness of the favorite star's roles and life on a film set more generally, reporting, for example, "I recently saw Lon Chaney partaking of a screen meal of light pink frankfurters and blue sauerkraut. If Lon's hot dogs had been photographed naturally, their too-vivid red would have made them appear black on screen. And the sauerkraut had to be tinted with huckleberry juice. And how would you like to drink pink milk?" Another moment in the same story on Hollywood tidbits features the star as an answer to the trivia question, "Who was the only movie star to ever make up his eyeball?"[36] The fan contest to win his makeup box evidences both Chaney's popularity and its threatening nature, suggesting a nationwide fanbase eager to transform as Chaney transformed himself. The magazine indicates that the violence, strangeness, and bodily difference of the adult actor's various characters would appeal to young boys even as, at odd moments, the magazine also works to manage this appeal, trying to render boy fans' appetites a tamer thing.

Distinguishing the star's appeal to different fan bases was crucial to the way the fan magazines worked to package his appeal, sensing, it would seem, his relatively straightforward appeal to the young boys who constituted much of his fan base as well as the sorrowful and gruesome image he seemed to present to the adults who also found meaning in his films. Bizarrely, for example, the children's magazine includes a tempting review of *Mr. Wu* while also warning that the film should not be shown to impressionable young fans: "'Mr. Wu,' Metro-Goldwyn-Mayer's exquisitely composed and photographed study of a high-caste

Chinese gentleman who uncompromisingly accepts the tremendous sacrifice his code of honor involves, is too intense and terrible in theme for juvenile audiences. Adults, however, will learn from it much of Oriental traditions and philosophy."[37] Bracketing the dubious claim about the film's educational value for the mature film fan, the warning uses language that would doubtless appeal to its youthful readers gobbling up details about Chaney's bodily modifications and strange on-set repasts.

Managing Chaney's stardom thus corresponded in part to managing boyish desires. In the opening to an article tied to the makeup box contest, the *Youth's Companion* rehearses the typical attributes of the Chaney star persona while also clarifying the necessity of this fundamentally incoherent characterization: "Lon Chaney hates interviews. . . . Because of this he is 'bad medicine' to any interviewer. But the Lon Chaney that I know is the most regular of fellows, and the most lonesome of lone wolves. Full dress and anything pertaining to society are his pet aversions. Yet he likes all athletic sports and is always to be seen at every big meet. His greatest hobby, though, is boys—real boys, and they love him."[38] Following the ambivalent characterization that insists that despite his antisocial tendencies, Chaney is a regular guy (a jock, even!), the article goes on to draw moral lessons that might be applied to daily life for Chaney's boy fans. For example, his habit of extreme makeup and preference not to appear out of costume becomes an example of discipline: "He achieved the title 'man of a thousand faces' by hard work, not by luck."[39] Later, discussing the extremities to which Chaney pushed himself physically, the magazine is at pains to recoup Chaney's work for normative masculinity. After describing the Hunchback transformation in all its masochistic glory—"The 'harness' he donned here was a type of straight-jacket which was so painful that it could be worn only for a limited time"—the author makes an abrupt and awkward turn: "I should like to bring out the point here that Chaney is by no means a contortionist, but a well-set-up, athletic type, as his appearance in "Tell it to the Marines," where he carried himself naturally, indicated. His characters are produced by clever acting rather than, as has been alleged, 'throwing his limbs out of joint.'"[40] In other words, Chaney is no freak. Rescuing

Chaney from the sideshow and casting the actor as a natural Marine, the *Youth's Companion* recognizes the dangers of Chaney's contagious sympathy and engages in a campaign to clean up the star's persona for the good of the nation's young men, much as the Code would clean up the pictures more broadly in the decade that followed.

Chaney's status as a role model for boys may have seemed particularly dangerous, in fact, because it suggested the only temporarily able-bodied status of all men, especially during the interwar era. As both David Skal and Karen Randall have argued, in films such as *The Penalty*, in which Chaney plays an amputee, the specter of maimed veterans haunts the film, reminding viewers that even the most masculine and normative bodies are susceptible to disability.[41] Further, as Gaylyn Studlar argues, while Chaney was a sort of one-man freak show, this was less a divergence from than a radical extreme of a kind of masculine masochism that linked him to stars like John Barrymore, who suffered romantically, and Douglas Fairbanks, whose films featured reckless self-endangerment.[42] Similarly, Alice Maurice notes that an "emphasis on pain also grounds his acting in physical labor," thereby lending Chaney "a certain working-class credibility."[43]

In the press, which sought to recoup his image and its appeal as normative, the fundamental disjuncture between Chaney's desires and those of magazine reporters is clear. Throughout his career, Chaney resisted requests for interviews, avoided making public appearances, and protested the coming of sound—fearing a unified voice would undo the work he had worked so hard to achieve through acting and makeup.[44] One *Photoplay* interview highlights both Chaney's reticence and the press's near-violent disregard for the actor's preference not to reveal himself:

> I did not get the story of Lon Chaney's childhood in a single talk with him. It took many hours of many days, but those days brought me something I value highly, Lon Chaney's friendship. He had told me succinctly that he hated interviewers. There were questions that I asked him which he flatly refused to answer. Yet after I had seen him several

times, after I had once got behind the barrier of his silence, his shyness was broken down and the friendliness that makes stagehands and every person with a hard luck story love him, stood revealed.[45]

Here, the language of breaking down barriers creates a sense of the other as a fort under siege—with the reporter forcing herself through Chaney's diffidence until she reaches the "revelation" of a relatable Chaney. As Maurice has suggested, Chaney's various disguises, including racial ones, suggested an authentic white performer underneath, so we might see this attempt to break down barriers as part of the ongoing attempt by the press to rescue Chaney's white masculinity.[46] Whereas the reporter insists on a sameness underneath—whether the idea that Chaney is like most people or that there is a consistency to the Chaney beneath the layers of makeup—Chaney's reticence to reveal his face out of character and his insistence on extreme visages might be understood as offering a very different proposition.

LOOKING, THINKING, AND FEELING WITH ERIK THE PHANTOM

In their films, Chaney and Browning undermine ideas of bodily and facial stability. Although there are many "born freaks" in Browning's film, he also shows the transformation of the classically beautiful Cleo into a freak; in the Browning-directed Chaney vehicle *The Unholy Three* (1925), disguises feature prominently; and Chaney's proximally disabled status defined his star persona and gave the actor an instability of bodily integrity that fascinated audiences across his career. Additionally, Chaney's and Browning's films explore the difficulty of building sympathy or identification between the nondisfigured spectator and characters with disfigurement, instead creating self-reflexive spaces for their audiences. This tendency is particularly notable in *The Phantom of the Opera* and *Freaks*, both of which explore struggles with point of view at the level of diegesis and at the level of form. Both, too, intervene in disability discourse by producing tales that bring into question the face as a site of stable signification.

The matter of the "big woman" Cleo's transformation into a sideshow attraction centers most of the controversy over *Freaks*'s seemingly contradictory first and second acts. Focused on domestic life behind the scenes at the circus, the first act works to establish for normative audiences that the freaks are—as the famous line goes—"one of us." The second act seems to undo this work by making the revenging members of the sideshow, who stalk their victim through a dark and stormy night, into the "horrible twisted things" that a prejudiced character early in the film insists they are. In addition to presenting the "freak" performers as monstrous—a charge the actress playing the bearded lady later brought against Browning in press coverage of the film—Cleo's punishment through enfreakment has troubled contemporary viewers and scholars, who find hypocrisy in the film's presentation of the nonnormative body as the ultimate punishment.[47]

Therefore, it is worth lingering on the particulars of Cleo's controversial transformation before moving on to Chaney's work with facial disfigurement. Mercifully, the culmination of the freaks' revenge on the duplicitous Cleo occurs off-screen. When she appears transformed, her enfreakment is hyperbolic, a metamorphosis that interprets the idea of the person with disability as quite literally inhuman. Half-bird and half-woman, Cleo previews Universal's transposition of disability onto movie monsters in the late 1930s and beyond.[48] This is not the extent of her change, however. The freaks have also disfigured Cleo, slashing or otherwise lacerating her face, a transformation that is in excess of or in addition to her new sideshow role as bird-woman.

Why this additional transformation? At the most banal level, Cleo's disfigurement might be understood as part of an overall transformation meant to make the once beautiful "normal" woman an "ugly freak"—an ableist metaphor suggesting her outer appearance has come to match her inner nature. More than this, however, by suddenly withdrawing her normative face, Cleo's transformation might also suggest something about the way disfigurement is read by others for whom disfigurement overpowers individuality. We might say that the film accepts the

FIGURE 3.1 Cleo's transformation.

typical prejudice against people with disabilities and assumes that if Cleo is evil, she might as well be transformed with a visible disability, thus clarifying her moral status in the minds of prejudiced viewers. However, given the film's otherwise sympathetic portrait of the sideshow performers, it remains unclear that the film holds such prejudices.

Instead, the film's notable staginess also suggests the possibility that the film believes its *audience* holds such views. Further evidence for this possibility comes in the form of a visual citation. Although viewers can only speculate about what Cleo has undergone during her transformation, a seam in the flesh on the right side of her face is visible. The skin of her cheek above the seam extrudes more than that of her lower jaw; it traces her cheekbone, giving the appearance of one layer overlapping another. In other words, Cleo appears in a kind of mask, one with a striking resemblance to Erik the Phantom's. With this posthumous tribute to his friend, Browning may have offered a key to the message he wished to convey in his muddled masterwork, visually echoing his longtime

FIGURE 3.2 The Phantom's mask.

collaborator's more sustained and thoughtful meditation on disfigurement and empathy.

The most famous story of disfigurement in the popular consciousness, *The Phantom of the Opera*'s many iterations ask readers and audiences to consider the Phantom as a figure of both horror and empathic feeling. The novel's 1925 adaptation provided an opportunity to transform the many binaries of Gaston Leroux's tale through visual metaphor: light and dark, surface and depth, clarity and obfuscation, above and below, insides and outsides. Most prominent among these is the opposition between revelation and concealment initiated by the film's opening shot, in which a man opens his lantern, establishing the film's chiaroscuro imagery and suspenseful atmosphere. Concealment matters to both the film's plot and the nondiegetic discourse around its star; the suspense leading up to the revelation of the Phantom's face would have titillated 1920s audiences eager to see Chaney's most recent transformation.[49] Audiences receive their first taste of the actor's latest metamorphosis in an early scene in which an opera house attendant who has seen him struggles to explain his appearance: "I have seen only the cloaked face of a man who hides his face and will not speak." This initial account of the Phantom resonates with Chaney's own star persona—an actor who resisted sound and tried to keep his naked face from the public eye.

Not until an excessively light, white, and gorgeous crowd of ballerinas asks a stagehand for the story of the opera's mysterious stranger does the film begin to detail the Phantom's disfigurement. The stagehand, Joseph Buquet, relishes in the details of the Phantom's gruesomeness, simultaneously titillating and horrifying the ballerinas. As Buquet gives his description, the film cuts between the teller and the crowd of ballerinas reacting in horror to his account. Clustered as a mini-audience to the story of the Phantom within the film's diegesis, the ballerinas'

FIGURE 3.3 The ballerinas' priming reaction.

reaction shots serve a pedagogical function for the viewer, contributing to the audience's identification with the ballerinas as well as an overall sense of what Julian Hanich calls "anticipatory disgust" as Buquet recounts, "his face is like leprous parchment, yellow skin strung tight over protruding bones!"[50] Through an accrual of details in Buquet's telling and the ever-escalating series of the ballerina's reactions, the film's audience, like Buquet's, has been primed for a first view of the Phantom.

The film individuates its pattern of priming reaction shots through a shift in focus to the heroine, Christine Daaé. Alone in her dressing room, Christine appears in a medium close-up, which allows the audience to see her eyes dart to the side of the frame, where, as an intertitle has explained, "from hidden places beyond the wall, a melodious voice, like the voice of an angel spoke to her." However, the source of the beautiful intonations remains mysterious to both Christine and the audience: the film shows the Phantom's cast shadow, a profile of the man, which contrasts with the fully lit, frontally presented Christine. The audience has been cued by the earlier conversations between the ballerinas and Buquet to try to pin down the image, to read disfigurement into the profile, but their curiosity remains as yet unsatisfied. Later, the film offers another turn of the anticipatory screw as the Phantom's hand appears, slipping a letter through the door of the opera house. Each of these little revelations acts as a kind of striptease, suspending disfigurement's ultimate exposure. The film's treatment of disability as well as its play with Chaney's star persona—how will the actor appear this time?—links fascination and fear while also articulating a fundamentally distanced viewing position. To look at the striptease, to look forward to the moment of revelation, will always be a looking at, rather than looking with.

The tease continues when the Phantom and Christine finally appear in the same frame. The Phantom's disembodied hand leads the way, appearing from the frame's edge to caress her. Spurred by this contact, Christine turns to look, and the characters appear in a two-shot for the first time. In her initial encounter, Christine reacts in horror to the Phantom's masked face. Perhaps hurt by Christine's reaction, Erik instructs, "Look not on my mask—think rather on my devotion." On the one hand, his words offer a banal look beyond or beneath the disability message. On the other hand, given the cinema's difficulty in representing character interiority without recourse to the facial close-up, Erik's plea for thinking rather than looking is an interesting one—a difficult proposition that the film explores from this point forward, as it stages looking versus thinking as opposed modes of interaction. The film has already identified Christine as a potentially sympathetic figure (we know she finds the Phantom's voice angelic), and she becomes its test subject for experiments in the limits of identification. After Erik makes his appeal to Christine, we get her point-of-view shot, and in the image, the Phantom's face goes out of focus, becoming blurred. While this may indicate that she is growing faint, the image distortion might also be read as an attempt to follow Erik's instruction.

But Christine's time underground with the Phantom shows the difficulty with thinking on devotion without access to a mask on which to visually read the emotion. Indeed, Christine slips quickly into the same mode of reacting as the ballerinas, and the film continues to build suspense through her responses. In the Phantom's underground hideout, Christine moves away from him while also trying to sneak a look, a pattern of behavior that exposes the messy proximity between disgust and desire. For Hanich, as for Carroll, disgust-inducing qualities preclude audience identification; instead, Hanich claims, audiences react "both to a disgusting object or act and a character's disgust response."[51] Among the reasons Hanich cites for the spectator's alignment with the disgusted character is the expressive power of the disgust response and its ripeness for mimicry (or, as I have been referring to it, a sympathy that involves bodily and emotional correspondence).[52] Given the identificatory power of the disgust response, the Phantom's hope to establish a sympathetic relationship seems all the more futile. When the Phantom tells Christine that he has brought her underground "so that which is good within me, aroused by your purity, might plead for your love," the staging makes clear Christine's refusal as she flees the two-shot, visually isolating each character in their own shot. He leans against the wall and receives front lighting, flattening him and eliminating any shadow, whereas Christine appears in side lighting, casting a hard shadow as she points at Erik and makes her accusation that he is the creature haunting the opera. The lighting and staging here enact visually what Christine's rhetoric achieves, pinning Erik down to a depthless figure of horror. Erik fights this flattening and responds to her accusation with one of his own: "If I am the Phantom, it is because man's hatred has made me so." This claim reverses the usual relationship between appearance and scapegoating. Although perhaps simply expressing that men have pushed him underground through their negative reactions to his appearance, Erik also suggests that there is something about being on the receiving end of hatred that strips one of one's humanity. This is the same logic that presumes love might restore humanity: "Your love will restore me." However, as the film plays out, it exposes the limitations in the relations among viewing subject, viewed object, and such redemptive affects.

The film explores these relations formally as well as thematically in its expressive use of two-shots and reaction shots. Whereas the Phantom and Christine perform an ongoing dance throughout the film in which he takes a step into her shot, they appear together, and she departs the shot, Christine and Raoul (her nondisfigured lover) appear repeatedly in the same shot. As they do, their faces touch, they embrace, and, in one late scene that involves kissing, drying tears, and the kissing of a wet handkerchief, the two lovers exchange an impressive quantity of bodily fluids, as if in a frenzy to circulate biological material.

Back in the Phantom's lair, seemingly overestimating the power of well-intended spirit over prejudiced responses to physical difference, Erik leaves Christine a note of instruction: "You are in no peril as long as you do not touch my mask. . . . The Spirit of Erik will overcome your fear." However, like her ability to "look not upon" his mask, her ability to follow this instruction is also limited. In the very next scene, her desire to see his disfigurement overcomes all else. The scene unfolds with the Phantom seated at the piano and Christine standing behind him. In a medium close-up, Christine appears thinking; the film then cuts back to a two-shot in which she reaches from behind to remove his mask. Such blocking may appear unnatural, but it allows both faces maximum exposure to the film's audience.[53] Because of this staging, the audience is the first to see Erik's face. As a result, the audience is also given the initial

FIGURE 3.4 Awkward unmasking.

opportunity to react. Then, following the spectator's moment for reaction, the film cuts to show Christine screaming in horror. It is worth noting that this is quite different from the way the film has preceded until this point; previously, reaction shots of Christine, the ballerinas, and others have done the work of preparing the audience's response to the Phantom. But given that the audience has already had the first opportunity to react, the possible redundancy of Christine's follow-up scream raises interesting questions. It can no longer serve a priming or pedagogical function because viewers have already experienced their own reactions.

In the scene that follows, Christine's redundant reaction provides an opportunity for spectators to compare their own responses to that of their horrified on-screen proxy. Once exposed, the Phantom cries out,

"Feast your eyes—glut your soul—on my accursed ugliness." Here, the invitation inverts the earlier plea to look not upon his mask, as the Phantom shows his awareness of the affective response that visual detail produces, knowing that this feast for the eyes will be digested and result in the soul's changed reaction to him. The scene bears out Peucker's evocative description of the conflation between eye and mouth as both characters respond to the climactic revelation. In the unmasking's fallout, both characters cover their faces. Christine covers her mouth—perhaps to avoid "ingesting" this sight—and the Phantom covers his whole face with both hands, effectively removing his visage as a source of affective stimulus.

With the Phantom's late-stage invitation to Christine (and viewers) to "feast your eyes," he acknowledges a fundamental perspectival problem. Throughout the film, audiences do not see things through the Phantom's eyes, despite several scenes in which he spies. The film's refusal to provide Chaney's Phantom with point-of-view shots—even when he is looking through a peephole or surveilling Christine and Raoul from his perch at the top of the opera house—means that the film enacts formally the same failings that Christine performs on an emotional level, visually expressing an inability to share a perspective with someone conceived of as monstrous.

While the film does not see things through Erik's perspective, it nonetheless insists that spectators see things through their own eyes, asking them to reflect on the process. In the moment when spectators react to the Phantom's face and then Christine's reaction to it, they have a chance to consider how they feel about feasting their eyes and glutting their souls and whether they want to identify—not with the Phantom, this appears to remain off the table—with people who respond to him as Christine does.

How, then, to read the ambivalent work of these films? Throughout Browning's and Chaney's filmographies, film audiences have repeated opportunities to compare their reactions to those of on-screen surrogates—whether the sideshow framing of *Freaks*, which begins and ends with an invitation to look at the transformed Cleo, Christine's reaction to the Phantom, or the theater scene climax of *The Unknown*. Further foregrounding the spectator's position, for example, *The Phantom of the Opera* ends with a scene similar to Christine's mask removal. After being chased through the streets of Paris by a lynch mob, Erik finds himself on the banks of the Seine, beset on both sides. When he turns to the portion of mob on his left, threatening them with an explosive ostensibly hidden in his raised fist, the camera is directly behind him. At first the audience sees only his back as he faces off against the angry rioters. Chaney then turns to face the camera so that he looks directly at the film's audience, now in the same perspectival position as the mob. He opens his hand to reveal his empty palm and laughs in our faces just before being overcome by the rioters. The film then cuts to reveal the crowd with which we have been sharing a point of view just as it rushes to consume Erik in its violent churn.

One might say that the film ends predictably and pessimistically, with the suggestion that no one within or without the film's diegesis is able to identify with Erik. In the final shots, Erik's body is quite literally cast out, as the mob throws it from the banks of the Seine to sink to the river's murky bottom. More interesting, and perhaps more hopefully, though, we might also understand the film as suggesting audiences should not need to identify with others to behave ethically. By repeatedly making its audience identify with prejudiced, fearful, and nondisfigured characters, *The Phantom of the Opera* does not ask audiences to overcome their fears of disfigurement. Instead, it asks them to consider how they feel about their feelings.

This double feeling, or thinking about structures of feeling, that Chaney's work encouraged took place alongside his experiments with radically destabilizing the face as a site of identification. This is the project Chaney undertook again and again, even as the journalists who covered him insisted on penetrating his shifting features to find a stable and normative visage. *The Phantom of the Opera* encourages an intellectual rather than emotional response by asking audiences to reflect critically on their more immediate affective reactions. At the same time that identification with the other is foreclosed, the one with whom audiences most identify, the self, is opened up to reflexive scrutiny. While the fan magazines demanded that Chaney show his true face, the play with masking, revelation, and ultimately rejection in *Phantom* shows that truly ethical behavior does not require this. Instead, the most ethical interaction with the other may involve self-reflection rather than the well-meaning and violent insistence that everyone be "one of us."

4

UNREAL REMEMBRANCE

Black Stars and Their White Audiences

Farina, the Phantom of the Opera, and even Shirley Temple are bogus, sham inventions of dreamland. Departing from the press's promotion of audience connection to these obviously synthetic beings, this chapter considers the way white nostalgia informed a discourse of realism surrounding some of the 1930s' most significant films and the actors who provided their "atmosphere." These men and women included both Black leads and supporting actors, sometimes known and applauded, sometimes censured in Black newspapers' coverage of the films, and often uncredited, both literally and figuratively, by white filmmakers and fan magazines. The use of white memory as test for verisimilitude was so prevalent when it came to Black performance, especially musical performance, that even in later films with Black leads the discussion of these characters and performers often recast them as the setting for white writers' recollections of a bygone era.

For an extended example of the interplay among fantastical white memories, the real, and Black performers, take the detailed preproduction materials for *Gone with the Wind* (Fleming, 1939), housed in the Wilbur G. Kurtz collection at the Margaret Herrick Library in Beverly Hills. Kurtz was the Atlanta historian called in to lend credibility to the epic. In these archives, a visitor can find a letter addressing the Negro Labor Battalion scene. Other letters and memos in the *Gone with the*

Wind files concern military regalia, firearms, and flag designs, all period-specific details to support an overall feeling of historical exactitude—an impulse not unlike that displayed by another notorious piece of revisionist filmmaking, D. W. Griffith's *The Birth of a Nation* (1915), which included "historical facsimile" scenes of Lee surrendering and Lincoln signing the Emancipation Proclamation that were meant to convey the authenticity of the filmmaker's history. In addition to their notoriety as the most noxious pieces of racist propaganda in U.S. film history, the two films are also notable for three overlapping characteristics: first, their use of Black actors; second, their attempt to verify their revisionist history through realistic details; and third, the way the first trait unravels the second, as the use of Black actors in stereotypical roles punctures the films' claims to historical realism. This is most clearly the case in Griffith's infamous scene from the South Carolina State House of Representatives, which receives the same "historical facsimile" tag as the iconic scenes with Lincoln and Lee, but plays as broad comedy.

When reflecting on the racist excess that punctures *Gone with the Wind*'s claims on historicity, the characterization of Mammy (Hattie McDaniel) and Prissy (Butterfly McQueen) may spring to mind, but the better corollary is the Negro Labor Battalion scene. This scene appears in the film's narrative and tonal arc as a part of the film's "serious" history rather than the antebellum "fun" that characterizes the early Mammy-Scarlett scenes. This conception of the scene as historical is evidenced by Kurtz's detailed prescriptions for the battalion members' clothing, tools, and, importantly for this chapter, their singing.[1] Kurtz's letter opens with a relatively staid historical justification for the scene, but shifts into semi-ecstatic description:

> When Atlanta was fortified in the early summer of 1864 the tremendous amount of labor required was beyond the quota of white labor available. At that time such organization of engineer corps that had been recruited, were at the front, outside the state of Georgia.
> Cap't. L.P. Grant of Atlanta was authorized to make plans and estimates for the chain of fortifications surrounding the city. An engineer by profession he did this work in a thoroughly efficient manner. His

plans were approved April 12th, 1864. Work began some weeks later. To do the heavy digging required, able-bodied slaves from all over Georgia were commandeered. The county sheriffs were instructed to round up their quota and then wire Cap't Grant for transportation. This hoard of Black men, descending upon the city, must have been a spectacular affair.

In addition to the language of the "hoard" (a misspelling of horde), familiar from racial panic narratives, the language of spectacle also appears here, emphasizing the inherent theatricality of a large group of Black men. This shift from descriptive historical recounting into spectatorial fantasy is a pattern in the letter, as historical revisionism's entertainment impulse when it comes to Black characters overtakes the drive for historical accuracy.

The letter also offers instruction for casting and costume design, and is worth quoting at length:

> These negroes wore no uniforms. They were field hands, and were dressed accordingly. Being summer, they wore shirts, trousers, coarse shoes and old straw or felt hats. All these articles should show signs of usage. The shirts, if white, should not be spotless affairs . . . they would show soil and certainly would be ragged. They would be open at the neck—or more or less open all the way . . . sleeves would be rolled up. The trouser legs would be a mass of "set" wrinkles, stained with red dust or mud—shoes likewise. The hats would be old "hickory"—straw and felt. Here and there a hat would be brimless and set at a rakish angle.
>
> They would carry pick-axes—axes—and shovels. These picks should not be the long, steel-forged picks of modern commerce. They should be the mattock or pick-axe type, for dirt digging in Georgia soil calls for the cutting of the roots. The shovels were long-handled affairs—mostly—with curved cutting edges. If short shovels are shown, they would be hand-grabs of bent wood—not the lunette cut-outs of modern shovel handles. Above all, these tools should not look as if they had just emerged from the hardware store. If desired, a few wagon-loads of odds and ends—mule equipment, such as pots, pans, skillets,

frying-pans, sacks of potatoes, and bales of empty sacks. The later would be meals sacks—or "cracker" sacks—better known as "gunny sacks." These, filled with sand or earth, were used as finishing touches to the earthen walls. They lined cannon embrasures with them. These wagons may be farm wagons with round canvas tops—or without canvas tops. The drivers would be negroes. The entire set-up can be built up as a rather barbaric spectacle—with a connotation of grim tragedy in the offing.

The negro laborers sang as they marched—and as they worked. The marching would not be with regular military precision—but rather a straggling progress of irregular formation. The song that Miss Mitchell has them sing: "Go Down Moses," is a well known "spiritual"; its melancholy air is particularly appropriate to a people in bondage. There would be plenty of dust in the air—the weather at this period was dry and hot.

Big Sam should be a giant of a negro—and one who would look as if he could sing loudly and melodiously—even if he doesn't.[2]

Of the many strange moments in this passage, the phrase "even if he doesn't" stands out as particularly bizarre among the many suppositions and "shoulds" that characterize Kurtz's letter.

This chapter focuses on the strange logic captured in the mention of a Big Sam who looks as though he would sing, even if he doesn't. I call this logic "counterfactual realism." The idea of a Black voice that could be real, even if it isn't—or, given the instructive nature of the letter, the idea of a Black voice that *should* be real, even if it isn't—stitches together white memories, Black voices, and reality claims. In the phrase, "looks as though he would sing," an absent subject appears. Looks to whom? As many scholars have noted, white fantasies about Black voices were not unique to plantation dramas. A vogue for Black voices came in with the talkies and lingered throughout the 1930s. The boom in Black singing represented by the films discussed in this chapter was already something of a rerun of a rerun. In her comprehensive study *Spirituals and the Birth of a Black Entertainment Industry*, Sandra Jean Graham traces a similar phenomenon that swept music halls and vaudeville stages in the late nineteenth century. In this case, Black singing authenticated a lie for white audiences, hungry for minstrel-style performances, who wanted the lie told in the most realistic way possible and demanded performances by Black musicians rather than white performers in blackface.[3] A similar desire plays out in *Gone with the Wind* and other plantation dramas, which used the presence of Black actors to vouch for their revisionist takes on antebellum life.

The discussions of recorded Black voices that followed the coming of sound also equated Black voices with an abstract sense of authenticity—an irony, of course, given the notoriety of *The Jazz Singer*, with its central blackface performance, as a sound film first. Nonetheless, a sense of Black voices as sounding better and more realistic remained. Arthur Knight, Ryan Jay Friedman, and Alice Maurice have all documented the significance to film history of the vogue for Black voices, with Friedman arguing for the importance of the Black talking picture to establishing a more highbrow film audience and Knight arguing for the importance of the musical genre to bringing Black performers into white theaters.[4] In her account, Maurice argues for a more fundamental integration of race and film technology: "the discourses of race and sound were intertwined during the transition to the talkie... because of what they already had in common: a dependence on popular expectations regarding authenticity, the alignment of internal and external characteristics, and the evidence of the senses."[5] By the time the white-directed and -targeted films such as *Gone with the Wind* and *Imitation of Life* premiered, white actors had settled into the new demands of sound films and anxieties about the recorded voice had largely settled. Nonetheless, a white fascination for Black singing remained. In the films discussed in this chapter—the earlier film *Hallelujah* (Vidor, 1929) and later films *Judge Priest* (Ford, 1934) and *Imitation of Life* (Stahl, 1934)—and the press around them, a pattern emerges as Black performance, especially singing, is made to do double work: both establishing a reality of milieu and providing ammunition for publicity campaigns that affirmed white nostalgia as similarly real.

For the first part of this argument, I am indebted to Charlene Regester's work on Black extras. She notes that "extra-roles were distinguished from other roles in that actors were required to provide the 'human backdrop' for pictures, to serve as supporting players to their more illustrious stars, and to lend authenticity to a picture's atmosphere," yet "these actors were rendered as unimportant, expendable, and merely embellishments to the enhancement of the white stars with whom they shared the screen."[6] While Regester focuses on the support Black extras provided to white stars, in this chapter I wish to extend her claims to consider the use the white press made of Black supporting players and leads alike. In the films discussed, Black performances and coverage of them not only authenticate filmic worlds, as Regester, Maurice, and others have argued, but white ideas about these worlds.

To examine the mobilization of Black performance on behalf of white nostalgia, the chapter traces a brief history of Black singing in mainstream Hollywood films. First, an examination of *Hallelujah* establishes the way Black singing was deployed in a landmark film to create a sonic mirage of a realist landscape. Next, a consideration of *Judge Priest* exemplifies this use of Black singing in its most conventional form as it confirms the reality of white memories. Lastly, a discussion of *Imitation of Life* traces the performance of Black suffering from the film's diegesis to its musical patterns to show how even an ostensibly progressive film with two stunning Black leads fell into this already-old Hollywood habit. Thus, even when Black actresses threatened to, in Miriam Petty's phrasing, "steal the show," an entrenched and consistent set of habits in both film and fan magazine discourse was working against them.

Finally, in tracking the function of Black singing across these three films, I wish to argue for the importance of what may seem like a formal mistake: a blurring of diegetic and nondiegetic sound. Early musicals, including *The Jazz Singer*, sometimes mixed the diegetic and nondiegetic, causing confusion about spatial relationships and the origin point of the sound in the image. Michael Slowik proposes the confusion may be a holdover from silent-era practices of playing music "suggested by the image," which was more important than "the clear delineation of diegetic or nondiegetic space."[7] Both *Hallelujah* and *Imitation of Life* share this type of "error," introducing a point of sonic confusion through Black singing. More than a holdover, I argue, the mixing of diegetic levels that occurs in these films may be understood as the sonic life of the discursive phenomenon this chapter traces: an ongoing blurring of foreground and atmosphere, diegetic and nondiegetic, white memory and Black performance.

SONIC LANDSCAPES AND REALITY SPECTACLES

While *Hallelujah* may be characterized as an example of Hollywood's more modernist filmmaking and *Judge Priest* as a more squarely nostalgic piece of Southern reminiscence, the two share a remarkably similar imaginative register when it comes to Black singing. Both exemplify the well-documented tendency of Hollywood films to feature Black singing either as atmosphere or as an innate and spontaneous aspect of racial expression to be uncovered by a white anthropological gaze. *Judge Priest* offers a clear case of the first, and *Hallelujah* offers an instance of the second, although each pulls from the other. In their portraits of Southern life, one modernist and primitivist and one historical revisionist, *Hallelujah* and *Judge Priest* both deploy Black performances of singing as authenticating atmospheric detail even as they simultaneously presented Blackness as inherently theatrical and spectacular. This paradoxical use of Black song created "reality effects" that supported white knowledge claims about Black Americans, as evidenced by both filmmakers and reviewers.[8]

As the many scholars working on *Hallelujah* and the history of early sound films have demonstrated, the film's simultaneous status as an important landmark in Hollywood's use of all-Black casts—it was the second major Hollywood film to do so, following *Hearts in Dixie* (Sloane, 1929)—and its status as the first fully synchronized film musical is no accident. As Maurice argues, "Claims that African American performers' voices could be reproduced more faithfully than others essentially promised that these voices would be 'in sync' with their bodies—and with audience expectations about what should emanate from those bodies."[9] *Hallelujah* and *Judge Priest* extend this promise to geographical reassurance: establishing that Black bodies and voices match white expectations while also affirming the location of Black bodies and voices in "the South" as a time and space distinct from broader American modernity. Specifically, *Hallelujah* is a folk musical, a genre that Desirée Garcia has suggested functioned to deny the realities of Black life at the time of filming, the labor involved in filmmaking, and the professional status of the cast members.[10] There is a particularly strong irony to this tendency in the case of *Hallelujah*, which populated its on-location Southern scenes with talent recruited from Harlem.

Nevertheless, white impressions of Blackness, and specifically white childhood memories, became central arguments for the film's authenticity. In her work on the film, Judith Weisenfeld extensively documents the way Vidor's recollections of his Southern childhood took on the status of sociological truth.[11] MGM's press materials are exemplary: "a native of a Southern State, and from his childhood, [Vidor's] background has been that of the cultured Old South in its days of glory. Knowing the negro, he has chosen a simple theme for 'Hallelujah,' a theme centered upon a humble negro farmer and his family, their lives and joys and sorrows. He has caught the rhythm of their existence and reproduced for the first time, a section of humanity so little understood by those who do not know this colorful race."[12] The claim of "reality" was also used to defend the film from censorship. In response to concerns about the film's depictions of adultery, gambling, and violence, Lamar Trotti, the MPPDA's resident Southerner, who would go on to pen *Judge Priest*, similarly confirmed that any licentiousness depicted was simply a truthful rendition of Black Southern life and its attendant promiscuity, and not a serious moral violation.[13]

Across Vidor's and MGM's proclamations, as well as Trotti's truth claims, a pattern emerges in which white memories of Blackness become the measure of representational veracity, and a film is judged more real and less open to censorship in relation to Black characters' proximity to white recollections. The Val Lewton review in *Screenland* captures this phenomenon particularly well, presenting Vidor and his film as neutral transmitters of racial truths. The review features the pattern of authentication between Black sounds and white memories that runs through much of the discourse on *Hallelujah* in particular and sound films set in the South more generally. Lewton claims the film "will bring the sweet sounds of plantation melodies, the furious cadences of revival meetings and the weird tones of Negro spirituals to those theatres which are equipped with sound devices." Here, Vidor's mind acts as a projector, resurrecting the stilled images of his youth, which in turn create the stuff of his motion picture: "Having once made up his mind to film a Negro story, Vidor . . . began to revive his memories of the South and of Negro life."[14]

Across early reviews and publicity pieces, a narrative materializes that suggests white audiences will identify with white memories, and specifically white Southern ones, rather than with Black characters or actors, thereby mitigating worries about whether or not, as a *Variety* review puts it, "Whites will accept it as a camera reproduction of the typical southland."[15] As *Motion Picture News*'s review puts it, "Even in the south where they are not willing to take the negro's artistic advancement into consideration they are going to like it. For the picture depicts negro life as they know it in that country and because of that they are going to be willing to accept it."[16] In industry publications, appeals to white Southern recollections—"negro life as they know it"—take on the role of both anticensorship strategy and epistemic appeal.

Unlike the later *Imitation of Life*, which would attempt to transmute Black feelings into white ones through its robust exercise of melodramatic techniques, *Hallelujah* attempted to create a "reality" of Blackness buttressed by preexisting white knowledge claims. The opening sounds that begin before the title and over the MGM logo demonstrate both the attempt and its counterfactual realism, as drums and chants blend into a medley of recognizable commercial spirituals.[17] Before the first filmed images appear on-screen, then, the film has already established its sonic business of validating white ideas about "real" Black life. When the first image of Vidor's film appears, it collaborates the sonic stereotype, opening onto a long shot of Black extras picking cotton in a field, an image that feels "real" for its familiarity from prior films as well as its framing. Over this tropological image can be heard a choral rendition of "Way Down Upon the Swanee River." The formal, choral singing style is clearly external to the film's diegesis, not coming from the laborers in the field. Despite the lack of human diegetic source, as Garcia has argued, it seems to come from the land itself, as sound and image establish the atmosphere for the film to follow.

As the film unfolds, the godly man Zeke (Daniel L. Haynes) strays from his love interest Missy Rose (Victoria Spivey) and his family, takes up with the nightclub floozy Chick (Nina Mae McKinney), undergoes a dramatic conversion, and starts a preaching career, only to be tempted by Chick once more—a fatal choice that leads to his murdering her gambler lover, being sent to prison, and finally reuniting with his family. While perhaps underinvested in its plot, which the film processes at an uneven pace (the chain gang sequence is remarkably short), *Hallelujah* demonstrates a fascination with the spectacle of Black singing, and, more particularly, large groups of Black singers. In a runtime that rapidly covers a number of wide-ranging events in Zeke's trajectory of sin and redemption, the film lingers over scenes in nightclubs, churches, and camp meetings, where sound and action are joined.

Although the world of *Hallelujah* offers numerous opportunities for showcasing musical performances, the film often pipes in sounds from outside the story's action. As a result, the sonic worlds of the film's nondiegetic soundtrack and the songs of the diegetic world blend together at times, indicating a promiscuity in delineation between what constitutes the film's story and what is part of a more affectual reality. This tendency reveals the lie behind the film's famed reputation as the first fully synchronized musical. While the diegetic world concerned with Zeke's temptation by Chick includes many performance scenes that cover a range of musical styles, including those of the night club, the chain gang, and the camp meeting, the nondiegetic soundtrack belongs entirely to the spiritual. Both the diegetic and nondiegetic sonic landscapes might thus be said to support a general stereotype of Black Americans as natively musical. However, the tendency of these two sonic realms to bleed together disturbs the film's claims to anthropological realism and instead bolsters a *feeling* of the real in which Blackness is pried from the body and moves to the soundtrack as atmospheric effect.

It is in the matter of the singing group that the film's blurring of diegetic and nondiegetic sound is most significant. The opening is worth considering in detail for the way it mixes diegetic levels. After the establishing shot of the cotton field, the choral rendition of "Swanee River" cuts out as the film individuates the fictional characters Zeke, Missy Rose, Mammy, and the rest of Zeke's family. Walking homeward from the cotton field, Zeke begins singing the song "Cotton," establishing it as part of his characterization as a friendly, eaasygoing man who loves to sing—a bit of sonic business located firmly in the story world. However, Zeke does not sing alone. Instead, his call, "Cotton," is met with a choral response. In this moment, diegetic call and nondiegetic response blend to form the distinctive spiritual style while also entangling the sonic worlds.

A similar bleed takes place a few scenes later, with a twist, as a character's voice departs his body in order to score a more realist scene; or, put otherwise, as the lead dissolves into atmosphere. When Zeke delivers his family's cotton to the mill, he begins singing Irving Berlin's "Waiting at the End of the Road" from atop his cart. The performance is

FIGURE 4.1 Song located in diegesis.

once again clearly located with Zeke. In the style of the stage and film musical appropriate to a Berlin song, an on-screen audience forms to watch Zeke, as do accompanying musicians, who play along on the banjo and jugs. However, unlike the cinematography of a typical Hollywood musical, the camera leaves Zeke mid-song to explore the cotton mill, examining the baler, the gin, and so on. While the song continues, the visual perspective changes, and the impossibility of the sonic and visual match becomes apparent: Zeke's singing could not come through as loudly or clearly as it does, nor does the camera's movement away from Zeke create a shift in aural perspective. As a result, Zeke's singing transfers briefly from the diegesis to the soundtrack as the film follows a different kind of realist interest: showcasing the space and processes of the cotton mill in documentary fashion. The shift of Zeke's singing from diegesis to sonic accompaniment thus belies the film's interest in showing the reality of Black lives and instead establishes the film's treatment of Blackness as a sign of the real.

A very different treatment of Black singing appears in the following scene, which introduces Nina Mae McKinney, the film's breakout star. McKinney's singing and dancing in the film appear in clearly demarcated club or performance spaces. McKinney, unlike the other characters, is treated as a professional, though this is a derogatory category in the film, as her singing and dancing are correlated with the nightclub vices of gambling, adultery, and drink. Nonetheless, her treatment by the camera suggests that McKinney is to be viewed as a star rather than atmosphere: her nightclub scenes feature a number of cuts and varied camera angles, and she appears in medium shots and medium close-ups that affiliate her with other movie stars rather than the more anthropological long and extra-long shots of cotton fields that attribute Black singing to the environment rather than to individual talent.[18] In fact, a number of white magazines refer to McKinney via comparisons to the white flapper star Clara Bow or ridicule her aspirations to dress like white stars such as Gloria Swanson or Peggy Joyce.[19] The condescending nature of the white fan magazines' treatment of McKinney's star power in contrast to their discussion of Haynes's "natural" performance is telling. The difference in reactions to McKinney and Haynes reflects the attitude toward Black professionalism and labor that appeared across publicity materials as well. In his interviews, Vidor waxed on about the authenticity of the Black performances he had captured, "the players lived through the episodes; they truly didn't act them. They felt them. . . . A Negro is a natural actor, singer, and born mimic. Any group of them can naturally sing and dance in harmony. They are born that way."[20] In contrast, Eva Jessye, who broke barriers as the first African American musical director for a Hollywood picture, gave her own interviews emphasizing her expertise and labor in organizing the film's musical numbers. Vidor's claims about the "natural" talent of *Hallelujah*'s performers also ignored the previous work of Haynes and Victoria Spivey, who brought experience from the stage and recording industry to the production.

Despite Vidor's stated intentions, as the film attempts to delve into character and racial psychology, its style departs the realist register in favor of the more modernist, expressionist images for which it has become known. For example, in the extended nighttime revival scene of the film's second half, white viewers positioned anthropologically in the film's first half consume spectacularly exteriorized Black feelings as religious and sexual feeling are expressed through fragmenting close-up shots of arms, strange cast shadows, and eerie wails.[21] At the same moment that the film's representation of Blackness is at its most spectacular, the individual Black characters and actors become most invisible, so dissolved are they into Vidor's formal experiment. However, it is also precisely at this moment that the viewer is most caught up by the sonic realm as editing and sound combine to form the scene's intense rhythm.

A handful of reviews suggest as much. White writers struggled to explain being emotionally moved by the experience of watching an all-Black cast on screen. One strategy they used was to insist on a kind of critical amnesia, a testament to the excellence of the film that also conveniently sidestepped the possibility of cross-racial identification. "When one can sit in a theatre and be so absorbed in a story that one forgets that it is being enacted by negroes," Freddie Schader wrote, "then the director and the author have turned out something. When one looks at the images of the negro players on the screen and forgets that they are Black then they too must be said to have contributed something far greater than anything that has been done before. That is the case with 'Hallelujah.'"[22]

In a long and positive review by the editors of the *National Board of Review Magazine*, Alfred Kuttner and Wilton Barrett similarly locate excellence in the film by evacuating Blackness of specificity. The film had been highlighted by the magazine's editors for special focus in its "Exceptional Photoplays" column, and the review opens with a familiar discussion of the appropriateness of Black American voices to the medium.[23] The lengthy review is notable both for the conservative magazine's discussion of white identification with Black characters and for its discernment among the film's various deployments of sound: "It would be wrong to call this film a study of just Negro life on the plantation; its imagination has lyric and dirge-like notes, those of sorrow and exultation, rarely has a film been so moving, so awakening to our own responsive inner experiences; the plantation becomes the world and its characters become ourselves, its story on the human side is a universal one."[24] Much as the fan magazines discussed earlier projected white feelings onto the Black children of *Our Gang*, this review places Zeke and Chick in a mythic time, a plantation chronotope that allows the white editors to position the Black sharecroppers as American everymen, not "just Negro." Indeed, the review goes so far as to declare "The plantation Negro is a national figure," an assertion that raises the question of what, by contrast, the modern, urban Black actors might be.[25]

Despite their invocation of a mythic national past, the reviewers object to stereotyped sound. "It would appear that Zeke's family were much given to close harmony and fancy shuffling," the review laments, "just because the audience out front expected it of them."[26] In contrast, the review favors

> the closing shots where the soundtrack is carried through successive scenes of the places which Zeke is passing on his way home. The tune of his banjo is heard continuously in the melody he is playing, as he sits on the roof of the moving train, as he walks through the fields to that

moment of silence when he stands waiting for his family to see him. Here the sound knits the pictures together in a double meaning. In the song of the banjo we pass back with Zeke over what he has been through, and in the picture we go with him toward the plantation he longs to see again.[27]

In other words, the reviewers prefer sound less grounded in the diegesis. Whereas the sound associated with "fancy shuffling" clearly emanates from a figure on-screen, when the song departs the body, leaving only the provocative voice, the white reviewers can better access a pleasurable nostalgic fantasy of plantation life.

In contrast to the high-brow *Hallelujah*, the Will Rogers vehicle *Judge Priest*, which featured Stepin Fetchit and Hattie McDaniel in broadly stereotyped comic roles, made none of *Hallelujah*'s anthropological claims and instead positioned itself as a straightforward nostalgia delivery mechanism. Adapted by Lamar Trotti from the Irvin Cobb "Judge Priest" sketches, the film was part of a Hollywood response to anxieties about the "Southern box office"—the threat of Southern theaters and audiences rejecting more racially progressive films.[28] *Judge Priest* features Rogers as a Kentucky judge in 1890, who presides over a small town busy making preparations to celebrate the twenty-fifth anniversary of the Civil War. We meet Priest at his bench in a scene that also introduces Poindexter (Fetchit), who has been wrongly accused of being a chicken thief. Priest and Poindexter bond over fishing and, with the case dismissed, head off to the river to test Poindexter's baiting technique. A widower who has lost both his wife and children, Priest looks fondly on his young nephew Jerome "Rome" Priest (Tom Brown), who has recently returned from law school and begun courting the neighbor girl Ellie May Gillespie (Anita Louise), much to the consternation of his snobbish mother. Meanwhile, Ellie May also receives romantic attentions from Flem Talley, who later brags about his intentions regarding Ellie May at his barbershop. Flem's rough talk draws the ire of a stranger to town, Bob Gillis (David Landau), who punches him, resulting in an attempted murder charge. When the charges are brought, prosecuting attorney Senator Maydew (Berton Churchill) asks Priest to step down for his lack of objectivity. Insulted, Priest recuses himself from the courtroom but does not stop meddling in the case. Much of the town becomes involved, with Rome acting as defense attorney, and the town reverend (played by *The Birth of a Nation*'s Henry B. Walthall) revealing that Gillis is, in fact, a Confederate hero and the father of Ellie May. Overcome by the defendant's battle for the honor of both daughter and Southland, the jury declares him innocent and all rejoice to the tune of "Dixie."

While the plot of the film is predictable, its sonic world is more interesting. As Matthew Bernstein documents, Southerners were brought in to consult on films not only to avoid insulting audiences below the Mason-Dixon line but also to ensure greater realism after the reaction of many to the accents of *Jezebel* (Wyler, 1938).[29] This realism without insult did not extend to the characters of Jeff Poindexter and Aunt Dilsey (McDaniel). However, through his interactions with these stereotyped Black characters, specifically vocal interactions, Rogers's Priest is established as a true Southerner with whom white audiences might identify. Although Rogers was mixed-race and a proud citizen of the Cherokee Nation, as Amy M. Ware has suggested, white audiences and critics often preferred to interpret the actor as white with some Cherokee blood, an admixture that nativists connected to authentic Americanness in the era.[30] Here, Rogers's casting as Dixieland judge suggests a performance of whiteness, even if his sly folksiness continues the actor's tradition of undermining social hierarchies. Furthermore, as James H. Cox demonstrates, Rogers's Cherokee identity did not necessarily entail feelings of cross-racial coalition against white supremacy. Rogers had come up on the vaudeville circuit singing "coon songs" and been protested by the NAACP in 1934, the same year as *Judge Priest*, for using a slur during a radio program.[31] Nonetheless, scholarship on the film highlights Priest's intimate relationship with the Black supporting characters, especially Fetchit's Jeff Poindexter. As Michael Charles Pounds points out, for example, both characters have the initials "JP." And while Pounds's assertion that Rogers's and Fetchit's vocal performances are indistinguishable as "thick drawl" seems dubious, given Fetchit's distinctive vocal style, the film does indeed build an intimacy between the two characters that allows them to exchange identities.[32]

Priest's comfort with Poindexter and Aunt Dilsey is a sign of his folksiness, as are his plain speech and rumpled clothing. Priest's homespun wisdom and warmth stand against the formal language and loquaciousness of Senator Maydew. Drawing a contrast between himself and his opponent, Priest explains, "First thing I learned in politics was when to say 'ain't.'" But beyond the contraction that marks Priest as a man of the people, his ability to communicate with and *as* Black Kentuckians marks him as a real Southerner. As Martin Rubin wrote in his *Film Comment* overview of Ford's "Will Rogers Trilogy," "the film suggests in Priest that the true Southerner becomes half-Negro himself."[33] In addition to trying on Poindexter's fishing technique, Priest also tries on his voice. When Flem Talley comes to court Ellie May, Priest hides in the nearby bushes and stages a dialogue between himself and Poindexter about the disgruntled family of another young lady coming to look for Talley. While Priest and Poindexter both speak in relatively unpolished Southern accents, their voices are of course distinct, allowing for a joke built on Rogers's imitation of Fetchit's iconic sound. This scene is the first of many that make self-aware use of the way off-screen Black sounds influence on-screen white actions.

Priest is himself quite aware of this, sometimes participating in and sometimes orchestrating Black performances. At the taffy pull party for Confederate veterans during which Rome and Ellie May initiate their flirtation, Aunt Dilsey and a chorus of Black women stand on a porch churning ice cream and singing. Over the course of the party, their song turns from "Massa Jesus Wrote Me a Note" to "My Old Kentucky Home." Singing the state song, Dilsey casts her benevolent gaze upon the scene of Rome and Ellie May picnicking in the grass, offering a soundtrack for young white love. Priest steps onto the porch and joins in the singing, the lone white voice in the chorus. If the supporting role of Black sonic performance to on-screen white action is still implicit here, it becomes explicit in the final act, in which Priest acts as director for the film's finale.

Before turning to the finale, however, it is worth mentioning a scene that was cut from the script that Trotti and his cowriter developed from Cobb's source materials. As Bernstein details in his work on the film, this scene featured a subplot including a rape accusation and threatened lynching. In the film, Priest sends Poindexter to buy more bait. The original script calls for Poindexter to be accosted by a lynch mob that has him confused with "a negro suspected of assault."[34] In the early script, Priest saves Poindexter by delivering a fiery speech at the jailhouse door. For fear of both insulting Southern audiences and distracting from the main plot line, these scenes were cut. However, a passing reference remains, oddly tied to Priest's orchestration of the film's final musical number. After learning of Gillis's true identity, Priest hatches his scheme, the first step of which involves asking Poindexter if he can play "Dixie." Poindexter responds that he can, and adds that he can play a second tune, too: "Marching through Georgia." Priest responds by saying, "I got you out of one lynching . . . catch you playing 'Marching through Georgia,' I'll join the lynching." Here, Priest violently rejects both Poindexter's musical idea (playing a song about Sherman) and ideas about Southern history, asserting his authority in programming the accompaniment for the action he is directing.

The courtroom scene that follows is explicitly cinematic and evokes the history of the South on film. The dramatic last-minute witness, Henry Walthall's Rev. Ashby Brand, recalls *The Birth of a Nation*; as Bernstein notes, the description Rev. Brand gives of Gillis's heroics could as easily describe the battlefield actions of his earlier *Birth of a Nation* character, the Little Colonel.[35] The testimony is accompanied by a subjective flashback sequence, during which Poindexter strikes up "Dixie." Although the pairing of "Dixie" with scenes that could have been taken directly from Griffith's 1915 film have the desired effect on the jury, the film is not straight nostalgia. Instead, the scene complexly and ironically reveals how easily manipulated the white jury is by sonic propaganda—propaganda derived from the minstrel stage no less—and how easily Poindexter (who has, incidentally, stolen at least one of his instruments from a Confederate veterans' band) plays upon their Confederate

FIGURE 4.2 Poindexter playing on white nostalgia.

sympathies. Despite this knowingness, the film nonetheless culminates in its own orgy of revisionist celebration as all members of the cast take to the streets for a parade, complete with a shift of the performance of "Dixie" from Poindexter's band to a white one and the waving of Confederate flags.

Although the film cleverly distances itself from the "not real" manipulations of Southerners presented in the trial sequence, it also establishes itself and Priest as really Southern through proximity to and manipulation of stereotyped Black performance. *Judge Priest*'s efforts to present a "true" Southern experience were appreciated by at least some audiences, and publicity materials in mainstream magazines retain the film's commitment to treating its Black performers in a different register than its white ones. In general, white fan magazines and trade papers treated the film as a mild but pleasant entertainment, sure not to offend censors or Southerners. For example, a *Screenland* review finds the film slow but suggests that "south of the Mason-Dixon line it is very likely to be the season's most popular picture."³⁶ Some reviews and fan responses were more positive, emphasizing in particular the role McDaniel's and Fetchit's stereotyped characters played in establishing a realistic South on-screen. For example, *Photoplay* notes, "The sleepy old Kentucky town is so real you can hear the June-bugs buzzing—and every character might have been born right there." In particular, the review highlights the "indispensable local color . . . provided by Hattie McDaniel and Stepin Fetchit in some grand scenes and music."³⁷

The language of "local color" is applied specifically to the film's Black actors, revealing the slippage between Blackness and ideas of regional atmosphere filled in by the performers' presence. For example, *Hollywood Filmograph* reports, "Big Hattie McDaniel, the colored Kate Smith, lent color to the picture and not only is she a good actress but her song with Will Rogers will knock them dead." The review concludes: "This picture should be a big hit and go over like wildfire all over the country and Europe. It gives a keen insight of the South and its lazy ways, lovable people and intense sectionalism."³⁸ The white fans who wrote in appeared to agree, with a native Kentuckian writing to the *New Movie Magazine*,

> Time's curtain rolled back and I relived the days of youth in 'My Old Kentucky Home.' Will Rogers in 'Judge Priest' finds his ideal role and the supporting cast is flawless. They appeared to me just like the folks with whom I was raised. I recognized the pool-room loafer, the farm clod-hoppers, the village gossip and the rest of the folks. There are no super thrills or extraordinary climaxes in this picture but you go away with that perfectly satisfied feeling. There are subtle tuggings of heart-strings, a little moisture in the eyes and many deep chuckles at the home-spun humor of the lovable old justice.³⁹

The nostalgic letter populates the film from the writer's memory, including the addition of characters not specifically present in *Judge Priest*, thereby illustrating much of the film's appeal: its corroboration of white ideas of the South and Southerners.

This corroboration is most offensive in the fan magazines' treatment of Hattie McDaniel, which disallowed the productive gap between star and performance that they extended, in however limited a fashion, to white actors. In order to function as authenticating "local color," Black actors and their characters needed to be one and the same. Moreover, as Petty has documented, with the exception of Fetchit/Perry, publicity reports "were rarely penned by major Hollywood studios for African American actors," an absence that may have compounded the zero-degree gap between performer and role in the relatively infrequent appearances of Black actors in the mainstream film magazines.[40] *Modern Screen*'s profile article on McDaniel's cooking exemplifies this trend, rendering her speech in stereotyped dialect:

> "Say," said Will to Hattie, eyeing her over the tops of his specs, "I'll bet you really *can* cook."
>
> "Can Ah cook? Mistah Rogers, can Ah cook!" answered Hattie with a grin. "You know, Mistah Rogers," she went on, encouraged by his friendly smile, "it's a funny thing about me. Ah was bo'n in Wichita, Kansas, but Ah talks just like the cullud folk from below the Mason-Dixie line and when it comes to cooking Ah's southern, too."[41]

Beyond the bizarreness of an article that simultaneously describes McDaniel's midwestern origins while insisting on her deep Southernness and rendering her speech in dialect, the article, like the film it promotes, allows for pleasurable and partial white identification with and occupation of Blackness. The article is addressed to the "modern hostess" who wants to serve "Hattie's dinner menu" of Southern chicken, candied yams, and greens in ham liquor. Here, the slipping on of a Black menu demonstrates the white hostess's "modernity," much as Rogers's slipping on Fetchit's voice demonstrates his "Southernness." In each case, Blackness is emptied of the subject in order for a white to occupy the performance position. Despite the emptying out, however, the Black actor and character must still be closely tied for the authenticating function to work. Hattie's menu and Dilsey's must be indistinguishable for the white hostess to demonstrate her modernity, and Poindexter and Fetchit must similarly be identical in order for Rogers to occupy a true "Black" voice and thus authenticate *Judge Priest*'s status as a "real" Southern film.

FEELING "REAL": BLACK SOUND AND
WHITE TEARS IN *IMITATION OF LIFE*

No film from the 1930s so obviously thematizes the nature of Black stardom's sidelining by the white establishment as does *Imitation of Life*. The narrative of parallel Black and white mother-daughter pairs has inspired criticism on melodrama, racial identification, and the cultural privileging of white women's feelings, even (especially) in a film about Black women, becoming a central text for scholars such as bell hooks and Miriam Thaggert to challenge the race neutrality of Laura Mulvey's theory of the gaze and for scholars such as Julie Grossman to theorize the fluidity of "textual and personal identities."[42] Still other scholars have taken up the film as a watershed moment for interactions among Black stardom, Black film criticism, and Black spectatorship, as well as the relationship between these discourses and mainstream (white) film coverage. Anna Everett, for example, notes that until John Stahl's *Imitation of Life* in 1934, the film industry had largely ignored Black audiences and press.[43] Matthew Bernstein's and Dana F. White's work on the film's distribution and reception in Atlanta has added regional specificity to the broader national debates Everett outlines, uncovering an even more varied response than the one Everett finds in northern Black newspapers.[44]

Finally, and most pertinent to this chapter's interest in how the white press rhetorically opened and foreclosed the possibility of connecting with Black characters and actors, Lauren Berlant, Sandy Flitterman-Lewis, and Miriam Petty have each taken up the question of cross-racial and intra-gender identification, as well as more complex and partial forms of connection, through the figures of Peola and Delilah. For example, Petty pinpoints the varying receptions of Louise Beavers's and Fredi Washington's characters and star personae as opportunities to consider emergent forms of Black identity in modernity.[45] Berlant and Flitterman-Lewis, in contrast, consider the various versions of *Imitation* as fantasies in which connections forged through shared experiences of labor (Berlant) or motherhood (Flitterman-Lewis) might temporarily allow the characters of Bea and Delilah to bridge racial difference.[46]

While Berlant reads Delilah's transition to brand "Aunt Delilah" as a problematic "solution" to her embodiedness—essentially a kind of leaning in to the spectacularization of Blackness through the national brand contra the disembodied abstract citizenship denied Black and female subjects—I want to consider the less frequent and but no less significant moments in which Blackness is disembodied in the film, whether through Delilah's death or the moments when Black sounds and bodies are disarticulated, as in the earlier *Hallelujah*.

While the significant criticism on *Imitation of Life* rightly focuses on the relationships among Bea, Jessie, Delilah, and Peola for the clear ways they stage problems of empathy and identification, less has been written about the way the deployment of Black sound as "atmosphere" and "local color" buttresses this elaboration of empathy and its limits. In addition to its diegetic exploration of identity, *Imitation of Life* mirrors filmic transformations in the 1930s as the representation of Blackness moves from on-screen spectacle to atmospheric support for white feeling, a transformation affected at least in part by a move from the visual to the aural.

Part of what differentiates *Imitation*'s exploration of race relations from, say, plantation dramas, is that the bulk of the witnessing falls to the white mother-daughter duo and very little to the Black mother-daughter pair. As Thaggert has argued, because of her commodification as "Aunt Delilah," Delilah is not available as a site of identification; instead, Thaggert posits Bea as "a privileged spectator and a character with whom the audience can identify."[47] Indeed, Bea is remarkably demanding as a spectator, crafting Delilah's image into the performance she most wants to see, acting as casting agent, director, and audience all in one.

As the film progresses, the spectacles of Blackness Bea demands of Delilah shift, tracking with the changing nature of Hollywood roles available to Black actors, as Bea recasts Delilah from comedic stereotype to symbol of universal maternal sorrow. Early in the film, Bea makes Delilah a mascot when she demands Delilah pose for a sign painter: "Smile, Delilah. No, not like that, a great big one." Here, Bea asks that Delilah conform to and thus confirm the jolly mammy type. In other words, despite Bea's and *Imitation*'s progressiveness, she recruits her friend into the kind of authenticating service seen in discussions of white memory and Southern Blackness in earlier films. She's also a cruel director, baiting Delilah into unsuspecting comedy, as when she explains her new love interest Stephen Archer (William Warren) is an ichthyologist. Knowing Delilah is unfamiliar with the word, Bea nonetheless leads her along, provoking her to make foolish statements about the lifestyle afforded by an unfamiliar profession. Later, Bea laughs over the joke with Stephen: "If you could have seen Delilah's face." Once again, Bea invokes Delilah's face as an image for white consumption. In these scenes from the first half of the film, Bea presses Delilah into a two-dimensional stereotype.

Unlike McDaniel's mammy figure in *Judge Priest*, however, Beavers's Delilah sings only occasionally. Delilah makes music a total of three times in *Imitation of Life*. The first instance appears relatively early in the film, in a scene set in the kitchen of Bea's house, where Delilah and Peola have come to live and work. Delilah stands over the kitchen stove humming and making pancakes for her white employer, serving her and providing an unobtrusive soundtrack for her breakfast. Notably, this scene in which Delilah provides support to Bea, feeding her and providing the sonic background, takes place just before Bea steals Delilah's culinary inheritance for her business venture. Commenting upon the delicious pancakes, Bea then proceeds to extract Delilah's "secret" family recipe. The very next scene features Bea beginning the pancake business that will make her fortune. Delilah will, over the course of the film, serve as background for all Bea's doings, and the sound of Blackness will come to be very important, both for the way Bea's character develops and for adding substance to the relatively thin plot of which she is the heroine.

The second time Delilah sings, she and Bea are together in the not-yet-open boardwalk pancake restaurant. Delilah stands at the plate glass window putting up paper and eavesdropping on Bea's charm offensive against the many vendors with whom she is establishing no-money-down installment plans. Here, Delilah's singing comments ironically and humorously on the action. Hearing the large sums being discussed, and knowing her employer has only a few dollars in her purse, she sings to herself, "I put my trust in Jesus." Delilah's third and final moment of song occurs in a brief, intimate moment of comforting her daughter. For a 1930s film that was noteworthy for the centrality of its Black characters, their scenes contain remarkably little of the singing that so characterized Black performances earlier in the decade. If Delilah sings little, Peola sings not at all. Instead, music transfers to the white characters for the majority of the film. Helpfully, Delilah and Peola have a brief exchange that glosses the phenomenon.

After the opening credits, the early scenes of the film contain no nondiegetic music. Only Delilah's two earlier moments of song, and a brief rhyme from baby Jessie could properly be called musical. But once the pancake fortune has been made, musical scoring begins to accompany the action, marking a shift in both the narrative and the sonic patterns of the film established to this point. First, a nondiegetic instrumental rendition of "Nobody Knows" accompanies a shot of the mass-produced boxes of pancake flour bearing Delilah's image. This is the only nondiegetic accompaniment Delilah's image will receive until she is dying. The scene is immediately followed by a celebratory party at which Bea meets her love interest, Stephen Archer, beginning a light romance plot of mistaken intentions that the film and Bea will both endow with great emotional weight. This scene also introduces the film's instrumental theme, inaugurating the presence of nondiegetic scoring for the second half.

In the party scene, the music has a source, although it will be repeated nondiegetically thereafter. Commenting on the music and its source, Delilah and Peola demonstrate what scholars have described as the film's depiction of generational difference, as Delilah looks on admiringly and Peola critically.[48] Peola and Delilah take on a spectator position for a moment, both figuratively and literally. As the help living downstairs, they are not invited to the party; physically, they are outside on the street, standing in the dark and gazing up at the well-lit rectangles of action in which white romance plays out. Delilah is enchanted by the entertainment before her, invested as she is in the story of a glamorous white woman's happiness. But when she turns to comment on the entertainment to her daughter, "Dems plays pretty good for white boys," Peola responds snappishly, "They ought to play well; they get paid enough."[49] This brief exchange offers a neat summary of the phenomenon of Black musical performance in Hollywood film as the on-screen jazz band becomes white, treated as professional, and well-paid.

As the film goes on, nondiegetic music echoing that of the party scene begins to accompany scenes involving the white actors. This music becomes the theme for scenes with Bea and Stephen and even carries over into the scene in which Stephen meets Jessie, inspiring the mistaken romance between this secondary white pairing. In addition to the instrumental jazz score, as mentioned above, the other song that repeats as nondiegetic music is the spiritual "Nobody Knows." It appears in the opening credits; as a sound bridge across the scene in which Delilah refuses her share of the pancake fortune and the one in which she is replicated as a logo on mass-produced pancake boxes; and again at the film's close, when Bea and Jesse reconcile. Scholars such as Berlant and Bernstein and White have seen the song's tracking through the film as a measure of its more progressive intentions, but placed against the history of atmospheric Black singing in Hollywood films, "Nobody Knows" looks much more like the kind of extractive relationship to Black tradition exemplified by Bea's commodification of Delilah's family recipe.

Interestingly, the one moment in which a Black character receives similar musical treatment to her white counterparts occurs when Peola is passing, having left her all-Black college for a job as a restaurant hostess. In this scene, Peola receives the instrumental nondiegetic scoring typically reserved for the romantic scenes between the white characters. As the scene opens on Jackson's restaurant, a light instrumental score plays. It continues as Delilah enters the restaurant; however, when Peola spots her mother, the music abruptly stops as the film cuts back and forth between the women's faces. As Peola's identity becomes clear to those around her, the score remains absent.[50] In an interaction across the film's diegetic levels, as Peola is racially recategorized, her musical treatment shifts as well.

Beyond the commodification of Black culture for white gain, shifting a Black song to background music for white characters also functions to transfer the film's emotional weight. As the Black cultural critic and author Sterling Brown noted at the time, "There is a scene where

Miss Bea goes upstairs while Delilah goes down. It is symbolic of many things. One is, that in *Imitation of Life* where Claudette Colbert has a role to bring out all that there is in her, both Miss Beavers and Miss Washington have, so to speak, to go downstairs."[51] That the gains in gravitas by Colbert's Bea come at the expense of Beavers's Delilah becomes increasingly clear as the film progresses.[52]

Across the film's runtime, Blackness becomes associated with tragedy rather than comedy at the same time it also becomes equated with the abstract qualities of seriousness and realism. When Peola returns briefly to the Pullman house to tell her mother that she is leaving forever to pass as white, Bea makes to leave and give Delilah and Peola their privacy. Delilah stops her, saying, "You stay. I want you to hear, too." When Bea emerges into the hall from witnessing Peola's rejection of Delilah, Jesse sees her stricken face and asks, "What's wrong mother?" "I've just seen such a tragedy," Bea replies. In addition to emphasizing Bea's role as a spectator to a new kind of Black performance, cuing white spectators of the film, the episode also grants emotional depth to the white conversation that follows, in which Jesse describes spending time with her mother's beau Steven. The frivolous misunderstanding that centers this plot is deepened by the Black tragedy playing out alongside it.

While Bea has been invited to hear something, she has not listened; instead, she translates the scene between Peola and Delilah into a tragedy she can understand, the universal tragedy of maternal heartache, rather than the particular heartache of a Black mother and her light-skinned daughter responding to life in a racist world.[53] Bea will go forward in the film interpreting her own relationship with her daughter in these terms, construing her daughter's affection for Stephen as a great tragedy, rather than the comedy of mistaken identities that is this plot's nearer generic fit. At the same time, because of her thin identification with Delilah, Bea can offer only superficial comfort. When Delilah tells Bea that she has lost Peola for good, Bea offers platitudes, telling Delilah, "She'll come back to you," evidencing her claim with an appeal to the universal relationship of children to their mothers. In this way, Bea's understanding predicts that of *Imitation*'s white critics and letter writers who would also voice their own limited empathy for Beavers's character.

White audiences responded in their letters to the movie magazines much as Bea does within the film, reporting that they had been moved by an encounter with the real. In these letters, audience members argue for the quality of the film as evidenced by the strength of their own emotional reactions to Delilah. In one letter objecting to the Academy Awards' snubbing of Beavers, a D. H. Chapman refers to her as "heartbreakingly real."[54] In an unusual letter from a Canadian theater manager, Walter H. Golding, the writer complains of Beavers being left out of American publicity. He contrasts Canadian fairness with American race prejudice, noting that Beavers is the true star of the film. However, he does so in terms that collapse the actress and the character in remarkably reductive terms, arguing "the new punch, the new angle of showmanship was the Negress mother—the kindly, loving, emotional, 100% natural mother."[55]

While Golding was correct about Beavers being largely left out of studio publicity materials, reviewers and columnists in U.S. fan magazines held her performance up for special recognition in terms nearly identical to Golding's, while also contrasting Beavers to white actresses, in the film and in Hollywood more broadly. For example, Norbert Lusk's "The Screen in Review" column for *Photoplay* highlights Beavers's performance as one of the strongest in current cinema, again appealing to her realism:

> It has the incontestable merit of a situation that has never been seen before in films. That of a Negro mother whose light-skinned daughter rejects her because her parent is black while she can pass for white. However, this powerful theme is subordinated and we are asked to give our greater interest to a mother who gives up her fiancé because her daughter loves him. Played by Claudette Colbert, Warren William, and Rochelle Hudson, these characters are not nearly so interesting as the colored couple of Louise Beavers and Fredi Washington, whose problem throbs with sympathy for both. Miss Beavers, whom you will

recognize as the maid in many films, is a finely natural actress who gives a performance that will be remembered a year from now. Something that cannot be said of Miss Colbert's well-dressed promenade.[56]

In a very different article, bemoaning feminine artifice in general and the effects of Technicolor on the appearance of actresses in particular, Herb Howe holds Louise Beavers out as an exception: "There is one, however, whom producers fail to remodel and upon whom technicolor [sic] will play no tricks. She suggests comfort rather than beauty and I have an idea this weary world is ready for her. I know I am. I refer to Louise Beavers, colored, whose hearty genuineness in "Imitation of Life" should put her white sisters to shame. Acting is easier for her than for white folks. She can concentrate on feeling. She hasn't the distraction of wondering if her nose is shiny. She knows it is."[57] In these pieces, white critics identify Beavers as giving them something different than her white counterparts; the term they use for this something is "the real."[58] As they did in reports on Black sound's authenticity, the reviews make a fetish of the Black actress as a reality effect. Significantly, however, the "authenticity" this particular review locates in Beavers's "shiny nose" may have been part of a relatively complex interplay between makeup and studio policy. As Adrienne McLean has written, one way studios met the Code's prohibition on miscegenation was to deny "glamour for Black performers."[59]

In contrast, Sterling Brown reads Delilah and, in particular, her musical treatment quite differently than white critics, who appeared not to notice the music. In his scathing review "Once a Pancake," Brown observes, "To the reviewer the shots nearest to truth are the Harlem funeral scenes; the most memorable is the flash of the electric sign after the death of Delilah. The good old heartbroken soul dies, having made Miss Bea's road an easy one, for little more return than comfort and affection; Miss Bea goes on to wealth, love and happiness, and Delilah gets her dubious immortality as an electrified trademark. The music of the quartette is stirring, although it is unfortunately synchronized with Delilah's dying, and is another instance of Hollywood's poor imitation of life."⁶⁰ For Brown, while the music accesses emotions, it does so in service of Hollywood's phony recollections of Black life.

As Brown's review indicates, Delilah's deathbed scenes are notable for the way they reveal the disturbing shallowness of the friendship as well as for the music that accompanies them. At her friend's bedside, Bea's witnessing is accompanied by Black sound as an instrumental rendition of "Nobody Knows" plays softly. The song continues through the rest of this first of two deathbed scenes, as Delilah describes to Bea the spectacular funeral she wants, noting, "I want those colored folks' eyes to bulge out." Delilah's dream funeral is a spectacle of her importance, directed toward a Black audience of which Bea seems remarkably ignorant.⁶¹ Delilah clarifies that she has membership in a number of important Black social organizations, including her lodge and church—spaces of Black civic life that remain off-screen. "You and your processions," Bea chides, changing the subject to something she finds more interesting: "Let me tell you some good news—I'm going to get married." Bea's line thus momentarily converts Delilah from the star of a Black tragedy to the spectator of a white comedy. When Bea exits the room, Delilah's deathbed music abruptly stops, but Bea carries with her a sense of seriousness that she applies to her own familial and romantic woes.

The film splits Delilah's death across two scenes. While the first is accompanied by the instrumental "Nobody Knows," the second features a nondiegetic choral performance of "Lord, Have Mercy." The second deathbed scene is unusual not just for granting nondiegetic music to Delilah but also because, with the exception of the opening credits, it is the only choral nondiegetic music in the film, with the words "Have Mercy" audible throughout the scene, transferring the film briefly into a timeless "other world" similar to *Hallelujah*'s mixed sonic diegesis.⁶² The characters present in the scene also break the film's typical staging patterns by including the adult Jessie, who has previously appeared primarily in the company of other white characters. Being in the presence of Black pain is thus presented as a necessary part of her maturation, a moment of contact with "the real." Over the course of the scene, Jessie stands as a silent audience member, witnessing Delilah and Bea's sorrowful discussion of Peola. As Delilah dies, the spiritual continues and the film cuts to Bea's and Jessie's reactions, as white mother and daughter turn away from Delilah's body and sob, accompanied by the music, breaking with the earlier deathbed scene's pattern of keeping the music associated with Delilah rather than the white characters. In the somber air of Delilah's death scene and the resonant tones of "Have Mercy," the white daughter and mother join in a shared feeling of sorrow. That Black music and Black death should remain as atmosphere at this moment, lingering to give reality and depth to white feeling, should come as no surprise, for Bea has already described her dying friend as a "mountain" and Jesse has named Delilah a "horsey" upon their first meeting, recastings that preview the violent metamorphosis of Delilah from woman to scenery, a transformation made literal by the neon sign of the film's finale. Even in a film with two Black leads, then, the Hollywood habit of treating Blackness as setting remains.

Delilah's death *does*, however, create a generic disturbance in the film. From the second deathbed scene, the film cuts to a Harlem church and Delilah's requested funeral. The change in venue takes place alongside a number of formal shifts. First, the screen fills with Black actors, a casting choice that was a matter of race pride and hope for future employment, with a *Chicago Defender* headline promising "Universal Partial to Race Since 'Imitation of Life.'"[63] Second, while most of the film relies on traditional Hollywood shot scales, Delilah's funeral procession uses long and extremely long shots to showcase the number of mourners and spectators gathered, at a camera distance from the action that has the effect of shifting tonal and generic registers away from the fictional melodrama that has preceded the scene. Delilah's funeral opens to a diegetically located choral performance of "There Is Rest for the Weary." In addition to the number of Black extras who appear, the scene is also noteworthy for the unusual framing and camera movement. The camera tracks backward from the open door of the church, leaving the choir inside, framed by the doorway. Having missed her mother's funeral, Peola stands between two white women on the street, witnessing the coffin being loaded into the hearse. One of the women notices Peola's tears and inquires, "Did you know her?"—the implication being that the white women do not but are gathered for the spectacle of the Black woman's funeral.[64] Peola rushes tearfully to the coffin and is taken into the awaiting car by Bea and Jesse. When Peola, Jesse, Bea, and Stephen pile into the hearse, the instrumental music associated with the funeral march begins. This music is neither clearly diegetic or nondiegetic, with a possible source in the procession's marchers who fill the Harlem streets, an ambiguity that further separates the scene from the rest of the film's diegetic world. With the camera framing, the distance from the funeral procession passing by, and the use of hundreds of Black extras with no lines or individualizing close-ups, the scene looks like one of the silent era's actuality films of parades and processions. And so, as Delilah achieves her dying wish, the film's equation of Blackness with a reality function is complete.

In its use of Black performers and performances of Black sound as a sign of the real that gives weight to insubstantial white feelings, the ostensibly progressive *Imitation of Life* tracks a similar pattern to the more conservative *Gone with the Wind*'s use of Blackness as atmosphere in the Negro Labor Battalion scene. As the nondiegetic refrain of "Nobody Knows" indicates, Black song could shorthand suffering in mainstream Hollywood pictures, so much so that in a 1935 novel, a suicidal white character's depression could be described through reference to the commercial spiritual. "I'm tired of living and I'm afraid of dying," complains a young white woman named Gloria.[65] Overhearing her, another white character responds sarcastically, "Say, that's a swell idea for a song. . . . You could write a song about an old nigger down on the levee who was tired of living and afraid of dying. He could be heaving cotton and singing a song to the Mississippi River. Say, that's a good title—you could call it Old Man River."[66] This brief exchange from Horace McCoy's *They Shoot Horses, Don't They?* and the development of white gravitas against the background of Black pain in *Imitation* both illustrate the racialization of unhappiness. Writing on depression, a topic addressed in the next chapter, Ann Cvetkovich notes that discussions of the malady "presume a white and middle-class subject for whom feeling bad is frequently a mystery because it doesn't fit a life in which privilege and comfort make things seem fine on the surface."[67] This emotional color line appears in the conversation about Gloria's unhappiness, which her interlocutor nastily suggests belongs to the provenance of Black song. This is the flip side of the stereotype of Black easygoingness, as Black unhappiness is likewise understood as a natural state under the rubric of the real—a stereotype evidenced by *Imitation of Life*'s ending, which leaves the Black women dead or in sorrow while returning its newly deepened white heroines to their natural state of happiness.

III
THE UNHAPPY

5

UNHAPPY VICTIMS

The Unreadability of Star Suicides

A *Silver Screen* column from 1939 illustrates the very behavior it ascribes to a gossiping public, as author Jeanne de Kolty hauls a trio of scandalous deaths, ranging from five years to more than a decade in the past, back into view:

> I recall another of Hollywood's laws, one of the most subtle and therefore one which is seldom recognized outside the industry: Never Reveal What Goes on Behind the Scenes. This law ties in with that old Jonah of scandal, since too frank revelations can result in the latter. Such cases as the William Desmond Taylor shooting and the untimely deaths of lovely Thelma Todd and Paul Bern are always cloaked in a shroud of mystery, even when the police decide on a suicide verdict, as in the Bern and Todd cases. It is almost invariably suspected that someone, somewhere in the industry might shed some light on these tragedies. Surely, somebody knows something about them. But Hollywood does not talk![1]

No one, it seems, can leave these bodies alone. They call for speculation.

If the star is a text, then the star suicide introduces an erratum that generates corrective narratives of extraordinary proportions. Nothing is so consistently generative of conspiracy theories as a star suicide. As a reading-too-much-into, an obsession with spurious connections, and a fixation on detail, the conspiracy theory is a particularly active form of fandom and entertainment reporting. This chapter considers two possible Hollywood suicides and the filmic and magazine discourse around them, arguing that the kind of misreading at the heart of the star suicide conspiracy theory schooled fans on the limits of empathy. Instead of extending empathic coverage toward the depressive, the fan magazines tended to open the door for conspiracy, forwarding narratives of relatable, unwitting victims over those whose unhappiness might prompt uncomfortable thinking about what in the world might be worth being unhappy about.

To take a brief example explored in the era's pulp fiction, Horace McCoy's 1935 Hollywood novel *They Shoot Horses, Don't They?* builds the tragic irony of its tale around a judicial act of misreading. The plot unfolds via alternating sections, the first made up of short lines across which the judge reads out the protagonist's sentence: death as punishment for the crime of murder. Between portions of the sentencing, the protagonist Robert offers his first-person retrospective narration of the events leading up to his mercy killing of Gloria, his partner in a Depression-era dance marathon. In these scenes, Gloria regales Robert with stories of failed suicide attempts, telling him that "she's tired of living, but afraid to die."[2] As the marathon drags on and Gloria grows increasingly disaffected, the novel achieves its climax with Gloria thrusting the fatal pistol into Robert's hands and begging him to help her. But despite Robert's attempts to explain what happened, the official legal narrative refuses his account of an assisted suicide and instead categorizes his act as murder.

As de Kolty's grouping of Todd and Bern alongside Taylor indicates, reading suicide as murder was not limited to the fictional realm in the 1920s and 1930s. Indeed, such misinterpretation of suicide was something of a phenomenon, especially when it came to famous Hollywood deaths. Although it is significant in *Horses* that Gloria is a film extra, not a star, the high-profile deaths of actress Thelma Todd and producer, and Jean Harlow's husband, Paul Bern became important sites for managing star discourse, a management strategy characterized by misreading, misdirection, and spurious interpretation rather than clarification.

ADJUDICATING PAIN AFTER THE CODE

As previous chapters have discussed, the 1920s and 1930s were a period of particularly intense reputational struggle for Hollywood. In these decades, the industry found itself spinning a number of star scandals, including the Pickford-Fairbanks divorce, the Fatty Arbuckle trial over the 1921 death of actress Virginia Rappe, and William Desmond Taylor's death, which pulled comedian Mabel Norman as well as actress Mary Miles Minter and her mother Charlotte Selby into its orbit. By the end of the thirties, in the face of increased public scrutiny and censorship pressures, the Code had emerged as the industry's most concerted effort to improve its reputation. But auxiliary businesses also had their part to play, including the various fan magazines, which operated in a reciprocal relationship with audiences, both responding to audiences' attitudes to various stars and shaping these attitudes through gossip columns, interview articles, and news items. Columnists in movie magazines were particularly savvy about raising the specter of scandal one minute only to piously dismiss salacious rumors as petty gossip in the next.

Pre-Code, speculations about suicide had marked some of the earliest star scandals, as in the 1920 case of former Ziegfield girl and actress Olive Thomas, who had married Mary Pickford's playboy brother Jack and died of an overdose of his syphilis medications. Rumors about the motivation for her consumption of the drug as well as the lifestyle of Thomas and Pickford circulated, although the most prominent fan magazines, such as *Photoplay*, worked to manage the industry's reputation by encouraging fans to read the tragedy in as wholesome a light as possible, as in this column by Cal York: "Her death occurred early in September following mercurial poisoning, a fatal potion which was taken by mistake for headache sleeping powder. She and her husband, Jack Pickford, were in the midst of their honeymoon trip, which had been planned repeatedly since 1917, the year of their marriage. Jack Pickford made a heroic effort to save his wife's life by forcing her to swallow thirty-two glasses of water as first aid treatment."[3]

In contrast to *Photoplay*'s coverage of this scandal, three years later *Screenland* covered actor Wallace Reid's morphine addiction, which soon led to his death, with an article bluntly titled "Dope" that raised rumors of "orgies" at the Reid household, even if to ultimately dismiss them.[4] The February 1923 issue of *Screenland* also teases the question "Is nudity immoral?" on its cover. Even *Photoplay*, the most influential of the fan magazines, tipped an editorial hand in pieces expressing that tragedies required a strong narrative cover and also risked producing counternarratives and conspiracies that needed managing. The same issue that presented Thomas's death as a terrible accident and Pickford as heroic, opened with an unusual editorial.

The editorial holds *Photoplay* readers, and filmgoers more broadly, responsible for the moral quality of Hollywood through a discussion of hypothetical child spectators.[5] Despite York's scrupulous avoidance of the rumors of sex and drugs that surrounded Thomas and Pickford, the editorial presents young children susceptible to corruption in terms that could not help but pique prurient curiosity: "Would you, day after day, send your eight-year-old Jack into a luxurious restaurant and let him choose at random, brandishing a little boy's barbaric appetite to his own eventual destruction, or at least serious discomfort?" Further, the editorial asks, "Would you permit your ten-year-old Mabel to wield her wild will in the shops of ready-made apparel, emerging thence to amaze the pedestrians, humiliate you and frighten the few remaining horses?" The editorial then makes its series of rhetorical questions pay in defense of the movies and an accusation against hypocritical filmgoers. "Yet in a general way, you make few attempts to guide their diversions," the editorial scolds. As a result, "every now and then, in consequence, some quack doctor of public morals talks about the 'pernicious movies.'" From here, the editorial reminds *Photoplay* readers that film exhibition is a business, and if they wish their children to see clean films, they must support such practices as "children's evenings" or "children's days." However, the editorial states, it would be a mistake to censor: "You never will shut out the honest, though ofttimes tragic stories of real life. Real life is the basis of art in shadowland as well as in literature and drama. But you don't cry down 'The Scarlet Letter' and 'The Easiest Way' because

The World's Leading Moving Picture Magazine

PHOTOPLAY

VOL. XVIII   *November, 1920*   No. 6

For Mabel and Jack

WOULD you, day after day, send your eight-year-old Jack into a luxurious restaurant and let him choose at random, brandishing a little boy's barbaric appetite to his own eventual destruction, or at least serious discomfort?

Would you permit your ten-year-old Mabel to wield her wild will in the shops of ready-made apparel, emerging thence to amaze the pedestrians, humiliate you and frighten the few remaining horses in our streets?

Would you encourage either child to read, or attempt to read, all our literary classics, or would you countenance a detailed study of every narrative in the Holy Bible?

You know you would do none of these things.

Yet, in a general way, you make few attempts to guide them in their film diversions. And every now and then, in consequence, some quack doctor of public morals talks about the "pernicious movies."

The mind of a child is the most susceptible, sensitive, permanent record in the world. There ought to be films especially for children, both educational and entertaining. There are such films now, but not enough of them, and there are no concerted attempts at children's evenings, children's afternoons, or children's programmes.

Your exhibitor is a business man. Prove that you want film education and film entertainment especially for your child, and you will get it. Many an enterprising picture-man has actually started children's days, only to abandon the practise because of neglect and non-appreciation.

You never will shut out the honest, though ofttimes tragic stories of real life. Real life is the basis of art in shadowland as well as in literature and the drama. But you don't cry down "The Scarlet Letter" and "The Easiest Way" because you know they are not proper pabulum for little sister and her brother. By demanding, you provide other books for Mabel and Jack.

You must do this in the photoplay.

FIGURE 5.1 *Photoplay* scolding parents.

you know they are not proper pablum for little sister and her brother. By demanding, you provide other books for Mabel and Jack."

Although likely intended to indicate generic little-boy-ness, Jack, this child of destructive "barbaric appetite," might well have called to mind the Jack deeper in the magazine's pages. The discussion of "real life" tragedies alongside fictional tales likewise brings to mind the Thomas case and further blurs the relationship between on- and off-screen, much as the scandals of the early twenties, of which Thomas's possible suicide was but one, resulted in not just decency clauses but also changes in representation, including, but not limited to, the depiction of suicide. The shift in depictions can be seen, for example, by comparing George Cukor's pre-Code *What Price Hollywood?* (1932)—which contains subjective images from the point of view of its depressive character leading up to his violent self-inflicted death by gunshot wound—with the scandalously similar post-Code *A Star is Born* (Wellman, 1937). By 1937, the scandal presented by *A Star is Born* is not about its depiction of the death of Esther Blodgett's mentor, Norman Maine—who simply walks into the Pacific one bright California day—but rather its near plagiarism of *What Price*. In the late 1930s, the psychology of the suicide was not to be explored on-screen, realism be damned.

When it came to the motion picture industry as a whole, the discourse about its role in public life alternated between describing the pictures as salubrious or perverse, family-friendly or sophisticated. Suicide within the industry obviously fell into the latter category, an act that the press, and sometimes the studio employing the person, framed as an unwholesome and unnatural act, even as suicide brought new attention to the individual's career. While a spectacular death differentiated posthumous stardoms at a time when there were perhaps too many actors competing for public attention, what Lisa Bode calls "an ever-expanding sea of past stars," suicide was a particularly thorny matter, and not just because it was scandalous in the manner of sex, drugs, or murder.[6] Instead, as the suicide rate reached a national peak and Americans took seriously the idea that economic Depression and psychological lows were linked, magazines promoted narratives of overcoming difficulty with good cheer.[7]

As discussed previously, the pint-sized emissary of good will Shirley Temple's 1934 breakout film *Stand Up and Cheer* makes explicit the connection between happy moods and a healthy national economy, with a plot that details the creation of an entertainment bureau, including a children's division, devoted to spreading "cheer" and creating "healthy-mindedness," thereby restoring faith in the market. Several song and dance numbers later, the film ends with a character announcing "The Depression is over!" and then detailing affective and economic responses to the entertainment division: "Factories are opening up! Men are going back to work by the thousands! Our byproducts are being sold the world over! Savings accounts are heaping up! The banks are pouring out new loans! There is no unemployment! Fear has been banished, confidence reborn! Poverty has been wiped out! Laughter resounds throughout the nation! The people are happy again! We're outta the red!" In the propaganda world of this film, the entertainment industry, audiences, and the nation work together to achieve market optimism through an unremarkable "let's put on a show" plot that makes feeling good a matter of patriotic duty. In films like Temple's, Hollywood offered a layman's account of and solution to the "animal spirits" John Maynard Keynes would identify in his 1936 work *The General Theory of Employment, Interest and Money*, which classified consumer confidence as an important economic measure.

By contrast, Angelenos were all too familiar with the metrics of suicide in the 1930s, when showboat coroner Frank A. Nance, who would oversee both the Todd and Bern inquests, was a regular fixture in the *Los Angeles Times*, where he reported monthly fatality numbers with a particular focus on car accidents and suicides. The latter category reached alarmingly high levels early in the decade, with Nance regularly noting record-setting and -breaking months. Headlines such as "Fifty-Six Die By Suicide"; "Suicides Set New Record in April, Coroner Reports"; and "July Killings Break Records" kept suicide in view as a public epidemic.[8] Suicide appeared in the paper as a problem for public works as well, with calls to eliminate the so-called suicide span of Pasadena's Colorado Street bridge.[9] If feeling good was part of national service, feeling bad, especially when bad feelings looked out of proportion or unearned, was not just unpatriotic but dangerous, a kind of public health crisis.

In this context, it is no surprise that fan magazines repeatedly probed and then foreclosed the possibility of celebrity suicides, often forwarding murder as a preferable explanation for mysterious deaths. While it might be explicable that life had become unbearable for the businessman or farmer who had lost everything, the unhappiness of celebrities raised the specter that wealth and well-being might be problematically detached from one another. Not just salacious, then, reading star suicides as murders was an interpretive act with ideological implications. Like many Hollywood deaths, those of actress Thelma Todd and Jean Harlow's husband Paul Bern have generated many such theories, some more and some less persuasive. It is not my intention to contribute to this discourse by making the diagnosis of suicide official in either case—indeed, Todd's death continues to produce speculation—but rather to consider what it means that suicide is the reading repeatedly refused, whether in fictional cases such as *They Shoot Horses, Don't They?* and Harlow's own film *Reckless* (Fleming, 1935) or in the newspapers and fan magazines covering real Hollywood deaths. The Todd and Bern cases played out differently in the papers, because of these movieland figures' different public personae as well as the clearer picture of Bern's death. Because the murder theory of the Bern death never had the traction of the many Todd theories, his case is particularly useful in judging public reactions to the high-profile suicide.

Whether clear or murky, famous or obscure, suicides provoke survivors and inspire judgment. In the case of the star suicide, survivors include the public and their stand-ins, the celebrity journalists and gossip columnists who claim to have known the celebrity. Following the star's death, these knowing survivors undertake the business of adjudicating pain. In the magazines, postmortem assessments of suffering very often find the star's pain lacking, and so the discourse turns to conspiracy. As living embodiments of such culturally laden values as joy, glamour, and energy, stars such as Todd gave no performance of suffering, and so their deaths demonstrate the nature of internal pain being a knowledge problem in the manner described by Elaine Scarry: an "absolute split between one's sense of one's own reality and the reality of other persons."[10] Scarry's work specifies that physical pain is different from emotional or psychological suffering that takes an object, such as lust *for* or anxiety *about*; instead, "pain is not 'of' or 'for' anything—it is itself alone."[11] By contrast, much of the recent work on negative affects has been interested in the political pointing done by darker emotional states that act as the smoke that indexes the fire of an unjust world.[12] Unlike Scarry's description of objectless pain, for example, Ann Cvetkovich accounts for depression as a political mode, an "affective register of . . . social problems."[13] But by losing depression's pain (in Scarry's physiological sense of the term) in her quest to destigmatize, deindividualize, and demedicalize the condition, Cvetkovich risks seeking external causes in order to make sense of depression, even if her "making sense" is much more radically inflected than that of the examples discussed in this chapter. This chapter thus builds on the important work of affect theorists like Cvetkovich to locate the political edge of bad feelings, particularly the way bad feelings activate a social response against the subject possessing such feelings, while also insisting on the disruptive significance of depression's sometimes directionless pain and retaining room for pain's opacity.[14] At least in part, responses to suicide register the provocation of the unknown as they express frustration with the suicide who does not make her pain legible and leaves behind a question.

Building from both Scarry's theory of objectless pain and affect theory's idea of unhappiness as political provocation, the remainder of this chapter tracks the way star suicides can raise the knowledge problem of the first and also the affective and political problems of the second. On the one hand, the suicide that is unexpected makes publics seek a reasonable cause; on the other, suicides that appear "undeserved" make publics hostile toward the suicide's attitude toward his life or world. Both reactions are at work in the cases gathered here. The coverage of Todd repeatedly refused the possibility that the actress may have been in pain, a refusal so total that elaborate mob conspiracies appear preferable. In the case of Bern, skepticism toward pain paired with a criticism of his suffering, as the suicide's pain is doubted (life should not have felt so unbearable) and his orientation toward the world is criticized (normal or happy things should not make him so unhappy). As Scarry writes, "pain comes unsharably into our midst as at once that which cannot be denied and that which cannot be confirmed."[15] In other words, pain looks a lot like the seeds of conspiracy.

THELMA TODD: THE DEATH OF A "REGULAR FELLOW"

Thelma Todd exited the world by playing an ironic trick on a movie industry that had held very different hopes for her. Todd's career was born out of the same need to rehabilitate Hollywood's reputation that had rocketed Temple to stardom. The actress made her way into the movies via a scouting contest that secured her a place in a Paramount finishing school as part of a high-publicity scheme to show that film stars could be and were made of wholesome American youths from Anytown, U.S.A.[16] Of the sixteen hopefuls the program tapped for fame, Todd was one of a small group, including "America's Boyfriend" Buddy Rogers, to make a film career. A beautiful young comedienne, she was known for her work with Hal Roach as one half of his attempt at a female comedy duo—first with ZaSu Pitts and then with Patsy Kelly—as well as appearances alongside Laurel and Hardy, Buster Keaton, and the Marx Brothers. Todd shocked the nation with her untimely death, even as she had started amassing a less than fully good girl reputation due to a bad marriage, an attachment to the married director Roland West (who had married the scandalous Jewel Carmen), and a love of nightlife. Nonetheless, Todd was known as a cheerful and stand-up kind of gal, appearing, for example, as a case in point for a *Silver Screen* article titled "The Troupers," which explains "Thelma Todd has been starred time and again in comedies, yet she is used to add fire or what have you to otherwise drab productions. She has 'built up' everything from Harold Lloyd to a cake of ice in one of the Marx Brothers' creations!"[17] In addition to her acting career, she was also known in town as a businesswoman who operated the popular Thelma Todd's Sidewalk Café with West.

Beyond her general good nature, there are a few other facts about Todd on which everyone agrees: The night she died, Todd had attended a party thrown by Ida Lupino at the Trocadero. The following morning, her Lincoln was parked in West's garage, where her maid discovered her body; it was determined that Todd had died of carbon monoxide poisoning. There are almost no other details on which the various Todd theorists have concurred, whether in the 1930s or the 1990s, when the Loni Anderson made-for-TV movie *White Hot: The Mysterious Murder of Thelma Todd* (Wendkos, 1991) suggested that gangster Lucky Luciano was behind Todd's death, a theory for which there is little evidence. Todd's December 1935 death raised immediate speculation, as even the relatively straightforward headline "Thelma Todd Found Dead in Her Auto" in *Motion Picture Daily* was followed by the presentation of two possibilities: "Police called it a homicide first, but later said death might have resulted from natural causes."[18] Three possibilities circulated: suicide, accidental death, and, because of ex-husband Pat DiCicco's possible Mafia ties and Todd's experience on the receiving end of a blackmail plot, murder.[19] While the autopsy surgeon declared the death accidental, a grand jury continued the investigation and leaned toward suicide, and others, including Todd's mother (though she later changed her mind), declared that the actress had been murdered. Further complicating matters, *Variety* reported that Todd's "friend and business associate" Roland West claimed that her noisy car would have been heard starting and that the patchy plaster of the garage would have allowed poisonous fumes to escape "before overcoming Miss Todd."[20]

In the *Independent Exhibitors Film Bulletin* review of Thelma Todd's final film, the Laurel and Hardy vehicle *The Bohemian Girl* (Horne and Rogers, 1936), the actress's recent death counts as yet another mark against what the reviewer L.J. sees as a very mediocre film. "Cross this one off your booking list!" the review opens, before detailing Todd's death as part of the picture's general shabbiness: "The usually funny Laurel and Hardy haven't a chance with the poor material placed in their hands and their antics are too patterned to bring about laughs without adequate 'business.' Parents will find plenty to object to for their children in the story, which has much to do with an unfaithful wife and some free and fancy stealing. It is all done crudely. The late Thelma Todd is seen in a brief singing sequence, with the voice obviously dubbed. This will bring low grosses everywhere."[21] The *Chicago Tribune* reacted to the film in no uncertain terms, opening its review with a frank, one-sentence paragraph: "This is a silly ass comedy based on the opera by Michael Balfe."[22]

Despite generally dismissive reviews, Todd's last film invites examination, raising the matter of evidence and interpretation in its storyline and its production history. *Bohemian Girl* is a film in which almost everyone is too stupid to see what's in front of them—this despite the plot's focus on the magic tricks, disguises, deceptions, and sleights of hand that characterize it as both a Laurel and Hardy and a "gypsy" picture. The main plot, such as it is, centers around an itinerant band including Stan and Ollie, who camp outside a palace from which Ollie's wife and her lover Devilshoof kidnap a child. They disguise the child with a bandana before running off together, leaving her unrecognizable to her kin and in the loving care of Stan and Ollie. From the disguised child's family to the pickpocket victims of scam fortune tellers to the cuckolded Ollie, dupes abound. Everyone is waiting for the turn of fortune's wheel that will make them the next fool—everyone except the wife, that is. Unlike her compatriots, the wife assesses the general lousiness of things, including her fool of a husband, and hightails it out of the camp. But she too is a body of evidence indicating something amiss beneath the film's surface.

We meet the wife after first encountering Stanley and Ollie at their campsite. The two men sit by a fire, peeling potatoes, while Ollie's wife carries on with Devilshoof behind the couple's painted wagon. When Stan comes upon the embracing couple and reports back, "You know what, I'm not going to say anything until I get positive proof, but I just saw Devilshoof kissing your wife," Ollie refuses to take in the information and goes to see for himself. Despite seeing his wife in the arms of her lover, he explains, "There was nothing to it. They were just having a little innocent fun," refusing the visible evidence as well as Stan's more plausible interpretation of the facts. The film then ratchets up the joke about the fool husband preferring a rosier narrative as the wife and Devilshoof walk to the front of the wagon, where they exchange tickles, loving looks, and a rose. The film cuts between the ostentatious display of adultery and the seated pair of onlookers, Stan and Ollie, creating an on-screen audience-proxy only to have Ollie come to the opposite conclusion of the film viewer. Throughout *The Bohemian Girl*, the wife taunts Stan and Ollie for their stupid acceptance of narratives in contradiction to obvious facts. When she kidnaps the aristocratic child, Devilshoof asks, "How are you going to account for her to your husband?" She replies, "Never fear, he'll believe anything I tell him." And, indeed, when Ollie demands to know from whence his spouse has conjured the young girl (played by *Our Gang*'s Darla Hood), she explains, "Well, if you must know, she's yours." He immediately embraces this preposterous lie, adopting the child as his own and demanding that Stanley congratulate him as a new father.

No bad trick of the movie, however, is as frustrating as Todd's disappearance. Todd was to have played the wife, and she had completed filming before she died. But, perhaps due to fear of bad publicity, Roach had the film reedited and Todd's scenes refilmed with another Laurel and Hardy regular, Mae Busch, taking the role. The last-minute recasting is like the mediocre severed thumb trick Stanley tries to teach Ollie in the bar: a poor substitution that leaves visible the missing object that's haunting the trick. Despite the film's effort to pull a quick switcheroo, the real violence behind Todd's disappearance would have been front of mind to her public. Details of the Todd case circulated rapidly and widely, with crime scene images of the actress's body slumped over the steering wheel making their way to fans across the nation. Additionally, Todd's funeral and the grand jury investigation into her death were well-publicized and well-attended media events, complete with guest stars such as ZaSu Pitts giving testimony.

The photos of Todd's body ran in major papers such as the *Los Angeles Times* and the *Chicago Daily Tribune*, thereby inviting Angelenos and the general public to become amateur sleuths, reading the images of Todd's body for conclusive evidence of the cause of her demise.[23] While the many unknowns in the Todd case doubtless contributed to the press's thorough chewing of conspiracy theories, as did the publicity enjoyed by officials such as coroner Frank Albert Nance during an election year, the disjuncture between her public persona and the possibility of a suicide verdict clearly generated much of the discussion.[24] The *LA Times,* for example, cited the presence in Todd's apartment of "more than 100 Christmas gifts, wrapped and addressed and ready for mailing" as primary evidence that the actress could not have taken her own life, a detail in keeping with her image as friend to many.[25] A number of papers ran stories emphasizing Todd's outwardly happy and helpful demeanor, offering a litany of anecdotes about the actress's cheery disposition to counter suicide speculations. For example, a bizarrely positioned tidbit in *Modern Screen*'s "Good News" section offers a narrative of Todd's smiling nature:

> The tragic death of beautiful Thelma Todd caused more genuine sorrow in Hollywood than the passing of any film personality in recent years, for Thelma had a quality about her that is rare out here—she was real. We saw her last at Paula Stone's cocktail party, just a week before her death, and she was, as always, lovely, radiant and full of the joy of living. Her eulogy wasn't shouted to the heavens by professional weepers, but her memory is held sacred by those she befriended—the prop boys, the extras and the has-beens of Hollywood. A florist, for instance, told us something about her just the other day. Whenever an extra girl of her acquaintance was ill Thelma sent a cheerful note, with a bouquet of roses—into which was tucked a $20 bill.[26]

The report portrays Todd as a healthy everygirl, attending parties, doing favors for other girls, and making real friends wherever she goes. Insisting that the actress was always "radiant and full of the joy of living," the paper makes it clear that girls like Todd simply are not suicides.

Equally important to foreclosing the possibility that a young woman might have been depressed beneath a veneer of vibrancy was the creation of conspiracy counternarratives. Whereas the suicide reading of Todd's death and even the accidental poisoning theory reflected poorly on the actress—as a depressive on the one hand and careless on the other—the murder angle allowed the picture of happiness to remain undisturbed and the stereotype of the depressive to remain similarly intact. The

Variety report immediately following Todd's death indicates an almost hopeful wish that the death might be understood this way: "Thelma Todd, 31, film actress for the past 11 years, died yesterday (Monday), in Santa Monica, Cal., from the effects of carbon monoxide poisoning. Undetermined whether accidental or suicidal. . . . Prior to the accidental death findings, daily papers over the country were sending in cries for yarns emphasizing the mystery and playgirl angle. If the mystery ingredient is kept alive it will be circulation and publicity for police officials connected with the case."[27] An editorial in *Hollywood* magazine offers a similarly coy dismissing and then raising of conspiracy theories:

> Forming another chapter in Hollywood's Mystery Book, the strange death of Thelma Todd undoubtedly will go down in history as another macabre puzzle without a solution. . . . Demon reporters built up every possible mystery angle: The possibility that she had been jabbed *inside* the mouth (the theory arose after the body had been cremated), the broken false tooth, the closed garage doors, the blood running from the mouth as she lay dead behind the wheel of the car, the motor switch on but the motor not running although there was gasoline left in the car, the argument over when she died, the person she told Martha Ford she was bringing to the latter's cocktail party (the coroner had said Thelma died hours before she assertedly called Mrs. Ford on the telephone)—these and a hundred other things.[28]

By framing their own reports against national newspapers, industry magazines accused newspaper reporters of whipping up salacious stories while simultaneously rehearsing the same gory details. Despite emphasizing the unlikeliness that Todd was murdered, the repeated rehashing of such theories suggests that conspiracy theories indicate more than public prurience around violent death. Indeed, as discourse around the Todd case reveals, it is nearly the opposite: entertaining murder theories evidences a profound distaste for suicide.

The squeamishness around this particular type of death would carry into the Code's flexibility regarding taking lives of others compared with depictions of taking one's own life. In the section detailing "Special

Regulations on Crime," murder is acknowledged as occasionally necessary to a film's story: "Because of the increase in the number of films in which murder is frequently committed, action showing the taking of a human life, even in mystery stories, is to be cut to a minimum. These frequent presentations of murder tend to lessen regard for the sacredness of life."[29] In contrast, the regulation immediately following specifies that "Suicide, as a solution of problems occurring in the development of screen drama, is to be discouraged as morally questionable and as bad theater—unless absolutely necessary for the development of the plot." Later, to further drive home the taboo on suicide, the MPAA would add a further sentence: "It should never be justified or glorified, or used to defeat the due process of the law."[30] Whereas the Code acknowledges the necessity, however distasteful, of showing murder, the regulations on suicide make clear that in all but the most exceptional cases, suicide was not a matter for the movies, a judgment that can be seen at play in the aforementioned shift in depiction from *What Price Hollywood?* to *A Star is Born*.[31]

The fan magazines appeared to concur, demonstrating a remarkable consistency in their treatment of Todd's death as they spun narratives around the tragedy to either recontextualize it—whether in relation to her vivacious nature or to murder theories—or decontextualize it entirely. An article titled "Hollywood's Tragic Trilogy" manages to do both at once by framing Todd's death against a series of "tragedies" loosely defined:

> A pall of tragedy lies over Hollywood these days.
>
> The trilogy of deaths which the stage and screen folk—always superstitious—believe in, has been fulfilled. First to go was gay, debonair Gordon Westcott, killed in a polo game. The second was Thelma Todd, a victim of monoxide gas. Who would be the inevitable third?
>
> John Gilbert, dying suddenly of a heart attack, closed the macabre record less than a month after Thelma's passing.
>
> Each time there has been a sudden, tragic death, two more have followed. Dorothy Dell began one such series; the great Will Rogers another. In time, Hollywood has come to believe firmly in this tragic trilogy.[32]

Here, Todd's death loses its specific meaning through its relocation into a narrative of Hollywood mystery and curses. Her death becomes significant to the degree that it develops a series, not for what it might say about the actress or her experience of life. By serializing her tragic death, the article flattens the particularity of her end into one instance of death broadly construed, which might have its source in causes ranging from polo accidents to heart attacks. Through such narrations or even de-narrations of Todd's death, the suicide possibility remains an absent cause that may not be narrated. As a result, the meanings of suicide stay off the table. The questions it might raise stay unasked.

Whether or not Todd died at her own hand remains an open question, but the periodicals clearly demonstrate an unwillingness to consider the possibility, despite the fact of a body in a car, dead from monoxide poisoning, and a grand jury report that the New York Times summarized as follows: "Most of the eighteen jurors believe she committed suicide by carbon monoxide poisoning. A few clung to the theory of foul play. Virtually none of the jurors, it was learned, believes that she lost her life accidentally."[33] In the time since the grand jury investigation, speculations have only increased, most notably with Kenneth Anger's *Hollywood Babylon*, which first introduced the Luciano conspiracy, and then with Andy Edmond's *Hot Toddy*, a highly imaginative account that pursued Anger's mobster angle and was then immortalized in *White Hot*.[34]

But despite the dramatic narratives that followed her death, as a comedian Todd depicted violence and mayhem as part of everyday life for a working girl. As mentioned previously, Todd's Hal Roach comedy shorts paired the actress first with ZaSu Pitts and then with Patsy Kelly as part of an effort to develop a female comedy duo along the lines of the studio's popular Laurel and Hardy team. In both the Pitts and Kelly comedies, the women are typically roommates and figured as working-class, single girls trying to get ahead in the world, whether by serving as typists (*Sealskins*, 1932), working as department store salesgirls (*Babes in the Goods*, 1934), driving ambulances (*War Mamas*, 1931), or fighting crowds to get a deal at a bedding sale (*Bargain of the Century*, 1933).[35] Throughout the shorts, Todd and her partner maintain loyalty to one another, keeping friendship intact while wreaking havoc on both the set and the costumes of their hapless male foils. The comedy short *Beauty and the Bus* (1933), for example, features Todd and Kelly as winners of a lottery drawing for a new car. Over the course of the film, the duo unleashes chaos across a series of run-ins with police officers, fellow motorists, and a truck driver, this last particularly ferocious as the driver destroys their automobile and Kelly responds with a wild, anarchic vengeance, throwing the contents of the truck into the street and starting a riot.[36] The film also deals with the threat of violence misperceived, deploying the classic trope of the car tire blowout, to which Todd, hearing the "gunshot," responds automatically by clutching her breast. But despite the general chaos and mayhem of the short, the pair of women are also resolutely normal gal pals with enough money to buy a raffle ticket but not an automobile. Trying to get out of a speeding ticket, Todd tells a traffic cop, "We're regular fellows, and you look like a regular guy." This is, of course, the problem with the possibility of a Todd suicide: that beneath a regular-fellow surface, there might be a violent sadness; or that, when dealt a regular-fellow life like the characters Todd portrayed, a person might respond with a total rejection of that life.

While Todd and her comedy partners tore the on-screen world apart to comic effect, in the modern world off-screen, responding to a regular life with suffering and violence qualified one as mad and criminal, as registered by the Code's ban on depicting suicide as well as the law's location of the unreachable suicide in the position of unpunishable posthumous criminality. The idea that excessive suffering must be remedied or punished, however bootlessly in a posthumous context, goes some way toward understanding the periodicals' preference for interpreting the potential suicide as a murder victim. While the unexplained corpse of a glamorous young person is dissatisfying, frustrating, and perhaps infuriating, the possibility of a living agent to blame and punish holds out the possibility of a satisfying conclusion to a tragic narrative. Even if the murderer remains mysterious, the conspiracy theory teases the prospect of balancing one instance of violence with its juridical other and restoring a neat sense of moral and legal order. The murder victim might be avenged at some future point, but the suicide evades her punishment for introducing disorder, for suggesting an inner emotional and psychological life that cannot be made tidy.

THE PATHOLOGICAL DEPRESSIVE AND HIS MODEL WIDOW: PAUL BERN AND JEAN HARLOW

Three years before Thelma Todd's death, Paul Bern's case played out quite differently in the press. Here was a clear suicide—though rumors of other causes still abound (notably, Ben Hecht brought new attention to the case in a 1960 *Playboy* article suggesting murder)—and, adding to the scandal, a suicide with a famous widow left behind.[37] Additionally, unlike the seemingly happy, all-American Todd, Bern was ethnic and melancholic, two qualities that the press wove together in its discussions of his death, which took a markedly different tone than discussions of Todd's unfortunate end. Much like Lon Chaney before him, Bern inspired two somewhat contradictory responses in the fan magazines. On the one hand, magazines cast Bern as a too-vulnerable figure doomed by both genetics and proximity to contagious sadness; on the other, some columns portrayed Bern's close company with sadness as symptomatic of a selfishly maudlin outlook, implying that suicide was the predictable, if unhappy, outcome of self-indulgent rumination over tragic matters. In both threads of the conversation, Bern's widow, Jean Harlow emerges contra her melancholy husband as a platinum phoenix, demonstrating to the world what a positive outlook can do.

More sympathetic reactions to Bern's death stripped him of his agency. Rather than holding the producer responsible, articles spun a narrative about a mysterious curse or positioned Bern as a particularly sensitive soul, susceptible to contagious suicidality. Such accounts played up Bern's reputation as "father-confessor of Hollywood"—language that also appears in *What Price Hollywood?* to describe Max Carey—and created an image of the producer as sacrificing himself on behalf of his penitents.[38] The salaciously titled "The Trail of Tragedy That Haunted Paul Bern" asks, "Did Paul Bern, movie executive and bridegroom of Jean Harlow, kill himself to save his platinum blonde bride from the malignant fate that pursued so many of the men and women he had befriended or loved?"[39] From the title of this article to the framing of the question, Bern and his loved ones are syntactically the passive recipients of a supernatural jinx devastating the innocent victims in its path. The article

FIGURE 5.2 Paul Bern's tragic associations.

goes on to detail the numerous deaths surrounding Bern, including his first wife Dorothy Millette, whose body was found in the Sacramento River shortly after his death, a likely suicide; the girl who was too beautiful to live, Barbara La Marr, whose deathbed he attended; his friend Rudolph Valentino; Lucille Rickson, whose death is understood to have been caused by tuberculosis but which this magazine reports as suicide; and Helen Carlisle, a Hollywood writer who committed suicide. Much like the description of Todd as one in a chain of Hollywood deaths, this list of the "father confessor's" dead confidants de-particularizes his death, thereby occluding any more specific account of the producer's unhappiness.

After rehearsing the many tragedies that occurred near Bern, noting his presence at a surprising—perhaps unseemly—number of deathbeds, and discussing his overly intense sympathy, the article modulates its compassion as it speculates upon his final act with a series of short hypotheticals:

Did Bern, in an introspective moment, ponder too long over this strange parade of death and misfortune in his life?

Did he convince himself that the same tragic fate that had overtaken so many of his friends and loved ones might pursue his beloved bride?

Did he, in a fit of oriental fatalism, believe that he could end this succession of tragic events by the supreme tragedy of his self-inflicted death?

And, therefore, did he kill himself to save the girl he loved above all else in the world?[40]

While the last question frames Bern's act as a romantic sacrifice, its combination with ethnic descriptors of Bern as "oriental" and "introspective" pulls another way. So, too, does his affiliation with the many female stars, a chain of association that is both feminizing and, with its inclusion of the "orchidaceous" Barbara Lamarr and Rudy Valentino, racially coded. Suggesting something fatal in his genetic makeup, the antisemitism here proposes a mulelike relationship between Bern and his wife, the famous platinum blonde. As the article puts it, "Few men had as many apparent reasons for wanting to live. A lovely and famous wife, professional success, money—what more could anyone ask of life?"[41] The rhetorical question casts Bern as one who—unlike the generic "anyone" who might be happy with such obvious blessings—counts as a bad match for the sexy blonde. Evidenced by his death, Bern's dissatisfaction with an obviously good life marks him as an oddity.[42]

While the first thread of conversation around Bern's death emphasized his passive succumbing, more critical accounts scold the deceased producer for his cultivation of exotic morbid tastes. The reproaches typically appear in specifically anti-intellectual and antisemitic terms, framing Bern as one whose various preoccupations prevented him from enjoying what—from the perspective of the fan magazines and, by extension, their readers—was so clearly enjoyable. For example, one installment of the "Close-Ups and Long-Shots" column notes, "A great man, tormented by doubts that sometimes possess the souls of deep thinkers, leaving them melancholy—such was Paul Bern."[43] Great man rhetoric aside, the article casts Bern's intellectualism as a source of suspicion, self-indulgent at best.

Dorothy Calhoun's *Motion Picture* article "Jean Harlow—Tortured by Tragedy" exhibits a more explicitly xenophobic blaming. She reports one source describing Bern as a "'student of suicide,' in a detached, philosophical way," and reports "David Selznick, producer, told of Bern's big collection of books on the subject. Lothar Mendes, director, said that he believed over study had caused Bern's 'delicately balanced sense of life to give way.' Lady Inverclyde, know on stage and screen as 'June,' said 'one could not help noticing that he was morbidly inclined.'"[44] The problem with Bern, as presented in the article, is both genetic and attitudinal, a matter of both inclination and study. Once again, Bern's typology is cast into greater relief because he is framed against the very blonde Harlow: "While Paul Bern was making glowing plans to marry the gorgeous platinum blonde who was just beginning her sensational screen rise, the shadow of the dark midnight hour that was to come two years later hovered over him. It was during the months when he knew that he was to marry Jean that he confided to a director-friend one day that he felt that he had inherited the family curse of suicide. 'My mother died by her own hand,' he said. 'Other close relatives have died the same way. *I shall probably kill myself some day.*"⁴⁵ With an unhappiness that appeared inexplicable and unearned but undeniable (unlike Todd's), the press fell into both racial and ethnic stereotyping, with the Calhoun article explaining, "He was a German. He was familiar with the unhappy philosophies of Nietzsche and Schopenhauer, and had delved into the morbid soul-searchings of German scientists and thinkers. His sensitive heart was sick with the sufferings of humanity. That sympathy of his led him to seek out grief and sorrow wherever he went.... Vicariously, Paul Bern must have died many times, in a life saddened by other people's pain. Death was no stranger to the man who had held so many dying hands in his."⁴⁶

Whereas the death of Todd demanded an explanation, the blaming narratives forwarded in the press make Bern's death at his own hands an inevitability, an outcome of both disposition and bloodline. In her 1952 memoir *From Under My Hat*, for example, Hedda Hopper recalls with admiration a Jim Tully remembrance published in *Script* that is shocking for its simultaneously antisemitic and admiring notes, "If he had a tendency toward the abnormal, so had every man of great mentality and sensitive heart through all the miserable ages.... He was ... an *old soul*. As the pearl is made through the hurt of the oyster, the hurts of the centuries made Paul Bern.... A great Jew, he made up for a million pawnbrokers."⁴⁷ Despite the racial inevitability these accounts offer, a final judgment of Bern's attitude as perverse remains: whether racially ingrained or not, with such obvious goods in his life, his attitude is all wrong.

In both the antisemitic, anti-intellectual accounts of Bern's death and the more sympathetic accounts of his fatal, even mystical, susceptibility to depression, one explanation remains off the table. Whether the papers describe Bern as cursed by a particular sensitivity to the lost souls around him or as morbidly and racially invested in dark thoughts, nowhere does the possibility of suicidal depression as a reasonable response to the world appear. Instead, the various articles repeatedly insist that Bern *should* have been happy and then go to lengths to explain how the producer veered offtrack from the appropriately happy life that a normal fellow would have made from Bern's lucky circumstances. Both the judgment that Bern *should* have been happy and the record-correcting insistence that Todd *was* happy show that the Hollywood suicide will always be framed as blameworthy for failing to react appropriately to what the magazines insist is a very fine world indeed—Bern by acting badly, and Todd by turning out not to be a suicide at all.

Retaining public sympathy postmortem requires being a pure victim, not being a party to one's own death. Even with the relatively clear-cut case of Bern's suicide, speculation remained surrounding the death of the heretofore well-liked Bern, with a grand jury investigation reopening the case, rumors in the paper, and, as late as 1990, conspiracy discussions of the producer's death. The 1934 grand jury investigation brought rumors of murder back into the public eye, with *Motion Picture Herald* reporting, "When records of the earlier grand jury were examined last week, the theory of Earl Davis, Bern's gardener, that the death was murder, not suicide, was revealed. It is understood, however, that the present grand jury has no interest in going further with the Bern case . . ."[48] The *Motion Picture Herald*'s hint at murder and then dismissal of the tantalizing possibility characterized movie magazines' tendency to position themselves as the voice of reason in salacious matters, speaking to similarly wise fans, at the same time they hinted at unreported matters. In 1935, for example, *Hollywood* magazine offered this tidbit:

> A grand jury in Los Angeles has dug up the old scandal behind the death of Paul Bern. They were disappointed in not being able to google over a true confession tale. The sworn statement that Jean Harlow had made to the police at the time was found to have mysteriously disappeared from the records.
>
> Every policeman and most of the people of Hollywood know the inside of this story; but it has never been made public; and never will be. It is not the kind of thing that is printed.[49]

While the first paragraph works to distinguish the paper and its readers from the grand jury who wanted to "google over true confession" tales, the rest suggests an inside scoop that allows a possible mystery, centered on Harlow, to remain alive. Calhoun's article, which accounts for the death as suicide, similarly maintains a mystery angle on the death, "The motives for Paul Bern's suicide became the greatest mystery of Hollywood since the baffling murder of William Desmond Taylor."[50] Across the many columns discussing the relatively clear case of Bern's cause of death, the authors repeatedly open room for mystery and conspiracy that might redeem Bern.

Though MGM, Millette, and Harlow would remain figures of suspicion in the eyes of some, most outlets offered a flattering take on Bern's young widow. For example, a number of fan letters to *Photoplay* offer sympathy to Harlow and warn the magazine's writers not to gossip about the mourning actress.[51] Columnists who followed this fan advice worked on reframing Harlow so that she appeared less the man-eating gold digger of her on-screen persona and more the devoted wife. The magazine discussions of Harlow are particularly interesting for their marked difference from coverage of her husband, as well as for how closely they echo the era's self-help accounts of the successful personality type. The distinction between Harlow's admirable attitude and the bad outlook of her dead husband is drawn with particular sharpness in a *Photoplay* article titled "To Be Happy—Give." The article details the way weathering Bern's suicide with her chin up improved Harlow's reputation, redeeming her from her tawdry screen roles. It begins by detailing the *Red-Headed Woman* star's reputation prior to the tragedy: "When Paul Bern, Jean's husband of a few months, was found dead on the floor of his bedroom, a tornado of gossip and trouble burst about the gleaming white head of his bride. But women, or at least a great majority of them, did not turn against her. They didn't need to then. They already loathed her."[52] The reporter goes on to explain, "She represented, on the screen, of course, the type of woman all feared and hated the most. The type of woman who can and may steal the other woman's man."[53] While reminding readers of Harlow's duplicitous roles, reporter Jane Hampton also begins the work of separating the actress from the characters she played, a distinction important to the article's redemption narrative. Hampton ends the article's opening provocation by noting, "Yet today Jean Harlow has hundreds of thousands of loyal followers and loyal friends."[54]

From here, Hampton details Harlow's changing public reception, explaining the transformation through the ratio of particular detail and didactic bromide typical of the self-help genre. As she explains, the key to Harlow's success is that "She made no bid for sympathy of any kind.... She never has." Harlow is then quoted uttering a series of platitudes: "What I am trying to say is that what we give out in this world, we are sure to get back twofold" and "Try, too, to remember that there are always so many things to be grateful for. The more things we're grateful for, the more things we have to be grateful about. It's an endless, swelling chain."[55] In both Harlow's statements and in the reporter's admiring recounting of them, we hear a precursor to the dogma of positivity Dale Carnegie would make famous two years later and that characterized schemes birthed out of the New Thought movement's focus on mindset more broadly.[56] The case of Harlow, the reporter suggests, is one of winning friends and influencing people through a cheery outlook and a staunch refusal of the type of self-pity of which the press found her husband guilty. Whereas Bern ruminated on sadness without reason, making those around him feel his depression, his widow soldiers on bravely in the face of real tragedy. The article closes with a laudatory description of the actress's fortitude: "Refusing to ask for sympathy. Refusing to utter the word which might bring her understanding and approval. Locking her grief and sorrow in her own heart. Closing the door and turning the key. Bearing it alone."[57] Importantly, in managing her negative emotional states, Harlow has taken double prophylactic measures, both sealing her sorrow in her own heart to prevent tragedy from infecting her broader outlook on the world and also sheltering the populace at large from her sadness. Harlow's sadness is admirable because, unlike the unhappiness of the depressive, it need not disturb the world.

The bodies in this chapter demonstrate the way the depressive's final act disturbs order and provokes a flurry of readings aimed at setting things right, especially when the suicide in question is a star. As a text that, as Richard Dyer has written, joins the special and the ordinary, the ideal star—the star type the figures in this book challenged—was both aspirational and relatable.[58] In death, possible suicides risked violating these norms and so generated recuperative projects in postmortem analyses that sought to reframe star deaths, as well as instructive articles about resilience in the face of tragedy. Better to "bear it alone," *Photoplay* magazine suggests, better not to make others feel one's pain. The various interpretations of the Todd case and the contrast between discussions of Bern and Harlow index a society that makes a virtue of transcending the particularities of one's outlook on the world—a society that makes a virtue of being the kind of person who does not let his or her own suffering point to the fact the world may not be a place where it is easy for such an individual to exist. While the murder victim is random or perhaps tragic, the body of the suicide is a far more uncomfortable object. It is a body of evidence for unhappiness: a body that testifies that the world, as it is, is intolerable; a body that, faced with the world as it is, has opted out.

The star suicide, particularly in the 1930s, registered a crack in the foundation of star discourse's disciplinary function. The star who turned out to be deeply unhappy—who, in death, had moved beyond being scrutinized and brought to order—punctured the truth claims offered up in the fan magazines of the 1920s and 1930s. In these decades, the magazines promoted stars under pressures exerted by studios and industry leaders to represent wholesome and uncontroversial stardoms, even as unrulier stardoms emerged due to a confluence of talent, timing, and fan activity. By the final run of the most famous of the fan magazines in 1980, star scandals had become the norm for Hollywood reporting. However, the role of star discourse in teaching fans how to both admire and admonish their objects of obsession remained.

CONCLUSION

If you were a regular *Photoplay* subscriber, the last issue to arrive in your mailbox was the May/June 1980 magazine. The cover featured *Dallas* stars Charlene Tilton and Victoria Principal. After this, the magazine would be absorbed into the relatively new *Us* (today's *Us Weekly*). Though the last issue reveals significant changes to the media landscape—with its focus on a television soap opera and a cover that promises to interview yet another TV star, Lou Ferrigno—much of the 1930s remains.

The very fact of a star magazine merger recalls the period of the 1920s and 1930s, when the magazines were finding their way. Additionally, *Us* sought to distinguish itself from competitors by being a celebrity-friendly magazine, very much in keeping with an earlier ethos characterized by, if not total cooperation with the studios, at least a sense that fan magazines were selling rather than exposing Hollywood.[1] Moreover, the particular issue I purchased from eBay still bears the mailing information of its original subscriber, a Mr. Williams of Manchester, MO, an indication of the ongoing national reach of star stories. But the echoes of the twentieth century's earlier decades in its later ones are not limited to the turbulence of a shifting media landscape—magazine mergers, sound films and silents, film and television—or the promotion of sanitized star narratives to nationally dispersed fans. The final issue of *Photoplay* makes explicit the presence of the 1930s in the 1980 magazine. The cover line announcing the magazine's highlighted "Star of the Month" proclaims its featured actress Meryl Streep "The Bette Davis of the '80s."[2]

Nor is the mention of Davis the only invocation of an earlier moment of film history. Coming to *Photoplay*'s final issue after spending years immersed in the magazine's archives, it is hard not to list the way stardoms of the 1920s and 1930s are *everywhere*. For example, the magazine features Lou Ferrigno reflecting on his largely silent performance as the Hulk in terms that resonate with Chaney's stardom: "Little kids are most interested in knowing if that's my real hair and how do I make my eyes white. . . . They see the sensitivity in the character that often adults miss. If the Hulk were to speak, it would make it a comedy show. I project so much emotion without speaking that I'd feel less communicative if the Hulk spoke."[3] Additionally, the composite celebrity gossip reporter Cal York (the name an amalgam of California and New York) still appears as a regular contributor. Cal York's column changed with the time, offering some of the more salacious details of the issue—including coverage of Bo Derek, her much older husband John, and a rumored feud with his daughter Sean—but the generally friendly insider perspective remains much the same.

The magazine also celebrated its place in film history with special feature sections titled "Photoplay Back Then" and "Out of the Pages of Photoplay." The latter was a monthly two-page spread that reran old star photos and appeared regularly throughout the magazine's final years; the former was a feature that reprinted an older article in its entirety. The first experiment with this recycling appeared in the February 1980 issue, which featured an October 1940 article "How Clark Gable and Carole Lombard Live" alongside the following explanation: "Hollywood's grand past and most memorable stars come back to vivid life again in Photoplay Back Then, a new feature of reprints from our 69-year history. Since 1980 is the 20th anniversary of his death, Clark Gable begins our series."[4] The article ends with a newly penned and very wholesome summary that, while describing Lombard's death by plane crash, finishes with an (admittedly macabre) emphasis on the couple's happy marriage: "He was buried in the crypt alongside his beloved Carole."[5]

Despite the announcement's claim to the magazine's storied continuity, the run of this particular feature was uneven, absent from the next issue in March 1980, perhaps a sign of the magazine's struggles. The last installation of "Photoplay Back Then," in the final May/June issue, reprints a December 1938 profile of Tyrone Power, again accompanied by a summary paragraph for readers who might want a snapshot of the actor's life. The final issues of *Photoplay* thus bear out Anthony Slide's assertion: "In response to the new competition, the fan magazines would often turn retrospective, believing, perhaps with some cause, that their readership was nostalgic for the golden age of not only moviemaking but also of the fan magazines."[6]

On the other hand, the material from the 1930s issues is presented with a modern spin, suggesting a facelift as well as continuity. This is particularly notable in the "Out of the Pages of Photoplay" section, which ran archival photographs with decidedly modern captions. The subtitle for the section "Rare Photos from Our Star-Studded Past" establishes the magazine's insider knowledge, implying that *Photoplay* was very much a part of Old Hollywood. While some of the newly written captions are respectful—"a former café singer and ice skater, Eva Gabor decided to try her hand at acting"[7]—others are not. One photo's caption encapsulates a moment in Hollywood history this way: "Seventeen-year-old Julia Jean Turner, later known as Lana, began her career as one of Hollywood's well-stacked starlets."[8] Another caption encapsulates the lives of Pat Patterson and Charles Boyer with none of the ambiguity of a 1930s magazine: "The happy couple stayed wed until 1978, when Pat died. Two days later, Boyer committed suicide."[9] While the photos in the final issue's spread, which span 1934–1966, reflect the prestige of decades firmly associated with old Hollywood, the captions offer a more modern, tell-all sensibility and suggest *Photoplay*'s long history of being in the know about stars' lives.

In addition to recontextualizing the past through a more modern sensibility, the magazine also interprets modern stardom through the lens of its long memory, most notably in this final issue with its memory of Bette Davis. As I have argued throughout *Hollywood's Others*, stardoms and their discursive management in the 1920s and 1930s offered glimpses of other ways of being while also policing these openings. This book began with an anecdote about Bette Davis receiving terrible advice about her looks and roles. The actress holds a place in the contemporary popular imagination as exacting, independent, iconic, queer. We think of Davis doing it her way, often against softer versions of femininity promoted in the magazines. She was simultaneously of classical Hollywood—the "fourth Warner brother"—and defined by her defiance of its norms. By the 1980s, the invocation of the 1930s had come to serve as part of star discourse's disciplining function, with actresses such as Davis used as simultaneous compliment and warning to their predecessors.

The May/June 1980 issue of *Photoplay* features a number of quite normative stars, most notably the conventionally attractive Charlene Tilton, who is photographed in front of a fireplace as well as in her kitchen, with a caption noting "Charlene does all her own chores around the house."[10] However, the magazine also features stars rising to prominence who are much more challenging to conventional notions of femininity: Meryl Streep, mentioned above, and a different Bette. In its coverage of Bette Midler and Streep, the magazine interprets their burgeoning stardoms through the 1930s to limn the edges of acceptable feminine behavior for the modern woman.

The coverage of both Midler and Streep is distinctly postfeminist, as is much of the issue in which it appeared. For example, a Q&A column featuring Laurence Olivier poses the actor a question about his wife: "You are now married to actress Joan Plowright, who is not as big a star as for instance, Vivien Leigh. Is it easier having a wife who is not a major star?" The actor answers: "It is. It may sound chauvinistic, but it is easier for a man to be in the superior position, careerwise and economically. Joan is a superb actress and we have acted together, but not terribly often. There are no conflicts. She is a superb mother as well and that is her primary role, by her own choice."[11] While the septuagenarian Olivier might have represented an old guard, he (and the magazine) emphasizes that Plowright is happy because she chooses to be so, calibrating the balance between family and work appropriately. Midler and Streep are also presented as modern, postfeminist women, with all the choices *and* all the gender policing that entails. As Bonnie Dow has argued, postfeminist popular culture of the 1980s is full of women who have it all and are dissatisfied, a marker that whatever is wrong must be their fault, since neither career nor family appears to make them happy and, as postfeminist ideology has it, the work of feminism is done.[12]

In its attempt to domesticate two women whose talent and work ethic threatened to swamp the magazine's reliance on the triumvirate of sex-romance-motherhood for promoting actresses, the issue ends up pitting Midler and Streep against one another. The Midler article follows much of the star reportage playbook discussed earlier in *Hollywood's Others*. The article opens with a discussion of Midler's "big break in a gay men's bath" and her "façade of bawdiness" but then defuses her association with queerness by transitioning to insider knowledge of Midler's strict upbringing and relentless work ethic: "Instead of boyfriends, which her father frowned on, Bette turned to work."[13] The article also emphasizes Midler's emotional vulnerability, describing her estrangement from her father and the death of her sister. The magazine presents this softness as a counter to another assessment of Midler, which it nonetheless rehearses: "Despite being tagged as a bitch by some who've worked with her, Bette is friendly and talkative, very frank, but also a little vulnerable. She reveals, 'I love being with people but I also tend to hear them and to be scared they might hurt me.'"[14] The article also recounts that while Midler's split from boyfriend Peter Riegart is amicable, "the bitch" Midler portrays in public has harmed her personal life. Echoing Joan Crawford's dictum that those who wanted to see the girl next door should go there, Midler identifies a desire for bitchy glamor in her fans: "People come to see me so they can live out their fantasies. . . . Honestly, they want to see somebody different, not the girl next door."[15] But life lived as Midler does, fully for her career, has hurt her: "No steps are being taken, though, to marry. Years back she kidded, 'Who'd marry *me*?' Today she won't even comment on marriage."[16]

The Midler profile thus echoes the more salacious version of a persona that had appeared on screen in *The Rose* (Rydell, 1979), a melodramatic rock musical loosely based on the life of Janis Joplin in which Midler had starred. In an early scene between Rose and her manager (Alan Bates), Rose complains: "I got no fucking life. I can't get laid.

Nobody wants me . . . I just got too much work." Interestingly, the film also connects Midler to both queerness and her namesake Bette Davis when Rose attends a drag show with performers impersonating both Davis's Baby Jane and Midler's Rose.[17]

The specter of the unhappy career woman who has sacrificed the womanly happiness of marriage and family on the altar of ambition appears in the Streep article as well, but with none of the Midler profile's sympathy. Instead, the profile promotes Streep as a counter to such unhappy women, an actress who knows her most important role is at home. The rhetorical work of the article is tricky to be sure, for Streep was both known as and promoted in the article as a great actress, which is to say a professional. Indeed, for her intelligence, the young Streep was sometimes compared to Katharine Hepburn, an appraisal the older actress did not appreciate. However, Streep is redeemed from her professionalism by her commitment to family, which was important to softening her intelligence and talent and creating distance from her recent role as Joanna Kramer in 1979's top-grossing *Kramer vs. Kramer* (Benton).

Today it is hard not to see *Kramer vs. Kramer* as a masculine hysterical reaction to *The Feminine Mystique* and its successors. Joanna Kramer is a fundamentally fickle woman who cannot be happy despite "having it all." During the famed courtroom scene, Joanna rehearses a CV that is both comically precise and typological: "When I first got out of Smith, I worked in the art department of *Mademoiselle* magazine," Joanna explains from the stand. From the alma mater she shares with Friedan to her vaguely feminist statements, "I've worked very hard to become a whole human being," the family-abandoning Joanna illustrates the collateral damage of a generation of women who grew up on "women's lib."

As a result, while the profile promotes Streep, it must do so without making her seem self-promotional, a feat it achieves through an act of comparison and warning. The "Star of the Month" feature cites an unnamed source on Streep's talent: "One critic says of Meryl, 'Quite simply, she is the best actress I've seen on the American stage, and I have no doubt she is going to be to movies in the '80s what Bette Davis was in the '40s.' "[18] The comparison is classic *Photoplay*, reminding readers of the magazine's long history and ties to classical Hollywood. At the same time, the comparison to a great star of an earlier moment is double-edged. In particular, it matters that the star of the past taken up here is Bette Davis. Although at the time the article's author Haddad-Garcia included this comparison, B. D. Hyman's salacious memoir *My Mother's Keeper* had not yet been published, the public would have known that Davis was married four times and largely raised her children as a single mother. The Davis comparison might thus be understood as a warning. Beyond this aspect of her private life, Davis is a notoriously mannered star, appearing in Susan Sontag's "Notes on Camp." As Julia A. Stern writes of Davis's performance style, "Davis was able to project competing ideas simultaneously: performing in a realist mode while also communicating her awareness that she was playing a part."[19] Davis thus makes a perfect comparison for the young Streep, an actress whose performance style a disparaging Katharine Hepburn described with the phrase "click, click, click."[20]

In contrast to the hardworking Midler or her predecessor and namesake Davis, Streep is established as the ideal woman for the postfeminist era, perfectly "having it all" in a way that enhances the happiness of all who come into her orbit. Unlike Joanna Kramer, "in the midst of the most spectacular and rapid rise to stardom in years, Meryl opted to take nearly a year off and accept no work at all for that period."[21] The article goes on to explain: "The reason why is simple: She got married and became a mother, two long-cherished dreams of hers."[22] Streep is happy because, of her own volition, she has kept her life in balance, not sacrificing family to work and fame. The profile reports her admirable decision-making in this regard: "I would not have had a baby if I didn't have the time to be a good mother. Mothering isn't something to squeeze into a busy schedule."[23] Taking what might be intimidating or alienating about Streep—the article mentions her high IQ—Haddad-Garcia frames Streep's intelligence as good sense.

In the pages of the final issue, this good sense distinguishes Streep from the overreaching Midler and Davis, whose careers overtake the personal and the feminine. Despite opening the article with a comparison to Davis's talents, Haddad-Garcia later distinguishes Streep from her predecessor, once again framing a warning as a compliment: "Meryl is *so far* extremely humble about her talents and achievements, noting earnestly that an actress cannot be good without good material and co-stars."[24] As a result of her good behavior—so far—Streep has been rewarded with men's professional attention: "Several male superstars have expressed a wish to work with Streep. Whether or not this will be the case after she is a bona fide superstar is another question. Talented actresses like Bette Davis (in her prime) and Streisand scare away more stars and potential costars than they attract, for men are intimidated by their magnetism and don't want to be overwhelmed on the screen."[25] Across the pages of its final issue, *Photoplay* triangulates Davis, Streep, and Midler, using stars past and present to alternately recuperate, elevate, and discipline one another.

The policing of Midler and Streep can be seen as a prelude to what would become the *Us/Us Weekly* ethos of the next millennium, which was, per Erin A. Meyers, "the extraordinarily ordinary," a kind of hyperaccentuation of the girl next door best embodied by reality star Lauren Conrad.[26] That Midler and Streep are the biggest stars in the final issue of *Photoplay*—and also, somehow, edge cases when compared to TV star Charlene Tipton, whose tame interview features an image of the star running a blender—encapsulates what has fascinated me over the course of writing *Hollywood's Others*. Difficult, nonnormative, and challenging stars have always *both* been audience favorites *and* created management problems for the star discourse that created and promoted them. They represent the simultaneous interplay of expansiveness and restriction that constitutes our star fantasies.

NOTES

INTRODUCTION

1. Whitney Stine, with Bette Davis, *Mother Goddam: The Story of the Career of Bette Davis* (New York: Hawthorn, 1974), 68.
2. Richard deCordova, *Picture Personalities: The Emergence of the Star System in America* (Urbana: University of Illinois Press, 2001), 98.
3. There were some notable exceptions; Emily Carman details the work of actresses such as Carole Lombard and Irene Dunne who managed to avoid such restrictive contracts. *Independent Stardom: Freelance Women in Hollywood* (Austin: University of Texas Press, 2016).
4. Eric Hoyt, *Ink-Stained Hollywood: The Triumph of American Cinema's Trade Press* (Berkeley: University of California Press, 2022), 3.
5. Hoyt, *Ink-Stained Hollywood*, 31–32.
6. Hoyt, *Ink-Stained Hollywood*, 151–153, 189.
7. Martin Quigley, "Editorial," *Exhibitors Herald-World* 100, no. 7 (August 16, 1930): 16.
8. Mary Desjardins, "'Fan Magazine Trouble': The AMPP, Studio Publicity Directors, and the Hollywood Press, 1945–1952," *Film History* 26, no. 3 (2014): 34.
9. Anthony Slide, *Inside the Hollywood Fan Magazine* (Jackson: University Press of Mississippi, 2010).
10. Sylvia Ulback, "Beauty and Personality Are Inseparable," *Photoplay* 46, no. 6 (November 1934): 48–49, 76.
11. Dorothy Manners, "Enter the Dixies," *Motion Picture Classic*, February 1929, 63.
12. Manners, "Enter the Dixies," 88.
13. Slide, *Inside the Hollywood Fan Magazine*, 11.
14. I need to thank Robert Jackson for drawing my attention to this moment in Baldwin. James Baldwin, *The Devil Finds Work* (New York: Vintage International, 2011), 7.

Jackson writes of Baldwin's ongoing evaluation of Davis in "James Baldwin and Film Beyond the American Century," *James Baldwin Review* 7, no. 1 (2021): 39–53. This moment also appears in Julia A. Stern's excellent book on cross-racial spectatorship, *Bette Davis Black and White* (Chicago: University of Chicago Press, 2021), 7.

15. Richard Dyer, *Heavenly Bodies: Film Stars and Society* (New York: Routledge, 1986).
16. Carl Plantinga, "The Scene of Empathy and the Human Face on Film," in *Passionate Views: Film, Cognition and Emotion,* ed. Carl Plantinga and Greg M. Smith (Baltimore, MD: Johns Hopkins University Press, 1999): 239–256, 239.
17. Highmore's examination of various experiences of disgust, particularly cross-cultural hostilities tied to this affect, turns to white Britons eating spicy vindaloo as an example of an exposure model that might retrain the sensorium. Ben Highmore, "Bitter Aftertaste: Affect, Food, and Social Aesthetics," in *The Affect Theory Reader,* ed. Melissa Gregg and Gregory J. Seigworth (Durham, NC: Duke University Press, 2010), 135–136.
18. bell hooks, *Black Looks: Race and Representation* (New York: Routledge, 2015), 23, 36.
19. Dyer, *Heavenly Bodies*; Sharon Marcus, *The Drama of Celebrity* (Princeton, NJ: Princeton University Press, 2019).
20. Sarah Polley, "A Spectrum of Individuals: U.S. Fan Magazine Circulation Figures from 1914 to 1965," *Star Attractions: Twentieth-Century Movies Magazines and Global Fandom* (Iowa City: University of Iowa Press, 2019), 69.
21. Tamar Jeffers McDonald and Lies Lanckman, "Introduction," *Star Attractions: Twentieth-Century Movies Magazines and Global Fandom,* ed. Tamar Jeffers McDonald and Lies Lanckman (Iowa City: University of Iowa Press, 2019), 2.
22. Jeffers McDonald and Lanckman, "Introduction," 3.
23. Slide, *Inside the Hollywood Fan Magazine,* chap. 3.
24. Mark Lynn Anderson, *Twilight of the Idols: Hollywood and the Human Sciences in 1920s America* (Berkeley: University of California Press, 2011), 59.
25. Marcus, *The Drama of Celebrity,* 4.
26. deCordova, *Picture Personalities,* 91.
27. deCordova, *Picture Personalities,* 10.
28. As Stamp argues, the feminization and thus uplift of the cinema was not a smooth process but one characterized by anxiety and not-always-successful attempts at containment, "for women were not always enticed by dignified, uplifting material." Similarly, Hansen's groundbreaking work on Valentino's appeal to his female fans as a site of not only "short-term marketing interests" but also broader cultural anxieties has been an important framework for my consideration of fan magazines' strenuous efforts to contain and manage the diverse appeals of stars both in and outside the cultural mainstream. Shelley Stamp, *Movie-Struck Girls: Women and Motion Picture Culture After the Nickelodeon* (Princeton, NJ: Princeton University Press, 2000), 7; Miriam Hansen, *Babel and Babylon: Spectatorship in American Silent Film* (Cambridge, MA: Harvard University Press, 1991); Miriam Petty, *Stealing the Show: African-American Performers and Audiences in 1930s Hollywood* (Berkeley: University of California Press, 2016); Anna Everett, *Returning the Gaze: A Genealogy of Black Film Criticism, 1909–1949* (Durham, NC: Duke University Press, 2001); Carrie Teresa,

Looking at the Stars: Black Celebrity Journalism in Jim Crow America (Lincoln: University of Nebraska Press, 2019); Agata Frymus, "Silent Film Era and Marginalised Spectatorship," *Early Popular Visual Culture* 21, no. 2 (2023): 183–188; Pardis Dabashi, "'There is No Gallery': Race and the Politics of Space at the Capitol Theater," *Early Popular Visual Culture* 21, no. 2 (2023): 208–222.

29. Teresa, *Looking at the Stars*, 20.
30. Everett, *Returning the Gaze*, 180.
31. Hary Levett, "Stepin Fetchit Moves O.K. Under Girl Boss," *Chicago Defender*, July 7, 1934, 6.
32. Levett, "Stepin Fetchit Moves O.K. Under Girl Boss," 6.
33. Michael Rogin, "'Make My Day': Spectacle as Amnesia in Imperial Politics," *Representations* 29 (Winter 1990): 99–123.

1. SEXING FARINA: *OUR GANG*'S "LITTLE FELLOW" AND OTHER FANTASIES OF BLACK CHILDHOOD

1. Herbert Howe, "Close-Ups and Long-Shots," *Photoplay* 28, no. 2 (July 1925): 14–36. In his foreword to Julia Lee's *Our Gang: A Racial History*, Henry Louis Gates Jr. reminisces about the syndicated *Little Rascals*' place in the 1950s as "a model of harmonious, localized integration" (vii), which, given that the syndicated episodes were made twenty to thirty years before *Brown v. Board of Education*, made the series, in the eyes of young Gates, "downright radical" (viii).
2. "Rand Lands Laugh Winner: Town Children as Our Gang Make 'Howling' Success of Stunt and 'Kidnap' Posters," *Exhibitors Herald*, February 13, 1926, 61.
3. "Novel Tie-Ups for Shorts," *Motion Picture News* 37, no. 26 (June 30, 1928): 2176.
4. "Start an 'Our Gang' Day," *Exhibitors Trade Review* 18, no. 9 (July 25, 1925): 37.
5. Julia Lee, *Our Gang: A Racial History of* The Little Rascals (Minneapolis: University of Minnesota Press, 2015), 202–203.
6. "This Is the Brownies' Book," *The Brownies' Book*, January 1920, 2.
7. Anna Everett, *Returning the Gaze: A Genealogy of Black Film Criticism, 1909–1949* (Durham, NC: Duke University Press, 2001), 286.
8. On one side, Leonard Maltin's *The Little Rascals: The Life and Times of Our Gang* appears to be an outgrowth of earlier progressive aspirations for the series, emphasizing the groundbreaking nature of the show's multiracial cast. Such accounts posit *Our Gang*'s on-and-off-screen schoolrooms as leading the way for *Brown v. Board of Education*. In contrast, in his discussion of the series, Tavia Nyong'o positions *Our Gang* as "Racial Kitsch" along the lines of lawn jockeys and other hateful tchotchkes. Leonard Maltin, *The Little Rascals: The Life and Times of* Our Gang (New York: Random House, 1977); Tavia Nyong'o, "Racial Kitsch and Black Performance," *Yale Journal of Criticism*, 15, no. 2 (Fall 2002): 371–391.
9. Lee, *Our Gang*, 39, 40.
10. Lee, *Our Gang*, 37.

11. The nineteenth-century origins of these tropes, particularly of the "pickaninny" as edible and insensate, have been thoroughly explored in the important work of Kyla Wazana Tompkins and Robin Bernstein. Kyla Wazana Tompkins, *Racial Indigestion: Eating Bodies in the 19th Century* (New York: New York University Press, 2012); Robin Bernstein, *Racial Innocence: Performing American Childhood from Slavery to Civil Rights* (New York: New York University Press, 2011).
12. William C. Lee, letter to W. E. B. Du Bois, July 15, 1919, W. E. B. Du Bois Archive, UMass Amherst.
13. Bernstein, *Racial Innocence*, 6.
14. Indeed, as Julia Lee notes, audiences at the time were happy to think of Buckwheat as a reincarnation of Farina. Lee, *Our Gang*, 156.
15. Paula Massood, "African American Stardom Inside and Outside of Hollywood: Ernest Morrison, Noble Johnson, Evelyn Preer, and Lincoln Perry," in *Idols of Modernity: Movie Stars of the 1920s*, ed. Patrice Petro (New Brunswick, NJ: Rutgers University Press, 2010), 229.
16. Bernstein notes the "absence of pain that unifies the construction of the pickaninny across differences." Similarly, Tompkins argues that the Black child's pain was crucial to white management of fear and desire for Black bodies. Bernstein, *Racial Innocence*, 34; Tompkins, *Racial Indigestion*, 90.
17. Maltin, *The Little Rascals*, 31.
18. Mary Winship, "Our Gang," *Photoplay* 25, no. 4 (March 1924): 40-41, 108.
19. Lee, *Our Gang*, 75; "Jackie Condon Is Signed Again for Our Gang," *Exhibitor's Herald*, December 4, 1926, 79; Myrtle Gebhart, "They Get Paid for Playing," *Picture-Play Magazine*, 19, no. 1 (September 1923): 52–54, 54.
20. For an extensive discussion of presenting Black children as food, see Tompkins, *Racial Indigestion*.
21. "Use Your Local Papers," *Exhibitor's Trade Review*, July 25, 1925, 39.
22. "Start an 'Our Gang' Day," *Exhibitor's Trade Review*, July 25, 1925, 37–38, 38.
23. Nyong'o, "Racial Kitsch and Black Performance," 371.
24. Jason Mittell, "Narrative Complexity in Contemporary American Television," *Velvet Light Trap*, no. 58 (Fall 2006): 32, 34; Jennifer Hayward, *Consuming Pleasures: Active Audiences and Serial Fictions from Dickens to Soap Opera* (Lexington: University Press of Kentucky, 1997), 150.
25. Maggie Hennefeld, "Slapstick Comediennes in Transitional Cinema: Between Body and Medium," *Camera Obscura* 29, no. 2 (2014): 85–117; 98, 97.
26. Ben Singer, *Melodrama and Modernity: Early Sensational Cinema and Its Contexts* (New York: Columbia University Press, 2001), 222.
27. Some have objected to this distinction between the episodic as static and conservative and the serial as both narratively and politically progressive. For example, Feuer has argued that "if the episodic series sitcom was static at the level of situation, it was not so at the level of character" (616). While *Our Gang* produced an enormous amount of audience engagement, the series tends to conform to the episodic's conservative tendencies. *Our Gang* depended on static characters as well as narrative arcs. With

the emphasis on types and the habit of replacing aging child actors with new, younger characters who slotted into the same typological role, *Our Gang* fantasized a world in which innocence was forever maintained and viewers would relate to the gang of scrappy types. Jane Feuer, "Narrative Form in American Network Television," in *Critical Visions in Film Theory*, ed. Timothy Corrigan, Patricia White, and Meta Mazaj (Boston: Bedford/St. Martins, 2011), 614.

28. In this reading, I depart from Julia Lee's account of the series' integrationist bent. For Lee, "If *Our Gang* was a miniature vision of one kind of America—one that was happily multiracial and multiethnic—its enemy was a vision of a different kind of America: one that was strictly segregated and nativist. For the *Our Gang* kids, the "hostile world" wasn't just the world of grownups and killjoys. It was also the world of Jim Crow" (40). I argue that the episodic structure of the series and the recurrent mule-and-cart gag present a highly limited version of integration.

29. The general structure of the series suggests that *Our Gang* shares much with what, deriving from Windsor McCay's comic strip, Scott Bukatman dubs Slumberland: a place of dreams and play, with a limit. As Bukatman notes, "An important aspect of the poetics of Slumberland, then, is that it's temporary. You wake up" (1). The delimited nature of Slumberland's dreams, whether those of Little Nemo or the Rarebit Fiend, may be seen as an important inspiration for the episodic container in which *Our Gang*'s children play. Scott Bukataman, *The Poetics of Slumberland: Animated Spirits and the Animating Spirit* (Berkeley: University of California Press, 2012).

30. Across a number of fields, scholars have linked seriality's temporal progression with that of selfhood. Presenting a different account of seriality and identity, Laura Horak's work on YouTube transgender transformation videos offers the term "hormone time" to describe the progress of images that present the completion of a temporal cycle in which the subject becomes his or her "true self" by the end (578). As Horak usefully reminds us, other scholars have noted that linearly progressive "straight" time is not always helpful for certain subject positions, most notably queer subjects (580). In her account of the social meanings of adolescence, Nicole Seymour offers this clarifying account: "Human development [is], first and foremost, a classical narrative paradigm—a forward-looking schema with strict criteria for progress and closure, and one that is exceedingly difficult to interrogate, precisely because of its natural appearance" (294). Laura Horak, "Trans on YouTube: Intimacy, Visibility, Temporality," Special issue on Trans Cultural Production, *TSQ: Transgender Studies Quarterly* 1, no. 4 (December 2014): 572–585; Nicole Seymour, "Somatic Syntax: Replotting the Developmental Narrative in Carson McCullers's *The Member of the Wedding*," *Studies in the Novel* 41, no. 3 (Fall 2009): 293–313.

31. Paul Wells, *Understanding Animation* (London: Routledge, 1998), 213 (emphasis original).

32. For example, Siobhan Somerville's *Queering the Color Line* traces the ways "the simultaneous efforts to shore up and bifurcate categories of race and sexuality in the late nineteenth and early twentieth centuries were deeply intertwined" (3), particularly through "expert discourses such as sexology [which were] part of the profound

reorganization of vision and knowledge in American culture between the 1890s and 1920s" (10). Mel Chen's work in animal studies focuses "on how animal-human boundaries are articulated *in terms of* sex and gender by examining perhaps the most consistent missing morphology in cultural representations of animals: the genitalia" (286, emphasis original). Siobhan B. Somerville, *Queering the Color Line: Race and the Invention of Homosexuality in American Culture* (Durham, NC: Duke University Press, 2000); Mel Y. Chen, *Animacies: Biopolitics, Racial Mattering, and Queer Affect* (Durham, NC: Duke University Press, 2012).

33. Chen, *Animacies*, 290.
34. Donna Haraway, for example, details the spatial creation of such a narrative in the organization of the American Museum of Natural History (24). Jolie Sheffer, in her study *The Romance of the Race*, discusses authors such as Pauline Hopkins who subvert the traditional "stereotypes of African backwardness and American progress" that positioned Africa as a place of savagery and the United States as a place of civilization (48). Donna Haraway, "Teddy Bear Patriarchy: Taxidermy in the Garden of Eden, New York City, 1908–1936, *Social Text* 11 (Winter 1984–85): 20–64; Jolie A. Sheffer, *The Romance of Race: Miscegenation, and Multiculturalism in the United States, 1880–1930* (New Brunswick, NJ: Rutgers University Press, 2013).
35. See Bernstein, *Racial Innocence*; Donald Bogle, *Toms, Coons, Mulattoes, Mammies, and Bucks* (New York: Continuum, 1989).
36. For a much deeper history of this phenomenon, see Hortense Spillers's groundbreaking "Mama's Baby, Papa's Maybe: An American Grammar Book," *Diacritics* 17, no. 2 (Summer 1987): 64–81.
37. Bernstein, *Racial Innocence*, 20.
38. Jacqueline Goldsby, *A Spectacular Secret: Lynching in American Life and Literature* (Chicago: University of Chicago Press, 2006), 5.
39. Goldsby, *A Spectacular Secret*, 22.
40. Goldsby, *A Spectacular Secret*, 20.
41. Indeed, this habit of selective remembering might be said to characterize attitudes toward the series as a whole. Describing critics' tendencies to forget *Our Gang*'s most racist moments, Tavia Nyong'o writes, "The cultural work it seems to do is less a bolstering of claims to white supremacy, and more a production of the appropriate ambience for the insinuation of a racially-unmarked innocence, an innocence predicated upon a forgetfulness of the past that is one of the greatest privileges of whiteness." Nyong'o, "Racial Kitsch and Black Performance," 381.
42. The movie fundamentally focuses on Farina's tremendous hunger; jokes about the child as simultaneously edible and insatiable frequently accompanied the pickaninny type. For more on this trope, see both Nyong'o, "Racial Kitsch and Black Performance," and Kyla Tompkins, *Racial Indigestion*.
43. Seymour, "Somatic Syntax," 294.
44. "T. W. Review of *Your Own Back Yard*, directed by Robert F. McGowan," *Moving Picture World* 76, no. 4 (September 26, 1925): 335.
45. "Our Gang Comedies," *Film Daily*, December 5, 1926, 15.

46. "Members of 'Our Gang'—'Cradle Robbers,'" in *Masters and Masterpieces of the Screen*, ed. C. W. Taylor (New York: Collier, 1927), 52; "Information Desk," *Modern Screen*, April 1936, 14.
47. B. M. Edith, "Review of *Are These Our Children*, directed by Wesley Ruggles," *Screenland*, no. 24 (February 4, 1932): 100 (emphasis original).
48. Huntly Carter, *The New Spirit of the Cinema: An Analysis and Interpretation of the Parallel Paths of the Cinema, Which Have Led to the Present Revolutionary Crisis Forming a Study of the Cinema as an Instrument of Sociological Humanism* (London: Shaylor, 1930), 129.
49. F. W. Sloane, "Paging Jackie's Barber," *Photoplay* 30, no. 1 (June 1926): 128 (emphasis original).
50. "The Newsreel," *Boy's Cinema*, no. 607 (August 1, 1931): 2.
51. Leonard Hall, "Retired at Eleven," *Photoplay* 40, no. 1 (June 1931): 35.
52. Hall, "Retired at Eleven, 35.
53. Hall, "Retired at Eleven," 35.
54. Robyn Wiegman, *American Anatomies: Theorizing Race and Gender* (Durham, NC: Duke University Press, 1995), 81.
55. Lee, *Our Gang*, 78–79.
56. "Players We Know," *Exhibitor's Trade Review*, March 8, 1924, 110.

2. FORGETTING SHIRLEY TEMPLE: AMNESIA, TECHNOLOGY, AND THE ABSTRACTED CHILD

1. Richard Dyer, "Four Films of Lana Turner," *Only Entertainment* (New York: Routledge, 2002), 80.
2. Arthur M. Loew, letter to Mary Pickford, October 13, 1943, Mary Pickford Papers at the Margaret Herrick Library, Beverly Hills, CA (hereafter Herrick Library).
3. Mary Pickford, letter to Shirley Temple, October 23, 1943, Mary Pickford Papers, Herrick Library.
4. In its joining of opposites and need for demonstration via performance, precocious cuteness is, as Lori Merish suggests, closely aligned with the freak. Lori Merish, "Cuteness and Commodity Aesthetics: Tom Thumb and Shirley Temple," in *Freakery: Cultural Spectacles of the Extraordinary Body*, ed. Rosemarie Garland Thomson (New York: New York University Press, 1996), 185–203.
5. "Hail Shirley Temple the New Queen," *Hollywood* 23, no. 7 (July 1934): 46.
6. Barbara Shaw, "Shirley Take a Bow," *Photoplay* 46, no. 3 (August 1934): 69.
7. Pamela Wojcik, for example, argues that child stars "worked to reassert the pricelessness and innocence of childhood at a time when the status of the child . . . was up for grabs." Pamela Wojcik, *Fantasies of Neglect: Imagining the Urban Child in American Film and Fiction* (New Brunswick, NJ: Rutgers University Press, 2016), 4.
8. John Kasson, *The Little Girl Who Fought the Great Depression* (New York: Norton, 2014), 9.

9. Aljean Harmetz, "What Makes Shirley Run, in Her Own Words: 'I've always been bossy...'" *New York Times*, October 25, 1988, C17.
10. Harmetz, "What Makes Shirley Run."
11. Richard Maltby, "The Political Economy of Hollywood: The Studio System," in *Cinema, Politics, and American Society*, ed. Philip Davies and Brian Neve (Manchester, UK: Manchester University Press, 1981), 42.
12. Tino Balio, *Grand Design: Hollywood as a Modern Business Enterprise, 1930–1939* (Berkeley: University of California Press, 1996), 13–14.
13. Graham Greene, "Wee Willie Winkie / The Life of Emile Zola," originally published in *Night and Day* October 28, 1937, reprinted in *The Graham Greene Film Reader: Reviews, Essays, Interviews & Film Stories*, ed. David Parkinson (New York: Applause, 1993), 233–235.
14. Brett Wood, "Lolita Syndrome," *Sight and Sound* 4, no. 6 (June 1994): 32–34. Molly Haskell's description of Temple as an "ideal post-Production Code sex kitten" has also been quite sticky. Molly Haskell, *From Reverence to Rape: The Treatment of Women in the Movies* (Chicago: University of Chicago Press, 1973), 123.
15. Gaylyn Studlar, *Precocious Charms: Stars Performing Girlhood in Classical Hollywood Cinema* (Berkeley: University of California Press, 2013), 58.
16. As Hatch argues, "children's performances of innocence functioned to neutralize the dangers that seemed to arise from the rapid social and cultural changes of the early twentieth century . . . transforming for the better the adults who came into [their] orbit." Kristen Hatch, *Shirley Temple and the Performance of Girlhood* (New Brunswick, NJ: Rutgers University Press, 2015), 21.
17. Studlar, *Precocious Charms*, 73.
18. Chad R. Newsom, "Temple of Youth," *Film Criticism* 39, no. 3 (2015): 6–25, 12.
19. Frank S. Nugent, "Miss Temple Plays Little Eva in 'Dimples,' at the Roxy—The Rialto Offers 'Lady Be Careful,'" *New York Times*, October 10, 1936, 21.
20. Andre Sennwald, "Review 1—No Title: The Paramount Presents Little Miss Temple in 'Now and Forever'—'Crimson Romance,'" *New York Times*, October 13, 1934, 10.
21. *Screen Book*, August 1936, Whalen scrapbook, Herrick Library.
22. Odec, "Dimples," *Variety* 124, no. 5 (October 14, 1936): 15.
23. Eric Ergenbright, "The Show Window," *Movie Classic* 10, no. 6 (August 1936): 17–19, 17.
24. C.A.W., "To-day's Cinema, London Film Reviews Poor Little Rich Girl," August 15, 1936, Whalen scrapbook, Herrick Library.
25. Rob Reel, "Shirley Sparkles as 'Poor Little Rich Girl,'" *Chicago American*, July 25, 1936, Whalen scrapbook, Herrick Library.
26. State care counts as a misfire of what Merish describes as cuteness's activation of "an erotics of maternal longing," which "generates an appropriative desire to 'rescue' the cute object by resituating it within a properly loving and appreciative (i.e., affectionally normative) family context" (188). But whereas Merish argues that "Shirley Temple's cuteness is linked with the transgression and benevolent recuperation of patriarchal law" (194), thereby emphasizing "the female child's vulnerability and powerlessness before the law and establish[ing] the benevolence of legal authority" (195),

this appears to be only partly true. While Temple is, as Merish suggests, associated with her own police force and, eventually, the FBI's J. Edgar Hoover and G-men (195), in both her press materials and her films Temple's stardom supports the familial, paternal part of patriarchal law more than the governmental side of things. Merish, "Cuteness and Commodity Aesthetics."

27. For a thorough explanation of Temple's role in lifting spirits during the Depression, see Kasson, *The Little Girl Who Fought the Great Depression.*
28. As Merish argues about such narratively disruptive moments in Temple films, "her cuteness is . . . directed at spectators both *within* and *without* the film's narrative." Merish, "Cuteness and Commodity Aesthetics," 197 (emphasis original).
29. Newsom, "Temple of Youth," 13.
30. Tom Gunning, "The Cinema of Attractions: Early Film, Its Spectator and the Avant-Garde," *Wide Angle* 8, no. 3/4 (1986), reprinted in *Early Cinema: Space, Frame, Narrative*, ed. Thomas Elsaesser (London: British Film Institute, 1990), 57.
31. Richard Dyer, "Entertainment and Utopia," in *Only Entertainment,* 2nd ed. (New York: Routledge, 2002), 19–35.
32. Merish, "Cuteness and Commodity Aesthetics"; Sianne Ngai, *Our Aesthetic Categories: Zany, Cute, Interesting* (Cambridge, MA: Harvard University Press, 2012).
33. It is not necessarily the case that 1930s audiences overlooked technological spectacles in Temple's films. For example, *Curly Top*'s cinematographer wrote an article about how to achieve the "living picture" shots for *American Cinematographer* magazine. John F. Seitz, "Can Amateurs Imitate Professional Tricks?," *American Cinematographer* 17, no. 6 (June 1936): 261, 269.
34. Hatch argues, "While today we might see children's precocious performances as posing a threat to the child's sexual innocence, in the early twentieth century . . . it was the child's economic innocence that was understood to be at risk." Hatch, *Shirley Temple and the Performance of Girlhood,* 147.
35. In her chapter on "economic innocence," Hatch explains Temple films instructed "audiences that happiness is free and bountiful, unlike money," thereby "critiquing the values promoted by modern capitalism without criticizing capitalism itself." As a result, Hatch argues, "much of Temple's film work was, therefore, devoted to erasing her status as a child laborer and promoting the illusion that, like any other innocent child, the only currency she recognized was love." Hatch, *Shirley Temple and the Performance of Girlhood,* 134, 144.
36. Kriste Lindenmeyer, *"A Right to Childhood": The U.S. Children's Bureau and Child Welfare, 1912–1946* (Urbana: University of Illinois Press, 1997), 132.
37. Viviana Zelizer, *Pricing the Priceless Child: The Changing Social Value of Children* (New York: Basic Books, 1985) 60, 80, 85.
38. Kasson, *The Little Girl Who Fought the Great Depression,* 51.
39. Kasson, *The Little Girl Who Fought the Great Depression,* 52.
40. Wojcik, *Fantasies of Neglect,* 80.
41. Gladys Hall Papers, untitled draft, April 1, 1939, Herrick Library, 1–14, 1.
42. Gladys Hall Papers, untitled draft, 3.
43. Gladys Hall Papers, untitled draft, 7.

44. Gladys Hall Papers, untitled draft, 10.
45. Gladys Hall Papers, untitled draft, 11.
46. Gladys Hall, with G. Temple corrections, "Shirley and the Quints," for April *Modern Screen*, n.d., Gladys Hall Papers, Herrick Library, 1–12, 4.
47. Hall, "Shirley and the Quints," 5.
48. Hatch, *Shirley Temple and the Performance of Girlhood*, 144–145.
49. Gladys Hall, telegram to Lester Grady, May 20, 1936, Gladys Hall Papers, Herrick Library.
50. Gladys Hall, notes on *Modern Screen* draft article, Gladys Hall Papers, Herrick Library.
51. Hall, notes on *Modern Screen* draft article, 8–9.
52. Hatch, *Shirley Temple and the Performance of Girlhood*, 77, 88.
53. Shirley Temple Black, *Child Star: An Autobiography* (New York: McGraw-Hill, 1988), 274.
54. Hedda Hopper was a particular fan of Temple—for example, writing to Brenda Helser (Olympic swimmer turned comtesse and columnist) about Temple's rejection from Stanford: "The Dean of Women, Mary Yost, now retired, was a jealous old maid, who hated all girls but ugly, dull ones who did nothing but study. It gave her the pride of her life to pass judgment on earnest little Shirley." Hedda Hopper, letter to Brenda Helser, April 20, 1951, Hedda Hopper Papers, Herrick Library.
55. Jack Hirschberg, "Miss Marker Grows Up," May 2, 1947, Jack Hirschberg Papers, Herrick Library, 1.
56. Hirschberg, "Miss Marker Grows Up," 1.
57. T.S., "'Kathleen,' With Shirley Temple, Is at Capitol," *New York Times*, December 19, 1941, 35.
58. In *Child Star*, Temple Black has this to say about kissing Dickie Moore: "Hardly a woman of the world, I was weary of his ineptness. After all, it was only on the cheek, and contrary to publicity hoopla indicating his as my initial kiss, months before someone had kissed me, and on the lips, in a horse corral" (341).
59. T.S., "'Miss Annie Rooney,' Starring Shirley Temple, Opens at the Rivoli," *New York Times*, June 8, 1942, 11.
60. Temple Black, *Child Star*, 340.
61. Temple Black, *Child Star*, 331.
62. "What the Picture Did for Me," *Motion Picture Herald* 149, no. 9 (November 28, 1942): 64–68, 66.
63. "What the Picture Did for Me," *Motion Picture Herald* 140, no. 3 (July 20, 1940): 40–42.
64. On *Kathleen*, a theater owner writes: "Played this the day before Labor Day one day only. I had to lower the admission on this picture, and at that I had to hide when the patrons left the theater"–Miss Edna Kelloff, Ute Theatre, Aguilar, Col. Small Town Patronage. "What the Picture Did for Me," *Motion Picture Herald*, 149, no. 2 (October 10, 1942): 50–52, 50.
65. "At Last," *Movie Makers* 15, no. 6 (June 1940): 295.

3. "FEAST YOUR EYES, GLUT YOUR SOUL": FEELING WITH LON CHANEY

1. Dick Hyland, "The Face of a Thousand Memories," *New Movie Magazine*, November 1930, 45, http://archive.org/stream/newmoviemagazineo2weir#page/n587/mode/2up/search/Chaney.
2. Hyland, "The Face of a Thousand Memories," 45.
3. "Funeral for Lon Chaney," *Nashua Telegraph*, August 28, 1930, 5.
4. This type of reading is exemplified in Ivan Butler's comment that "it is the ordinary, the apparently normal, the beautiful which horrify—the monstrous and distorted which compel our respect, our sympathy, ultimately our affection." Ivan Butler, *Horror in the Cinema*, 2nd ed. (London: Zwemmer, 1970), 65, quoted in Joan Hawkins, "'One of Us': Tod Browning's *Freaks*," in *Freakery: Cultural Spectacles of the Extraordinary Body*, ed. Rosemarie Garland Thomson (New York: New York University Press, 1996), 267.
5. For example, Joan Hawkins reads the film's shift to a more traditional horror picture in the second half as reasserting the freaks' monstrosity, effectively undoing the work of the film's first half (269). She also identifies Cleo's punishment as problematically linking moral monstrosity and physical difference. Others, such as Rachel Adams, read the film's incoherence as central rather than pitting the first and second halves against each other. For Adams, the film's fundamental ambiguity is in keeping with the cinema's transition to respectability and the freak show's transition to the margins of society. Rachel Adams, *Sideshow U.S.A.: Freaks and the American Cultural Imagination* (Chicago: University of Chicago Press, 2001).
6. Carl Plantinga offers a useful rejection of our fixation on the differences between sympathy and empathy. For the purposes of this chapter, I use "sympathy" because of the resonance between the term's etymological roots and the contagion anxieties at play in Chaney's star discourse. See Carl Plantinga, "The Scene of Empathy and the Human Face on Film," in *Passionate Views: Film, Cognition, and Emotion*, ed. Carl Plantinga and Greg M. Smith (Baltimore, MD: Johns Hopkins University Press, 1999), 245–247. As ethics and affects increasingly interest film scholars, pre-Code horror films of the 1920s and 1930s offer a crucial site for investigation, particularly when it comes to ethically loaded affects such as disgust. Scholars working in this area include William Brown, Amy Coplan, Berys Gaut, Tarja Laine, Carl Plantinga, Daniel Shaw, and Greg Smith, as well as Noël Carroll, who has argued against assumptions that audiences take on characters' feelings. For example, Tarja Laine makes explicit a link between affect and ethics. See Tarja Laine, "Affective Telepathy, or the Intuition of the Heart: Persona with Mulholland Drive," *New Review of Film and Television Studies* 7, no. 3 (September 2009): 326. See also Noël Carroll, *The Philosophy of Motion Pictures* (London: Blackwell, 2008).
7. In particular, this chapter seeks to counter accounts that imagine activities such as role taking or sensorial retraining as uncomplicated or necessarily ethical activities.
8. Noël Carroll, *The Philosophy of Horror; or, Paradoxes of the Heart* (New York: Routledge, 1990), 10, 161.

9. "Right off the Reel," *Boys' Life* 17, no. 10 (October 1927): 36, 55.
10. Indeed, the "elevated horror" of contemporary director Ari Aster trades in markedly low horror tropes of disfigurement for its scares.
11. Ato Quayson, *Aesthetic Nervousness: Disability and the Crisis of Representation* (New York: Columbia University Press, 2007), 19.
12. Martin Norden, *The Cinema of Isolation: A History of Physical Disability in the Movies* (New Brunswick, NJ: Rutgers University Press, 1994), 99. More recently, Angela Smith's *Hideous Progeny* offers a more complicated account of disability in horror. Here, she argues, "classic horror films also disrupt the neat correlations of surface appearance and innate or genetically determined character. As well as emphasizing social and environmental causes and exacerbations of physical deviance, classic horrors repeatedly associate hideous facial features with illusion, performance, and cinematic trickery, suggesting the misleading and ableist conclusions drawn from surface traits" (126–7). Angela Smith, *Hideous Progeny: Disability, Eugenics, and Classical Horror Cinema* (New York: Columbia University Press, 2011).
13. Norden, *The Cinema of Isolation*, 115.
14. Brigitte Peucker, *The Material Image: Art and the Real in Film* (Stanford, CA: Stanford University Press, 2007), 1.
15. Susan Schweik, *The Ugly Laws: Disability in Public* (New York: New York University Press, 2010).
16. Quoted in Adrienne Phelps Coco, "Diseased, Maimed, Mutilated: Categorizations of Disability and an Ugly Law in Late Nineteenth-Century Chicago," *Journal of Social History* 44, no. 1 (Fall 2010): 23–37.
17. Laura Marks, *The Skin of the Film: Intercultural Cinema, Embodiment, and the Senses* (Durham, NC: Duke University Press, 2000).
18. Peucker, *The Material Image*, 35.
19. Thomas Doherty, "The Motion Picture Production Code of 1930," in *Pre-Code Hollywood* (New York: Columbia University Press, 1990), 347–359.
20. Smith, *Hideous Progeny*, 2. Importantly, Smith considers that while horror films delight in the horrific display of the disabled body, they also make clear the horrifying nature of eugenics, revealing "eugenics' disability discourse as perverse and unstable, traversed by superstitious and unscientific concepts it claimed to have left behind, and obsessively fascinated with the deviance it claimed to abhor" (7).
21. The cinema lagged behind other realms of popular entertainment. For example, the "freak show," once the staple of late nineteenth-century carnivals, came under regulations simultaneous to the "unsightly beggar," with some cities' ordinances grouping the disabled and "freaks" together as those seeking to make a profit by inflicting their difference on the general public. Schweik, *The Ugly Laws*, 102.
22. Dwight Codr, "Arresting Monstrosity: Polio, Frankenstein, and the Horror Film," *PMLA* 19, no. 2 (2014): 176.
23. Robin Larsen and Beth A. Haller, "The Case of Freaks: Public Reception of Real Disability," *Journal of Popular Film and Television* 29, no. 4 (Winter 2002): 168.
24. Adams, *Sideshow U.S.A.*, 63; Meira Cook, "None of Us: Ambiguity as Moral Discourse in Tod Browning's Freaks," in *Screening Disability: Essays on Cinema and Disability*,

ed. Christopher R. Smith and Anthony Enns (Lanham, MD: University Press of America, 2001), 48. Writing of the film's negative reception, Adams observes that "the carnival setting and characters of *Freaks* recalled too vividly the low origins of the cinema in storefront theaters and on the vaudeville circuit" (63).
25. For more on Browning's biography, see Bernd Herzogenrath, ed., *The Cinema of Tod Browning: Essays of the Macabre and Grotesque* (Jefferson, NC: McFarland, 2008); and David J. Skal and Elias Savada, *Dark Carnival: The Secret World of Tod Browning* (New York: Anchor Books, 1995).
26. Adams, *Sideshow U.S.A.*, 60.
27. Eugenie Brinkema, "Browning. Freak. Woman. Stain," in Herzogenrath, *The Cinema of Tod Browning*, 160.
28. Maude S. Cheatham, "Meet the Frog," *Motion Picture Classic*, January 1920, 38, http://lantern.mediahist.org/catalog/motionpicturecla1920broo_0262.
29. Ruth Waterbury, "The True Life Story of Lon Chaney," *Photoplay*, February 1928, 56, http://archive.org/stream/photoplay3334movi#page/n37/mode/2up.
30. Even contemporary criticism tends to view Chaney's distinctive performance style as grounded in his family's history with disability. For example, Matthew Jarron reinscribes the Chaney origin myth when he argues that Chaney's mother's deafness "certainly gave Chaney a power of visual expression which served as the basis of his art: When you watch him on screen you can see him act with his whole body." Matthew Jarron, "Paying the Penalty: Alienation Through Disability in the Films of Lon Chaney," *Alienation and Resistance: Representation in Text and Image*, ed. Gordon Spark et al. (Newcastle upon Tyne, UK: Cambridge Scholars, 2010), 57.
31. Waterbury, "The True Life Story," 57.
32. Other scholars have also seen Chaney as interested in problems of identification. For example, Aviva Briefel argues, "Masochism is central to the construction of male monsters, who initiate their sadistic rampages with acts of self-mutilation. These 'masochistic moments' close off the film to viewer identification and draw our attention to the *process* of identification itself" (16). But whereas Briefel argues that the monster's tendency toward self-mutilation creates a profound moment of disidentification in spectators, the censors of the era seemed wary that this might not be the case and that the actor's seeming perversion might transfer to audiences who identified with him. Aviva Briefel, "Monster Pains: Masochism, Menstruation, and Identification in the Horror Film," *Film Quarterly* 58, no. 3 (Spring 2005): 16–27.
33. "Questions and Answers," *Photoplay*, 1921, 118.
34. Waterbury, "The True Life Story," 56.
35. "Who Will Win Lon Chaney's Make-up Box?," *Youth's Companion* 102, no. 11 (November 1928): 564, https://archive.org/details/sim_youths-companion_1928-11_102_11/page/564/mode/2up.
36. Fred Gilman Jopp, "If It Can't Be Done—He Does It!," *Youth's Companion* 103, no. 5 (May 1929): 261, ProQuest, http://unr.idm.oclc.org/login? https://archive.org/details/sim_youths-companion_1929-05_103_5/page/260/mode/2up.
37. "The Best Motion Pictures," *Youth's Companion* 101, no. 27 (July 7, 1927): 465, https://archive.org/details/sim_youths-companion_1927-07-07_101_27/page/464/mode/2up.

38. Fred Gilman Jopp, "Lon Chaney Wants to Know," *Youth's Companion* 102, no. 11 (November 1928): 564, https://archive.org/details/sim_youths-companion_1928-11_102_11/page/564/mode/2up.
39. Jopp, "Lon Chaney Wants to Know," 564.
40. Jopp, "Lon Chaney Wants to Know," 564.
41. Karen Randell, "Mad Love: The Anxiety of Difference in the Films of Lon Chaney Sr.," in *Screening the Dark Side of Love: From Euro-Horror to American Cinema*, ed. Karen A. Ritzenhoff and Karen Randell (New York: Palgrave Macmillan, 2012), 69–82, 72.
42. Gaylyn Studlar, *This Mad Masquerade: Stardom and Masculinity in the Jazz Age* (New York: Columbia University Press, 1996), 200, 202.
43. Alice Maurice, "The Death of Lon Chaney: Masculinity, Race, and the Authenticity of Disguise," *Hollywood at the Intersection of Race and Identity*, ed. Delia Malia Caparoso Konzett (New Brunswick, NJ: Rutgers University Press, 2019), 41.
44. For more on Chaney's proprietary relationship to his makeup, see Adrienne McLean's *All for Beauty*, in which she persuasively connects Chaney's various looks to Tom Gunning's idea of the "attraction." Adrienne L. McLean, *All for Beauty: Makeup and Hairdressing in Hollywood's Studio Era* (New Brunswick, NJ: Rutgers University Press, 2022), 40.
45. Waterbury, "The True Life Story," 36.
46. Maurice, "The Death of Lon Chaney," 40.
47. Hawkins, "'One of Us,'" 266.
48. For example, while the studio featured Chaney's *Hunchback* and *Phantom* in the early 1930s, the later 1930s and early 1940s were boom years for the Boris Karloff *Frankenstein* franchise, which referenced disability less directly through the monster's awkward physical motions.
49. Building on Karen Randell's arguments about Chaney, I argue that his stardom was in part based in an identification with the body in transformation. As she explains, "Audiences went to see 'who' he was going to be in this movie and 'how' he was going to achieve this. The display of deformity and disfigurement became a 'must see' spectacle in the same way that the nineteenth-century 'freak show' displayed its characters to a paying audience. Deformity here becomes a site of entertainment rather than a site of anxiety. In this way, the films of Lon Chaney act as an interpolation (an insert that both alerts one to, and distracts one from, the traumatic event) between the spectator and the trauma." Thus, we might understand Chaney as constantly reminding able-bodied and nondisfigured audiences of the instability and impermanence of their status; as his proximally disabled status reminds spectators, the able-bodied subject as always at risk of acquiring disability. And while I do not necessarily disagree with Randell's argument that Chaney allows anxieties about injured veterans to play out on-screen, I do disagree about the necessarily prophylactic function of the film screen when she argues that, through Chaney, anxiety about maiming "is displaced into the safe space of another (fantasy) space, namely the cinematic space." Karen Randell, "Masking the Horror of Trauma: The Hysterical Body of Lon Chaney," *Screen* 444, no. 2 (Summer 2003): 216–221, 218.

50. Julian Hanich, "Toward a Poetics of Cinematic Disgust," *Film-Philosophy* 15, no. 2 (2011): 11–35, 16. In his work on emotion and identification, Gaut also emphasizes the importance of the reaction shot: "The reaction shot can be a more effective vehicle for affective and empathic identification than is the point-of-view shot. The reaction shot shows the human face or body, which we are expert at interpreting for signs of emotion." Berys Gaut, "Identification and Emotion in Narrative Film," in *Passionate Views: Film, Cognition, and Emotion*, ed. Carl Plantinga and Greg M. Smith (Baltimore, MD: Johns Hopkins University Press, 1999), 210.
51. Hanich, "Toward a Poetics," 23.
52. Hanich, "Toward a Poetics," 23.
53. Linda Williams reads this scene differently. Building on Mary Ann Doane's claim that a woman in cinema can control the gaze if it is part of her eventual victimization, Williams interprets the unmasking scene as part of a horror movie habit of linking the monstrous and the feminine, "in which her look at the monster recognizes their similar status within patriarchal structures of seeing" (18). Discussing the strange blocking in which Christine and the Phantom are both positioned to face the camera, Williams argues, "the audience's belated adoption of the woman's point of view undermines the usual audience identification and sympathy with the look of the cinematic character. But it may permit a different form of identification and sympathy to take place, not between the audience and the character who looks, but between the two objects of the cinematic spectacle who encounter one another in this look—the woman and the monster" (19–20). Linda Williams, "When the Woman Looks," in *The Dread of Difference: Gender and the Horror Film*, ed. Barry Keith Grant (Austin: University of Texas, 1996), 15–34. Angela Smith, in reading this scene, argues that in *Phantom* and other films that foreground disability "revelations," "impairment is framed in ways that uncover the subjective, contradictory, and dynamic nature of cultural narratives about disability. While the revelations work to excite shock and horror in viewers, they also confuse genetically determinist narratives: they foreground impairments that may be acquired rather than congenital; they illuminate cultural and mythic interpretations of impairment that continue to attach to and undercut the scientific claims of eugenic discourse; and they bring to light the spectacular, manipulated, and performative—that is, the culturally and textually generated—elements of disability." Smith, *Hideous Progeny*, 121.

4. UNREAL REMEMBRANCE: BLACK STARS AND THEIR WHITE AUDIENCES

1. As Steve Wilson documents, the film's producer David Selznik fought against too much historical accuracy, arguing, "we have seriously hurt the beauty of our production by letting authenticity dominate theatrical effects." Steve Wilson, *The Making of Gone with the Wind* (Austin: University of Texas Press, 2014), 112. Writing more broadly of the relationship between the South and the movies, Robert Jackson notes

of films such as *Gone with the Wind*, "These films and others in their tradition were not historically accurate, despite their pretensions; but in their subtle emotional longings, empire-building dreams, and racial fantasies, they were half true, which proved, for modern American culture, far more important." Robert Jackson, *Fade In, Crossroads: A History of the Southern Cinema* (New York: Oxford University Press, 2017), 11.

2. Wilbur G. Kurtz, Letter to Messrs. Stacey, Lambert, Coles, and Forbes, January 1, 1939, Wilbur G. Kurtz Collection, Herrick Library, 1–2.
3. Sandra Jean Graham, *Spirituals and the Birth of a Black Entertainment Industry* (Urbana: University of Illinois Press, 2018), xiii.
4. Ryan Jay Friedman, *Hollywood's African American Films: The Transition to Sound* (New Brunswick, NJ: Rutgers University Press, 2011); Arthur Knight, *Disintegrating the Musical: Black Performance and American Musical Film* (Durham, NC: Duke University Press, 2002).
5. Alice Maurice, "'Cinema at Its Source': Synchronizing Race and Sound in the Early Talkies," *Camera Obscura* 17, no. 1 (2002): 32.
6. Charlene Regester, "African-American Extras in Hollywood During the 1920s–1930s," *Film History* 9, no. 1 (1997): 95, 99.
7. Michael Slowik, *After the Silents: Hollywood Film Music in the Early Sound Era, 1926–1934* (New York: Columbia University Press, 2014), 56.
8. The term "reality effect" comes from Barthes's essay of the same title, in which he describes the function of the atmospheric detail in realist literature. As Barthes writes, "just when these details are reputed to *denote* the real directly, all that they do—without saying so—is *signify* it." Roland Barthes, "The Reality Effect" (1969), in *The Rustle of Language*, trans. Richard Howard, ed. François Wahl (Berkeley: University of California Press, 1989), 148 (emphasis original).
9. Maurice, "'Cinema at its Source,'" 33.
10. Desirée Garcia, *The Migration of Musical Film: From Ethnic Margins to American Mainstream* (New Brunswick, NJ: Rutgers University Press, 2014), 54.
11. Judith Weisenfeld, *Hollywood Be Thy Name: African American Religion in American Film, 1929–1949* (Berkeley: University of California Press, 2007), 20.
12. Weisenfeld, *Hollywood Be Thy Name*, 21.
13. Weisenfeld, *Hollywood Be Thy Name*, 28.
14. Val Lewton, "Hallelujah: About King Vidor's New Picture," *Screenland* 17, no. 3 (January 1929): 83.
15. Ruth Morris, "Hallelujah," *Variety* 96, no. 7 (August 28, 1929): 18, 31.
16. Freddie Schader, "Hallelujah," in "Opinions on Pictures," *Motion Picture News* 40, no. 8 (August 24, 1929): 735.
17. Sandra Jean Graham's term "commercial spiritual" encompasses most of the songs mentioned in this chapter. She describes the commercial spiritual as characterized by three principal traits: "First, the songs were written for personal financial profit and mass market appeal, attributed to a composer, and usually published. Second,

although the lyrics typically display minstrel humor and stereotypes, they index traditional spirituals through idiomatic words and phrases (e.g. 'golden chariot,' 'Gabriel's trumpet,' 'gospel train/raft/ship,' 'hallelujah') and themes (getting to heaven, judgment day). Third, most commercial spirituals bear at least a superficial musical resemblance to folk spirituals, most commonly manifested in internal refrains, call and response, and gapped-scale melodies." Graham, *Spirituals and the Birth of a Black Entertainment Industry*, 145.

18. Garcia gives a thorough discussion of the film's affiliation of Black performance with the landscape, thereby naturalizing the talents of Black actors and fixing the Black characters in place.
19. Morris, "Hallelujah"; Herbert Howe, "The Hollywood Boulevardier," *New Movie Magazine* 3, no. 6 (June 1931): 40–41, 114; Delight Evans, "Hallelujah! Review," *Screenland* 20, no. 1 (November 1929): 50; Dorothy Manners, "Enter the Dixies," *Motion Picture Classic* (February 1929): 63, 88.
20. Weisenfeld, *Hollywood Be Thy Name*, 43.
21. See Maurice's important diagnosis of the scene as an apotheosis of pure film form. Maurice, " 'Cinema at Its Source,' " 62.
22. Schader, "Hallelujah."
23. Alfred B. Kuttner and Wilton A. Barrett, "Hallelujah," *National Board of Review Magazine* 4, no. 9 (November 1929): 5–8.
24. Kuttner and Barrett, "Hallelujah," 5.
25. Kuttner and Barrett, "Hallelujah," 6.
26. Kuttner and Barrett, "Hallelujah," 7.
27. Kuttner and Barrett, "Hallelujah," 8.
28. The "Southern box office," Thomas Cripps has argued, was an invention used to limit the portrayals of African Americans, but which had little grounding in documented evidence about Southern audiences. Thomas Cripps, "The Myth of the Southern Box Office: A Factor in Racial Stereotyping in American Movies, 1920–1940," in *The Black Experiences in America: Selected Essays*, ed. James C. Curtis and Lewis J. Gould (Austin: University of Texas Press, 1970).
29. Matthew H. Bernstein, "A 'Professional Southerner' in the Hollywood Studio System: Lamar Trotti at Work, 1925–1952," *American Cinema and the Southern Imaginary*, ed. Deborah Barker and Kathryn McKee (Athens: University of Georgia Press, 2011), 124.
30. Amy M. Ware, *The Cherokee Kid: Will Rogers, Tribal Identity, and the Making of an American Icon* (Lawrence: University Press of Kansas, 2015), 6–7.
31. James H. Cox, " 'Learn to Talk Yaqui': Mexico and the Cherokee Literary Politics of John Milton Oskison and Will Rogers," *Western American Literature* 48, no. 4 (Winter 2014): 411.
32. Michael Charles Pounds, "What's Black and White and Misread All Over? Race, Identity, and Community in Judge Priest," *American Journal of Semiotics* 11, no. 3 (1994): 179–201. For a brilliant account of Stepin Fetchit/Lincoln Perry's sound, see Miriam J. Petty's chapter "Lincoln Perry's 'Problematic Stardom,' " in *Stealing the*

Show: African-American Performers and Audiences in 1930s Hollywood (Oakland: University of California Press, 2016).

33. Martin Rubin, "Mr. Ford & Mr. Rogers," *Film Comment* 10, no. 1 (January–February 1974), 56.
34. Bernstein, "A 'Professional Southerner,'" 133.
35. Bernstein, "A 'Professional Southerner,'" 130.
36. Delight Evans, "Reviews of the Best Pictures," *Screenland*, December 1934, 54–55, 54.
37. "The Shadow Stage," *Photoplay* 47, no. 1 (December 1934): 56–57, 56.
38. Lindy, "Judge Priest Review," *Hollywood Filmograph* 14, no. 3 (September 22, 1934): 3.
39. N. H. Young, "Old Kentucky Home," letter in "You Tell Us," *New Movie Magazine* 11, no. 1 (January 1935): 42, 62.
40. Petty, *Stealing the Show*, 190.
41. Marjorie Deen, "The Modern Hostess," *Modern Screen* 8, no. 5 (October 1934): 6, 72–73.
42. Julie Grossman, *Literature, Film, and Their Hideous Progeny* (London: Palgrave Macmillan, 2015), 84.
43. Anna Everett, *Returning the Gaze: A Genealogy of Black Film Criticism, 1909–1949* (Durham, NC: Duke University Press, 2001), 193.
44. While most scholarship on the reception of the film across Black and white audiences has focused on big national newspapers and trades such as *Variety*, or major northern Black papers such as *The Defender* or the *New Amsterdam News*, White's and Bernstein's study of the film's reception in Black and white Atlanta communities sheds light on regional differences in reactions to the film, particularly toward the light-skinned Peola and the passing subplot. For example, while national papers and film magazines praised Beavers and Washington and held the Delilah-Peola plot up for special recognition, white Atlanta papers remained silent on these aspects of the film. Matthew H. Bernstein and Dana F. White, "'Imitation of Life' in a Segregated Atlanta: Its Promotion, Distribution and Reception," *Film History* 19 no. 2 (2007): 152–178, 157.
45. Petty, *Stealing the Show*, 130.
46. Flitterman-Lewis argues, "So concerned is Stahl with the recuperation of difference into an idealized maternal unity, that by the close of his version of the film, race as an issue has disappeared entirely." Sandy Flitterman-Lewis, "*Imitation(s) of Life*: The Black Woman's Double Determination as Troubling 'Other,'" *Literature and Psychology* 34, no. 4 (1988): 44–57, 48. See also Lauren Berlant, *The Female Complaint: The Unfinished Business of Sentimentality in American Culture* (Durham, NC: Duke University Press, 2008).
47. Miriam Thaggert, "Divided Images: Black Female Spectatorship and John Stahl's *Imitation of Life*," *African American Review* 32, no. 3 (Autumn 1998): 484.
48. Donald Bogle has argued, "Peola was the New Negro demanding a real New Deal"; Everett has extended this claim in terms of Washington's own criticism of Hollywood Jim Crow. Donald Bogle, *Toms, Coons, Mulattoes, Mammies, and Bucks* (New York: Continuum, 1989), 60. Everett, *Returning the Gaze*, 222.

49. Petty also reads this scene as central to establishing generational and political difference between Delilah and Peola, noting the way Peola's "play well" corrects her mother's ungrammatical "plays good." Petty, *Stealing the Show*, 154.
50. Miriam Thaggert has described this scene as illustrating "the fluidity of the color line," as Delilah gazes from outside "into the white world her daughter occupies." Flitterman-Lewis also reads this scene, describing Delilah's position outside the window looking in as "the repressed background of Peola." Thaggert, "Divided Images," 486; Flitterman-Lewis, "*Imitation(s) of Life*," 51.
51. Sterling A. Brown, "Imitation of Life: Once a Pancake," *Opportunity: Journal of Negro Life*, March 1935, 87–88, 88.
52. Valerie Smith reads the shifts between musical themes and mother-daughter pairs differently, arguing that the alternations naturalize pleasure as belonging to the white pairing and naturalize the suffering of the Black pairing. Valerie Smith, "Reading the Intersection of Race and Gender in Narratives of Passing," *Diacritics* 24, no. 2/3 (Autumn 1994): 43–57.
53. Bea's appropriation of Delilah's suffering is thus an even more superficial form of empathy than that Berlant describes in "Poor Eliza" as she universalizes the effects as well as the feelings of suffering.
54. D. H. Chaman, "Rebellion in the Ranks," in "Just as You Say," *Movie Classic* 8, no. 4 (June 1935): 82.
55. Walter H. Golding, "No Color Line in Film," *Motion Picture Herald* 118, no. 4 (January 26, 1935): 70.
56. Norbert Lusk, "The Screen in Review," *Picture Play* 41, no. 6 (February 1935): 48–49, 48.
57. Herb Howe, "Coloring the Hollywood Beauties," *New Movie Magazine* 10, no. 3 (March 1935): 28–29, 29.
58. As Miriam Petty has demonstrated, some Black critics also found value in white tears. Describing Bernice Patton's *Pittsburgh Courier* article on a screening at which white critic Louella Parsons and other white audience members cried, Petty writes, "Patton conjures the image of a theaterful of weeping white patrons to signal Imitation's power to move and transform white perceptions and behavior, one screening at a time." Petty, *Stealing the Show*, 157.
59. Adrienne L. McLean, *All for Beauty: Makeup and Hairdressing in Hollywood's Studio Era* (New Brunswick, NJ: Rutgers University Press, 2022), 178.
60. Brown, "Imitation of Life," 88.
61. See Thaggert, "Divided Images," 486.
62. See Michael Slowik on the way confusion at the level of diegesis can invoke sonic "other worlds." Slowik, *After the Silents*, 196.
63. "Universal Partial to Race Since 'Imitation of Life,'" *Chicago Defender*, June 29, 1935, 6.
64. In her reading of this exchange, Kirsten Lew notes the importance of this scene to the film's intervention into the construction of racial difference. She writes that it is hard to determine whether "they are shocked because they are standing next to the daughter of *the* Delilah, or because they didn't expect someone who looks like Peola

to be the daughter of Delilah." Kirsten Lew, "From Social Problem to Maternal Melodrama: The Lost Lynching Scene in John M. Stahl's Imitation of Life," *Film History* 30, no. 4 (Winter 2019): 122 (emphasis original).

65. Horace McCoy, *They Shoot Horses, Don't They?* (London: Serpent's Tail, 1995), 76.
66. McCoy, *They Shoot Horses, Don't They?*, 77.
67. Ann Cvetkovich, *Depression: A Public Feeling* (Durham, NC: Duke University Press, 2012), 115.

5. UNHAPPY VICTIMS: THE UNREADABILITY OF STAR SUICIDES

1. Jeanne de Kolty, "Behave or Else," *Silver Screen* 9, no. 3 (January 1939): 28–29, 29.
2. Horace McCoy, *They Shoot Horses, Don't They?* (London: Serpent's Tail, 1995), 76.
3. Cal York, "Plays and Players," *Photoplay* 18, no. 6 (November 20, 1920): 82.
4. Eunice Marshall, "Dope," *Screenland from Hollywood* 6, no. 6 (March 1923): 61–63.
5. "Editorial: For Mabel and Jack," *Photoplay* 18, no. 6 (November 20, 1920): 27.
6. In Bode's discussion, death by suicide, while scandalous, also marked certain stars as "special": "these deaths, more so than deaths from illness or accident, place a retrospective filter over how a person's character is remembered." Lisa Bode, "Fade Out/Fade In: Dead 1920s and 1930s Hollywood Stars and the Mechanisms of Posthumous Stardom," *Celebrity Studies* 5, no. 1 (2014): 91.
7. Feijun Luo et al., "Impact of Business Cycles on US Suicide Rates, 1928–2007," *American Journal of Public Health* 101, no. 6 (June 2011): 1139–1146.
8. "Fifty-Six Die by Suicide," *Los Angeles Times*, August 18, 1930, A14; "Suicides Set New Record in April, Coroner Reports," *Los Angeles Times*, May 12, 1932, A7; "July Killings Break Records," *Los Angeles Times*, August 29, 1932, A14.
9. "Experts Ask New Bridge to Eliminate Suicide Span," *Los Angeles Times*, April 30, 1935, A1; "Pasadena Span Claims Seventy-Second Suicide," *Los Angeles Times*, December 30, 1935, A1.
10. Elaine Scarry, *The Body in Pain: The Making and Unmaking of the World* (New York: Oxford University Press, 1985), 4.
11. Scarry, *The Body in Pain*, 161.
12. Sianne Ngai, for example, speaks of the political nature of dissatisfaction and the way it can point to the uneven distribution of goods. Sianne Ngai, "Jealous Schoolgirls, Single White Females, and Other Bad Examples: Rethinking Gender and Envy," *Camera Obscura* 16, no. 2 (2001): 177–228.
13. Ann Cvetkovich, *Depression: A Public Feeling* (Durham, NC: Duke University Press, 2012), 12.
14. Ahmed's model of the unhappy affect alien is especially useful for clarifying the responses to suicide this chapter tracks, for the refusal to empathize with the suicide is a defense of American capitalism and Hollywood as the happy organ of that system. Of these affect aliens, Ahmed explains, "Some bodies are presumed to be the

origin of bad feeling insofar as they disturb the promise of happiness." The real Paul Bern and the fictional Gloria both originate this kind of "bad feeling." Sara Ahmed, "Happy Objects," in *The Affect Theory Reader*, ed. Melissa Gregg and Gregory J. Seigworth (Durham, NC: Duke University Press, 2010), 29–51, 39.

15. Scarry, *The Body in Pain*, 4.
16. As Karina Longworth suggests in her Thelma Todd episode of *You Must Remember This*, it seems that the short-lived program was almost certainly more about the publicity generated than the careers of the aspiring young actors and actresses, who were charged for the privilege of attending Paramount's talent school and very few of whom made it into the industry. For more on the program and the talent film it produced, *Fascinating Youth* (1926), see J. B. Kaufman, " 'Fascinating Youth': The Story of the Paramount Pictures School," *Film History* 4, no. 2 (1990): 131–151.
17. Jeanne de Kolty, "The Troupers," *Silver Screen* 5, no. 7 (May 1935): 32–33, 66.
18. "Thelma Todd Found Dead in Her Auto," *Motion Picture Daily* 38, no. 142 (December 17, 1935): 1.
19. "Thelma Todd Dead; In Films 8 Years," *Motion Picture Herald* 121, no. 12 (December 21, 1935): 26.
20. "Thelma Todd Death Probe Pushed; Jury Calls Cicco, Others," *Variety*, December 25, 1935, 3.
21. L.J., "The Bohemian Girl," *Independent Exhibitors Film Bulletin*, March 4, 1936, 11.
22. Mae Tinée, "Laurel-Hardy Use a Story from an Opera: *The Bohemian Girl*," *Chicago Daily Tribune*, February 27, 1936, 17.
23. George Shaffer, "Gas from Auto Kills Thelma Todd," *Chicago Daily Tribune*, December 17, 1935; "Pictures Tell Story of Tragic and Mysterious Death of Thelma Todd," *Los Angeles Times*, December 17, 1935.
24. Longworth, *You Must Remember This*, draws attention to the importance of the high-publicity Todd case for elected officials.
25. "Body of Thelma Todd Found in Death Riddle," *Los Angeles Times*, December 17, 1935, republished as part of "From the Archives" series, https://www.latimes.com/local/obituaries/archives/la-me-thelma-todd-19351217-story.html.
26. Leo Townsend, "Good News," *Modern Screen* 12, no. 4 (March 1936): 106.
27. "Thelma Todd, 31, Dies, Monoxide Poisoning; No Mystery Angles," *Variety* 18 (December 1935): 2, 20.
28. Ted Magee, "Today in Hollywood," *Hollywood* 25, no. 3 (March 1936): 5.
29. Thomas Doherty, *Hollywood's Censor: Joseph I. Breen & the Production Code Administration* (New York: Columbia University Press, 2007), 355.
30. Doherty, *Hollywood's Censor*, 355.
31. The power and ongoing influence of this prohibition can be seen as late as the Elizabeth Taylor-led 1960 adaptation of John O'Hara's 1935 novel *Butterfield 8*.
32. John Winburn, "Hollywood's Tragic Trilogy," *Hollywood* 25, no. 3 (March 1936): 10.
33. "Grand Jury Divides on Miss Todd's Death: Most of Them Favor Suicide Theory, but None Believes It Was Accidental," *New York Times*, January 4, 1936, 34.

34. Kenneth Anger, *Hollywood Babylon* (New York: Dell, 1975); Andy Edmonds, *Hot Toddy: The True Story of Hollywood's Most Sensational Murder* (New York: William Morrow, 1989).
35. For a full overview of the Todd-Pitts and Todd-Kelly shorts, see James L. Neibaur, *The Hal Roach Shorts of Thelma Todd, ZaSu Pitts and Patsy Kelly* (Jefferson, NC: McFarland, 2019).
36. With a focus on both the dangerous nature of everyday life for young women *and* the comedic chaos wrought by these women, the shorts recall the type of silent comedy films discussed by Maggie Hennefeld in *Specters of Slapstick & Silent Film Comediennes* (New York: Columbia University Press, 2018).
37. In his biography of Jean Harlow, Irving Shulman overviews the murder conspiracies that centered on the idea that MGM staged Bern's death scene to look like a suicide in order to protect Harlow's reputation from the damage that would have resulted from the public's knowing that her husband had been murdered by another woman. In addition to Hecht's piece, famed gossip columnist Hedda Hopper also contributed to this theory. Irving Shulman, *Harlow: An Intimate Biography* (1964) (Lincoln, NE: iUniverse.com, 2000), 194–195.
38. James A. Daniels, "The Trail of Tragedy That Haunted Paul Bern," *New Movie Magazine* 6, no. 6 (December 1932): 32–33, 95–96.
39. Daniels, "The Trail of Tragedy," 32.
40. Daniels, "The Trail of Tragedy," 96.
41. Daniels, "The Trail of Tragedy," 32.
42. As Longworth, *You Must Remember This*, recounts, speculations about Bern's possible homosexuality or impotence haunted his death.
43. Kathryn Dougherty, "Close-Ups and Long-Shots," *Photoplay* 42, no. 6 (November 1932): 25–26, 26.
44. Dorothy Calhoun, "Jean Harlow—Tortured by Tragedy," *Movie Classic* 3, no. 3 (November 1932): 16–17, 66, 71, 73; 66.
45. Calhoun, "Jean Harlow," 66 (emphasis original).
46. Calhoun, "Jean Harlow," 66.
47. Tully quoted in Hopper, ellipses and emphasis original to Hopper. Hedda Hopper, *From Under My Hat* (Garden City, NY: Doubleday, 1952), 216.
48. "This Week," *Motion Picture Herald* 117, no. 7 (17 November 1934): 8 (ellipses original).
49. Harry Carr, "Shooting Script," *Hollywood* 24, no. 2 (February 1935): 30–31, 30.
50. Calhoun, "Jean Harlow," 16–17.
51. "The Audience Talks Back," *Photoplay* 42, no. 1 (December 1932): 6–8.
52. Jane Hampton, "To Be Happy—Give," *Photoplay* 44, no. 3 (August 1933): 72, 105; 72.
53. Hampton, "To Be Happy," 72.
54. Hampton, "To Be Happy," 72.
55. Hampton, "To Be Happy," 105.
56. For a detailed accounting of self-help culture at this time, see Beth Blum, *The Self-Help Compulsion: Searching for Advice in Modern Literature* (New York: Columbia University Press, 2020).

57. Hampton, "To Be Happy," 105.
58. Richard Dyer, *Stars* (London: British Film Institute, 1999), 35.

CONCLUSION

1. Alex Kucczynski, "Striking Back at the Empire: Wenner Media Takes on the Mighty Time Inc. in Transforming Us to a Monthly Magazine, *New York Times*, September 27, 1999, https://www.nytimes.com/1999/09/27/business/striking-back-empire-wenner-media-takes-mighty-time-transforming-us-monthly.html?pagewanted=all.
2. Mary Desjardins's work on the return of classical Hollywood stars suggests the importance of taking seriously the use of Davis as a mediating force. As she argues, "the sign of the female star . . . is central to understanding many of the anxieties, as well as pleasures that recycled stars invoke through their public, multi-mediated emergence, loss, and return." Mary R. Desjardins, *Recycled Stars: Female Film Stardom in the Age of Television and Video* (Durham, NC: Duke University Press, 2015), 3.
3. Craig Modderno, "The Incredible Hulk's Lou Ferrigno," *Photoplay* 94, no. 3 (May/June 1980): 46–47, 68–69; 68.
4. "Photoplay Back Then: How Clark Gable and Carole Lombard Live," *Photoplay* 93, no. 11 (February 1980): 58–62, 58.
5. "Photoplay Back Then," 62.
6. Anthony Slide, *Inside the Hollywood Fan Magazine: A History of Star Makers, Fabricators, and Gossip Mongers* (Jackson: University Press of Mississippi, 2010), 221.
7. "Out of the Pages of Photoplay," *Photoplay* 94, no. 3 (May/June 1980): 36–37, 36.
8. "Out of the Pages of Photoplay," 37.
9. "Out of the Pages of Photoplay," 37.
10. Mikki Dorsey, "Dallas's Charlene Tilton," *Photoplay* 94, no. 3 (May/June 1980): 4.
11. "Laurence Olivier: Straight Talk," *Photoplay* 94, no. 3 (May/June 1980): 22–23.
12. In films like *Fatal Attraction*, which Dow analyzes, the unhappy career woman appears pitted against the traditional stay-at-home mother: "This is the archetypal postfeminist duel to the death, neatly encapsulating the dichotomies that postfeminist media fed upon in the 1980s: femininity versus feminism, careerism versus motherhood, equality versus difference, selfishness versus sacrifice." Bonnie Dow, "The Traffic in Men and the *Fatal Attraction* of Postfeminist Masculinity," *Women's Studies in Communication* 29, no. 1 (2006): 124.
13. George Haddad-Garcia, "The Rose's Bette Midler," *Photoplay* 94, no. 3 (May/June 1980): 24–27, 60; 26. As Mitchell Morris argues, Midler embodied multiple, sometimes conflicting identities, in part through her channeling of various performance styles, which can be seen in her portrayal of the Joplinesque Rose: "For Bette Midler, an overlaying of earlier performers and types allowed her a capacious representational space to summon and reaccentuate historical notions of gender, race, and sexual desire, and it did so with a loud insistence on fun." Mitchell Morris, "The

Blacks, the Jews, and the Gays: Bette Midler's Third-Order Vaudeville," *Women and Music* 22, no. 1 (2018): 108.

14. Haddad-Garcia, "The Rose's Bette Midler," 26–27.
15. Haddad-Garcia, "The Rose's Bette Midler," 60.
16. Haddad-Garcia, "The Rose's Bette Midler," 60 (emphasis original).
17. Melissa Bradshaw reads this scene as a warning about the fate of divas such as Midler and Davis: "The scene begins with the emcee impersonating Bette Davis as Baby Jane, an allusion to the plight of the diva who has outlived her fame. This functions as well as a compacted tribute to Davis, Midler's real-life namesake, whose iconic performance as the sadistic former child star attempting a comeback (only a decade after staging a similar comeback herself by playing the aging diva Margo Channing in All About Eve) turned a moment of personal desperation into a lasting triumph." Melissa Bradshaw, "Devouring the Diva: Martyrdom as Feminist Backlash in The Rose," *Camera Obscura* 23, no. 1 (2008): 76–77.
18. George Haddad-Garcia, "Meryl Streep: Photoplay's Star of the Month," *Photoplay* 94, no. 3 (May/June 1980): 42–45, 42.
19. Julia A. Stern, *Bette Davis Black and White* (Chicago: University of Chicago Press, 2021), 12.
20. A. Scott Berg, *Kate Remembered* (New York: Penguin, 2005).
21. Haddad-Garcia, "Meryl Streep," 42.
22. Haddad-Garcia, "Meryl Streep," 43.
23. Haddad-Garcia, "Meryl Streep," 43.
24. Haddad-Garcia, "Meryl Streep," 43 (emphasis added).
25. Haddad-Garcia, "Meryl Streep," 43.
26. Erin A. Meyers, *Extraordinarily Ordinary: Us Weekly and the Rise of Reality Television Celebrity* (New Brunswick, NJ: Rutgers University Press, 2020), 2.

SELECTED BIBLIOGRAPHY

Adams, Rachel. *Sideshow U.S.A.: Freaks and the American Cultural Imagination.* Chicago: University of Chicago Press, 2001.
Ahmed, Sara. "Happy Objects." In *The Affect Theory Reader*, ed. Melissa Gregg and Gregory J. Seigworth, 29–51. Durham, NC: Duke University Press, 2010.
Anderson, Mark Lynn. *Twilight of the Idols: Hollywood and the Human Sciences in 1920s America.* Berkeley: University of California Press, 2011.
Baldwin, James. *The Devil Finds Work.* New York: Vintage International, 2011.
Balio, Tino. *Grand Design: Hollywood as a Modern Business Enterprise, 1930–1939.* Berkeley: University of California Press, 1996.
Barthes, Roland. "The Reality Effect" (1969). In *The Rustle of Language*, trans. Richard Howard, ed. François Wahl, 141–148. Berkeley: University of California Press, 1989.
Berlant, Lauren. *The Female Complaint: The Unfinished Business of Sentimentality in American Culture.* Durham, NC: Duke University Press, 2008.
Bernstein, Matthew H. "A 'Professional Southerner' in the Hollywood Studio System: Lamar Trotti at Work, 1925–1952." In *American Cinema and the Southern Imaginary*, ed. Deborah Barker and Kathryn McKee, 122–147. Athens: University of Georgia Press, 2011.
Bernstein, Matthew H., and Dana F. White. "'Imitation of Life' in a Segregated Atlanta: Its Promotion, Distribution and Reception." *Film History* 19, no. 2 (2007): 152–178.
Bernstein, Robin. *Racial Innocence: Performing American Childhood from Slavery to Civil Rights.* New York: New York University Press, 2011.
Black, Shirley Temple. *Child Star: An Autobiography.* New York: McGraw-Hill, 1988.
Blum, Beth. *The Self-Help Compulsion: Searching for Advice in Modern Literature.* New York: Columbia University Press, 2020.
Bode, Lisa. "Fade Out/Fade In: Dead 1920s and 1930s Hollywood Stars and the Mechanisms of Posthumous Stardom." *Celebrity Studies* 5, no. 1 (2014): 90–92.
Bogle, Donald. *Toms, Coons, Mulattoes, Mammies, and Bucks.* New York: Continuum, 1989.

Bradshaw, Melissa. "Devouring the Diva: Martyrdom as Feminist Backlash in the Rose." *Camera Obscura* 23, no. 1 (2008): 69–87.
Briefel, Aviva. "Monster Pains: Masochism, Menstruation, and Identification in the Horror Film." *Film Quarterly* 58, no. 3 (Spring 2005): 16–27.
Brinkema, Eugenia. "Browning. Freak. Woman. Stain." In *The Cinema of Tod Browning: Essays of the Macabre and Grotesque*, ed. Bernd Herzogenrath, 158–173. Jefferson, NC: McFarland, 2008.
Bukataman, Scott. *The Poetics of Slumberland: Animated Spirits and the Animating Spirit*. Berkeley: University of California Press, 2012.
Carman, Emily. *Independent Stardom: Freelance Women in Hollywood*. Austin: University of Texas Press, 2016.
Carroll, Noël. *The Philosophy of Horror; or, Paradoxes of the Heart*. New York: Routledge, 1990.
———. *The Philosophy of Motion Pictures*. Malden, MA: Blackwell, 2008.
Chen, Mel Y. *Animacies: Biopolitics, Racial Mattering, and Queer Affect*. Durham, NC: Duke University Press, 2012.
Codr, Dwight. "Arresting Monstrosity: Polio, Frankenstein, and the Horror Film." *PMLA* 19, no. 2 (2014): 171–187.
Cook, Meira. "None of Us: Ambiguity as Moral Discourse in Tod Browning's Freaks." In *Screening Disability: Essays on Cinema and Disability*, ed. Christopher R. Smith and Anthony Enns, 47–56. Lanham, MD: University Press of America, 2001.
Cox, James H. "'Learn to Talk Yaqui': Mexico and the Cherokee Literary Politics of John Milton Oskison and Will Rogers." *Western American Literature* 48, no. 4 (Winter 2014): 400–421.
Cripps, Thomas. "The Myth of the Southern Box Office: A Factor in Racial Stereotyping in American Movies, 1920–1940." In *The Black Experiences in America: Selected Essays*, ed. James C. Curtis and Lewis J. Gould. Austin: University of Texas Press, 1970.
Cvetkovich, Ann. *Depression: A Public Feeling*. Durham, NC: Duke University Press, 2012.
Dabashi, Pardis. "'There Is No Gallery': Race and the Politics of Space at the Capitol Theater." *Early Popular Visual Culture* 21, no. 2 (2023): 208–222.
DeCordova, Richard. *Picture Personalities: The Emergence of the Star System in America*. Champaign: University of Illinois Press, 2001.
Desjardins, Mary. "'Fan Magazine Trouble': The AMPP, Studio Publicity Directors, and the Hollywood Press, 1945–1952." *Film History* 26, no. 3 (2014): 29–56.
———. *Recycled Stars: Female Film Stardom in the Age of Television and Video*. Durham, NC: Duke University Press, 2015.
Doherty, Thomas. *Hollywood's Censor: Joseph I. Breen & the Production Code Administration*. New York: Columbia University Press, 2007.
———. *Pre-Code Hollywood: Sex, Immorality, and Insurrection in American Cinema, 1930–1934*. New York: Columbia University Press, 1990.
Dow, Bonnie. "The Traffic in Men and the *Fatal Attraction* of Postfeminist Masculinity." *Women's Studies in Communication* 29, no. 1 (2006): 113–131.
Dyer, Richard. "Entertainment and Utopia." In *Only Entertainment*, 2nd ed., 19–35. New York: Routledge, 2002.

———. "Four Films of Lana Turner." In *Only Entertainment*, 2nd ed., 79–111. New York: Routledge, 2002.
———. *Heavenly Bodies: Film Stars and Society*. New York: Routledge, 1986.
———. *Stars*. London: British Film Institute, 1998.
Everett, Anna. *Returning the Gaze: A Genealogy of Black Film Criticism, 1909–1949*. Durham, NC: Duke University Press, 2001.
Feuer, Jane. "Narrative Form in American Network Television." In *Critical Visions in Film Theory*, ed. Timothy Corrigan, Patricia White, and Meta Mazaj, 610–619. Boston: Bedford/St. Martins, 2011.
Flitterman-Lewis, Sandy. "*Imitation(s) of Life*: The Black Woman's Double Determination as Troubling 'Other.'" *Literature and Psychology* 34, no. 4 (1988): 44–57.
Friedman, Ryan Jay. *Hollywood's African American Films: The Transition to Sound*. New Brunswick, NJ: Rutgers University Press, 2011.
Frymus, Agata. "Silent Film Era and Marginalised Spectatorship." *Early Popular Visual Culture* 21, no. 2 (2023): 183–188.
Garcia, Desirée. "The Musicals of Black Folk." In *The Migration of Musical Film: From Ethnic Margins to American Mainstream*. New Brunswick, NJ: Rutgers University Press, 2014.
Gaut, Berys. "Identification and Emotion in Narrative Film." In *Passionate Views: Film, Cognition, and Emotion*, ed. Carl Plantinga and Greg M. Smith, 200–216. Baltimore, MD: Johns Hopkins University Press, 1999.
Goldsby, Jacqueline. *A Spectacular Secret: Lynching in American Life and Literature*. Chicago: University of Chicago Press, 2006.
Graham, Sandra Jean. *Spirituals and the Birth of a Black Entertainment Industry*. Champaign: University of Illinois Press, 2018.
Grossman, Julie. *Literature, Film, and Their Hideous Progeny*. London: Palgrave Macmillan, 2015.
Gunning, Tom. "The Cinema of Attractions: Early Film, Its Spectator and the Avant-Garde." *Wide Angle* 8, nos. 3/4 (1986). Rpt in *Early Cinema: Space, Frame, Narrative*, ed. Thomas Elsaesser, 56–62. London: British Film Institute, 1990.
Hanich, Julian. "Toward a Poetics of Cinematic Disgust." *Film Philosophy* 15, no. 2 (2011): 11–35.
Hansen, Miriam. *Babel and Babylon: Spectatorship in American Silent Film*. Cambridge, MA: Harvard University Press, 1991.
Haraway, Donna. "Teddy Bear Patriarchy: Taxidermy in the Garden of Eden, New York City, 1908–1936." *Social Text* 11 (Winter 1984–1985): 20–64.
Haskell, Molly. *From Reverence to Rape: The Treatment of Women in the Movies*. Chicago: University of Chicago Press, 1973.
Hatch, Kristen. *Shirley Temple and the Performance of Girlhood*. New Brunswick, NJ: Rutgers University Press, 2015.
Hawkins, Joan. "'One of Us': Tod Browning's *Freaks*." In *Freakery: Cultural Spectacles of the Extraordinary Body*, ed. Rosemarie Garland Thomson, 265–276. New York: New York University Press, 1996.

Hayward, Jennifer. *Consuming Pleasures: Active Audiences and Serial Fictions from Dickens to Soap Opera*. Lexington: University Press of Kentucky, 1997.

Hennefeld, Maggie. "Slapstick Comediennes in Transitional Cinema: Between Body and Medium." *Camera Obscura* 29, no. 2 (2014): 85–117.

———. *Specters of Slapstick & Silent Film Comediennes*. New York: Columbia University Press, 2018.

Highmore, Ben. "Bitter Aftertaste: Affect, Food, and Social Aesthetics." In *The Affect Theory Reader*, ed. Melissa Gregg and Gregory J. Seigworth, 135–136. Durham, NC: Duke University Press, 2010.

hooks, bell. *Black Looks: Race and Representation*. New York: Routledge, 2015.

Horak, Laura. "Trans on YouTube: Intimacy, Visibility, Temporality." Special issue on Trans Cultural Production. *TSQ: Transgender Studies Quarterly* 1, no. 4 (December 2014): 572–585.

Hoyt, Eric. *Ink-Stained Hollywood: The Triumph of American Cinema's Trade Press*. Berkeley: University of California Press, 2022.

Jackson, Robert. *Fade In, Crossroads: A History of the Southern Cinema*. New York: Oxford University Press, 2017.

———. "James Baldwin and Film Beyond the American Century." *James Baldwin Review* 7, no. 1 (2021): 39–53.

Jarron, Matthew. "Paying the Penalty: Alienation Through Disability in the Films of Lon Chaney." In *Alienation and Resistance: Representation in Text and Image*, ed. Gordon Spark et al., 56–68. Newcastle upon Tyne, UK: Cambridge Scholars, 2010.

Jeffers McDonald, Tamar, and Lies Lanckman, eds. *Star Attractions: Twentieth-Century Movies Magazines and Global Fandom*. Iowa City: University of Iowa Press, 2019.

Kaufman, J. B. "Fascinating Youth: The Story of the Paramount Pictures School." *Film History* 4, no. 2 (1990): 131–151.

Knight, Arthur. *Disintegrating the Musical: Black Performance and American Musical Film*. Durham, NC: Duke University Press, 2002.

Larsen, Robin, and Beth A. Haller, "The Case of Freaks: Public Reception of Real Disability." *Journal of Popular Film and Television* 29, no. 4 (Winter 2002): 164–173.

Lee, Julia. *Our Gang: A Racial History of The Little Rascals*. Minneapolis: University of Minnesota Press, 2015.

Lew, Kristen. "From Social Problem to Maternal Melodrama: The Lost Lynching Scene in John M. Stahl's Imitation of Life." *Film History* 30, no. 4 (Winter 2019): 107–126.

Longworth, Karina. "Thelma Todd." *You Must Remember This*. Podcast episode, February 6, 2017.

Kasson, John. *The Little Girl Who Fought the Great Depression*. New York: Norton, 2014.

Laine, Tarja. "Affective Telepathy, or the Intuition of the Heart: Persona with Mulholland Drive." *New Review of Film and Television Studies* 7, no. 3 (September 2009): 325–338.

Luo, Feijun, et al. "Impact of Business Cycles on US Suicide Rates, 1928–2007." *American Journal of Public Health* 101, no. 6 (June 2011): 1139–1146.

Maltby, Richard. "The Political Economy of Hollywood: The Studio System." In *Cinema, Politics, and American Society*, ed. Philip Davies and Brian Neve, 42–58. Manchester, UK: Manchester University Press, 1981.

Marcus, Sharon. *The Drama of Celebrity*. Princeton, NJ: Princeton University Press, 2019.
Marks, Laura. *The Skin of the Film: Intercultural Cinema, Embodiment, and the Senses*. Durham, NC: Duke University Press, 2000.
Massod, Paula. "African American Stardom Inside and Outside of Hollywood: Ernest Morrison, Noble Johnson, Evelyn Preer, and Lincoln Perry." In *Idols of Modernity: Movie Stars of the 1920s*, ed. Patrice Petro, 227–249. New Brunswick, NJ: Rutgers University Press, 2010.
Maurice, Alice. "'Cinema at Its Source:' Synchronizing Race and Sound in the Early Talkies." *Camera Obscura* 17, no. 1 (2002): 31–71.
———. "The Death of Lon Chaney: Masculinity, Race, and the Authenticity of Disguise." In *Hollywood at the Intersection of Race and Identity*, ed. Delia Malia Caparoso Konzett, 39–57. New Brunswick, NJ: Rutgers University Press, 2019.
McLean, Adrienne L. *All for Beauty: Makeup and Hairdressing in Hollywood's Studio Era*. New Brunswick, NJ: Rutgers University Press, 2022.
———. *Being Rita Hayworth: Labor, Identity, and Hollywood Stardom*. New Brunswick, NJ: Rutgers University Press, 2004.
Merish, Lori. "Cuteness and Commodity Aesthetics: Tom Thumb and Shirley Temple." In *Freakery: Cultural Spectacles of the Extraordinary Body*, ed. Rosemarie Garland Thomson, 185–203. New York: New York University Press, 1996.
Meyers, Erin A. *Extraordinarily Ordinary: Us Weekly and the Rise of Reality Television Celebrity*. New Brunswick, NJ: Rutgers University Press, 2020.
Mittel, Jason. "Narrative Complexity in Contemporary American Television." *Velvet Light Trap*, no. 58 (Fall 2006): 29–40.
Morris, Mitchell. "The Blacks, the Jews, and the Gays: Bette Midler's Third-Order Vaudeville." *Women and Music* 22, no. 1 (2018): 108–116.
Neibaur, James L. *The Hal Roach Shorts of Thelma Todd, ZaSu Pitts and Patsy Kelly*. Jefferson, NC: McFarland, 2019.
Newsom, Chad. "Temple of Youth." *Film Criticism* 39, no. 3 (2015): 6–25.
Ngai, Sianne. "Jealous Schoolgirls, Single White Females, and Other Bad Examples: Rethinking Gender and Envy." *Camera Obscura* 16, no. 2 (2001): 177–228.
Norden, Martin. *The Cinema of Isolation: A History of Physical Disability in the Movies*. New Brunswick, NJ: Rutgers University Press, 1994.
Nyong'o, Tavia. "Racial Kitsch and Black Performance." *Yale Journal of Criticism* 15, no. 2 (Fall 2002): 371–391.
Petty, Miriam J. *Stealing the Show: African-American Performers and Audiences in 1930s Hollywood*. Berkeley: University of California Press, 2016.
Peucker, Brigitte. *The Material Image: Art and the Real in Film*. Stanford, CA: Stanford University Press, 2007.
Plantinga, Carl. "The Scene of Empathy and the Human Face on Film." In *Passionate Views: Film, Cognition and Emotion*, ed. Carl Plantinga and Greg M. Smith, 239–256. Baltimore, MD: Johns Hopkins University Press, 1999.
Polley, Sarah. "A Spectrum of Individuals: U.S. Fan Magazine Circulation Figures from 1914 to 1965." In *Star Attractions: Twentieth-Century Movies Magazines and Global Fandom*, ed. Tamar Jeffers McDonald and Lies Lanckman, 61–80. Iowa City: University of Iowa Press, 2019.

Pounds, Michael Charles. "What's Black and White and Misread All Over? Race, Identity, and Community in Judge Priest." *American Journal of Semiotics* 11, no. 3 (1994): 179–201.

Quayson, Ato. *Aesthetic Nervousness: Disability and the Crisis of Representation*. New York: Columbia University Press, 2007.

Randell, Karen. "Mad Love: The Anxiety of Difference in the Films of Lon Chaney Sr." In *Screening the Dark Side of Love: from Euro-Horror to American Cinema*, ed. Karen A. Ritzenhoff and Karen Randell, 69–82. New York: Palgrave Macmillan, 2012.

Regester, Charlene. "African-American Extras in Hollywood During the 1920s–1930s." *Film History* 9, no. 1 (1997): 95–115.

Rogin, Michael. "'Make My Day:' Spectacle as Amnesia in Imperial Politics." *Representations* 29 (Winter 1990): 99–123.

Rubin, Martin. "Mr. Ford & Mr. Rogers." *Film Comment* 10, no. 1 (January–February 1974): 54–57.

Scarry, Elaine. *The Body in Pain: The Making and Unmaking of the World*. New York: Oxford University Press, 1985.

Schweik, Susan. *The Ugly Laws: Disability in Public*. New York: New York University Press, 2010.

Seymour, Nicole. "Somatic Syntax: Replotting the Developmental Narrative in Carson McCullers's *The Member of the Wedding*." *Studies in the Novel* 41, no. 3 (Fall 2009): 293–313.

Sheffer, Jolie A. *The Romance of Race: Miscegenation, and Multiculturalism in the United States, 1880–1930*. New Brunswick, NJ: Rutgers University Press, 2013.

Slide, Anthony. *Inside the Hollywood Fan Magazine*. Jackson: University Press of Mississippi, 2010.

Slowik, Michael. *After the Silents: Hollywood Film Music in the Early Sound Era, 1926–1934*. New York: Columbia University Press, 2014.

Smith, Angela. *Hideous Progeny: Disability, Eugenics, and Classical Horror Cinema*. New York: Columbia University Press, 2011.

Smith, Valerie. "Reading the Intersection of Race and Gender in Narratives of Passing." *Diacritics* 24, nos. 2/3 (Autumn 1994): 43–57.

Somerville, Siobhan B. *Queering the Color Line: Race and the Invention of Homosexuality in American Culture*. Durham, NC: Duke University Press, 2000.

Spillers, Hortense. "Mama's Baby, Papa's Maybe: An American Grammar Book." *Diacritics* 17, no. 2 (Summer 1987): 64–81.

Stamp, Shelley. *Movie-Struck Girls: Women and Motion Picture Culture After the Nickelodeon*. Princeton, NJ: Princeton University Press, 2000.

Stern, Julia A. *Bette Davis Black and White*. Chicago: University of Chicago Press, 2021.

Studlar, Gaylyn. *Precocious Charms: Stars Performing Girlhood in Classical Hollywood Cinema*. Berkeley: University of California Press, 2013.

———. *This Mad Masquerade: Stardom and Masculinity in the Jazz Age*. New York: Columbia University Press, 1996.

Teresa, Carrie. *Looking at the Stars: Black Celebrity Journalism in Jim Crow America*. Lincoln: University of Nebraska Press, 2019.

Thaggert, Miriam. "Divided Images: Black Female Spectatorship and John Stahl's *Imitation of Life*." *African American Review* 32, no. 3 (Autumn 1998): 481–491.

Tompkins, Kyla Wazana. *Racial Indigestion: Eating Bodies in the 19th Century*. New York: New York University Press, 2012.

Ware, Amy M. *The Cherokee Kid: Will Rogers, Tribal Identity, and the Making of an American Icon*. Lawrence: University Press of Kansas, 2015.

Weisenfeld, Judith. *Hollywood Be Thy Name: African American Religion in American Film, 1929–1949*. Berkeley: University of California Press, 2007.

Wells, Paul. *Understanding Animation*. New York: Routledge, 1998.

Wiegman, Robyn. *American Anatomies: Theorizing Race and Gender*. Durham, NC: Duke University Press, 1995.

Williams, Linda. "When the Woman Looks." In *The Dread of Difference: Gender and the Horror Film*, ed. Barry Keith Grant, 15–34. Austin: University of Texas Press, 1996.

Wilson, Steve. *The Making of Gone with the Wind*. Austin: University of Texas Press, 2014.

Wojcik, Pamela. *Fantasies of Neglect: Imagining the Urban Child in American Film and Fiction*. New Brunswick, NJ: Rutgers University Press, 2016.

Zelizer, Viviana. *Pricing the Priceless Child: The Changing Social Value of Children*. New York: Basic Books, 1985.

INDEX

aesthetic nervousness, 82
affective administration, 10–12
Agar, John, 72
Aid to Dependent Children (ADC), 69
Anderson, Mark Lynn, 12
Anger, Kenneth, 155
anticipatory disgust, 97
Associated Press, 80
Association of Motion Picture Producers (AMPP), 3
authenticity, 2, 105, 108–9, 111, 116, 132, 189n1

Baby Burlesks (Educational Film Exchanges, Inc.), 50–51, 54
Balázs, Béla, 8
Balfe, Michael, 150
Barett, Wilton, 117
Barrymore, John, 91
Beauty and the Bus (1933), 156
Beavers, Louise, 125, 130–32
Berkeley, Busby, 64
Berlant, Lauren, 9, 125–26
Bern, Paul, 2, 10, 12, 17, 140, 146, 157–65, 158*f*
Bernhardt, Sarah, 9
Bernstein, Matthew, 119, 121, 125

Bernstein, Robin, 16, 24
Birth of a Nation, The (Griffth, 1915), 105, 121
Black child stars, 16, 21–46, 117. See also Farina character in *Our Gang*
Black dancers, 51
Black extras, 108–9, 112, 134–35
blackface, 108
Blackness, 18, 29, 36, 110–30, 134–36
Black singing, 17, 107–24, 129
Black stars and White audiences: connection between, 125–36; counterfactual realism, 107, 112; impact of, 104–10; reality spectacles, 110–24; sonic landscapes, 110–24; white nostalgia, 17, 104, 108–9, 122*f*
Black voice, 107–8, 124
Blue Bird (Lang, 1940), 75
Bode, Lisa, 144
Bohemian Girl, The (Horne and Rogers, 1936), 149–51
Boles, John, 59–60
Bow, Clara, 6, 115
Boyer, Charles, 169
Brown, Sterling A., 132–33
Brownies' Book, The (NAACP), 22

Browning, Tod, 16–17, 80, 85–86, 92–103
Buquet, Joseph, 96–97
Busch, Mae, 151

Calhoun, Dorothy, 160, 163
Carlisle, Helen, 159
Carroll, Noël, 81–82
Carter, Hunter, 40
celebrity suicides. *See* suicide
censorship, 3, 9, 111–12, 141. *See also* Motion Picture Production Code
Chaney, Lon: cast transformation in *Freaks*, 92–103; death of, 79–80; introduction to, 2–3, 8, 16–17, 79–83; nonnormativity of films, 83–85; sympathy for disabled persons, 85–92
Chapman, D. H., 131
Chen, Mel, 34
Chicago Defender, 134
Chicago Tribune, 150, 151
child labor, 9, 16, 50–51, 55, 64, 67–71, 183n35. *See also* Farina character in *Our Gang*; Temple, Shirley
child stars, 9, 15–16, 21–46. *See also* Hoskins, Allen; Temple, Shirley
Child Star (Temple), 72
Cinema of Isolation, The (Norden), 82
Cobb, Irvin, 118
the Code. *See* Motion Picture Production Code
Codr, Dwight, 85
Colbert, Claudette, 130
Condon, Jackie, 26
Conrad, Lauren, 174
conspiracy theories, 17, 139–41, 151–56
Coogan, Jackie, 40
counterfactual realism, 107, 112
critical race theory, 8
cross-group identifications, 7–9
Cukor, George, 144
Curly Top (Cummings, 1935), 59, 60*f*, 63–65, 68
Cvetkovich, Ann, 135, 147

Daniels, Mickey, 40
Darling, Jean, 26, 32
Darmour, Larry, 22
Davis, Bette, 1–2, 5–7, 168, 169–70, 172–74
deCordova, Richard, 2
de Kolty, Jeanne, 139
Dell, Dorothy, 154
del Río, Dolores, 53
Dempsey, Jack, 51
depression, 10, 135, 147, 157–65
Desjardins, Mary, 3
DiCicco, Pat, 149
Dietrich, Marlene, 51–52
Dimples (Seiter, 1936), 56
disabled persons, 2, 6, 9, 17–18, 80–92, 186nn20–21, 188n49
disfigurement, 17, 80–81, 84–86, 92–102, 188n49
disidentification, 10, 14, 43, 187n32
Dow, Bonnie, 170–71
Downs, Johnny, 40
Du Bois, W. E. B., 22–24
Dyer, Richard, 7, 9, 47, 62, 164
Dyer Anti-Lynching Bill, 24

eating the Other, 9
Edmond, Andy, 155
Educational Film Exchanges, Inc., 51
Everett, Anna, 125
Exhibitors Herald World, 3–4
Exhibitor's Trade Review, 22, 26, 44

Fairbanks, Douglas, 91
Fair Labor Standard Act (1938), 50
fan identification, 9, 89
fan magazines: affective administration, 10–12; cross-group identifications, 7–9; individualizing stars, 13–15; studio relationships with, 3–6
Farina character in *Our Gang*: aging out of, 39–45, 41*f*; end of, 45–46; gendering of, 25–39, 28*f*; Hoskins, Allen, 15–16, 21, 25–27, 39–44, 72; seriality of, 27–31, 28*f*;

sexual development, 31–39; significance of, 21–24; slapstick and, 31–39
feminism, 8–9, 170–74
Fetchit, Stepin, 118
Feuer, Jane, 30
Fitzgerald, F. Scott, 86
Flitterman-Lewis, Sandy, 125
Fog Over Frisco (Dieterle, 1934), 1
Ford, John, 17
Frankenstein (1931), 85
Freaks (Browning, 1932), 80–82, 86, 92–94, 94*f*
Friedman, Ryan Jay, 108
From Under My Hat (Hopper), 161

Gable, Clark, 168
Gabor, Eva, 169
Garcia, Desirée, 17, 111
Garland, Judy, 9
gender ambiguity, 16, 21–46
General Theory of Employment, Interest and Money, The (Keynes), 145
Gilbert, John, 154
Golding, Walter H., 131
Goldsby, Jacqueline, 37
Gone with the Wind (Fleming, 1939), 104–5, 108, 135
Gordon, Mack, 62
Graham, Sandra Jean, 107–8
Great Depression, 2, 6, 10, 16–17, 48, 54, 59, 66–69, 140, 144–45
Greene Graham, 54
Griffth, D. W., 105
Grossman, Julie, 125
Gunning, Tom, 61

Haddad-Garcia, George, 173–74
Hall, Gladys, 71
Hallelujah (Vidor, 1929), 6, 17, 108, 109–15, 117–18
Hampton, Jean, 163–64
Hanich, Julian, 97–98
Harlow, Jean, 2, 4, 10, 17, 157–65, 158*f*

Hartman, Saidiya, 9
Hatch, Kristen, 54
Haynes, Daniel L., 113, 115–16
Hays, Will, 3–4
Hays Code. *See* Motion Picture Production Code
Hearts in Dixie (Sloan, 1929), 110
Hennefeld, Maggie, 28–29
Hepburn, Katharine, 173
Herriman, George, 34
Highmore, Ben, 8
Hollywood Babylon, 155
Hollywood Code. *See* Motion Picture Production Code
Hollywood Filmograph, 123
Hollywood (magazine), 153, 162
hooks, bell, 9
Hopper, Hedda, 161
Hoskins, Allen, 15–16, 21, 25–27, 39–44, 72
Hot Toddy, 155
Howe, Herbert, 21
Hoyt, Eric, 3
Hudson, Rochelle, 59–61
Hyman, B. D., 173

Imitation of Life (Stahl, 1934), 17, 108, 109, 112, 125–36
Independent Exhibitors Film Bulletin, 149
individualizing stars, 13–15
interracial love, 18

Jeffers McDonald, Tamar, 11
Jessye, Eva, 116
Jezebel (Wyler, 1938), 119
Jim Crow era, 9, 16, 34, 43
Joyce, Peggy, 115
Judge Priest (Ford, 1934), 108, 109–11, 118–23

Karloff, Boris, 85
Kathleen (Bucquet, 1941), 73–74, 76
Kelly, Patsy, 148
Keynes, John Maynard, 145
Knight, Arthur, 108

Kornman, Mary, 40
Kramer vs. Kramer (Benton, 1979), 172
Ku Klux Klan (KKK), 24, 43
Kuttner, Alfred, 117

La Marr, Barbara, 159
Lanckman, Lies, 11
Lantern project, 12
Lee, Julia, 22–23
Lee, William, 24, 43
Leigh, Vivien, 170
Lewton, Val, 111–12
Little Colonel, The (Butler, 1935), 65
Lochner v. New York, 67
Loew, Arthur, 47–48
Los Angeles Times, 145, 151–52
Love Bug, The (1925), 26
Lupino, Ida, 149
lynching, 23–24, 37, 43–44, 102, 121

Maine, Norman, 144
Maltby, Richard, 53–54
Manners, Dorothy, 6–7
Marcus, Sharon, 9
Massood, Paula, 25
Maurice, Alice, 17, 91, 108, 110
McCoy, Horace, 135
McDaniel, Hattie, 118, 123–24, 127
McKinney, Nina Mae, 6, 115–16
McLean, Adrienne, 132
melodrama, 28–29, 79, 112, 125, 134, 171
Mendes, Lother, 160
Merish, Lori, 49, 54–55
#MeToo movement, 8
Meyers, Erin A., 174
Midler, Bette, 170–71, 173–74
Millette, Dorothy, 159
Minter, Mary Miles, 141
Miss Annie Rooney (Marin, 1942), 52–53, 55, 74–75
Modern Screen, 11, 71, 152
Moore, Dickie, 52
Morrison, Ernie, 25

Motion Picture, 160
Motion Picture Classic, 87
Motion Picture Daily, 149
Motion Picture Herald, 162
Motion Picture News, 22, 112
Motion Picture Production Code, 2–4, 9, 12, 18, 51–54, 83–85, 91, 132, 141–48, 153–56
Motion Picture Story Magazine, 10
Movie Classic, 58
movie-struck girl, 11, 13–14
Mulvey, Laura, 125
murders, 17, 37, 44, 140, 146–63, 165, 196n37
My Mother's Keeper (Hyman), 173

NAACP, 22, 119
Nance, Frank Albert, 145, 151–52
National Board of Review Magazine, 117
Negro Labor Battalion scene, 104–7, 135
New Movie Magazine, 79, 123
Newsom, Chad, 56, 60
New York Times, 56, 73, 155
Ngai, Sianne, 9
nonnormativity of films, 83–85
No Noise (1923), 34
Norden, Martin, 82
Norman, Mabel, 141
Now and Forever (Hathaway, 1934), 57
Nugent, Frank, 56–57, 62

Of Human Bondage (Cromwell, 1934), 1
Olivier, Laurence, 170
on-screen personality, 3, 163
Our Gang: A Racial History of the Little Rascals (Lee), 23
Our Gang (Roach, 1922). *See* Farina character in *Our Gang*

Patterson, Pat, 169
Penalty, The (Worsley, 1920), 87–88
Petty, Miriam, 109, 125
Peuker, Brigitte, 82–83, 84
Phantom of the Opera, The (Julian, 1925), 81, 82, 83, 92, 95–103, 95f, 100f

Philosophy of Horror, The (Carroll), 81
Photoplay Magazine, 1, 5, 7, 10–11, 87, 88, 91–92, 123, 141–42, 143f, 167–70
Pickford, Jack, 141
Pickford, Mary, 47–48, 141
picture personality, 2–3, 13, 48
Pitts, ZaSu, 148, 151, 155
Plantinga, Carl, 8
Plowright, Joan, 170
Polley, Sarah, 10–11
Poor Little Rich Girl (Cummings, 1936), 57–62
Pounds, Michael Charles, 119
Power, Tyrone, 169
Principal, Victoria, 167
public display of visible disability, 83–84

Quayson, Ato, 82
queer identification, 8–9, 170–72, 179n30
Quigley, Martin, 3–4
Quirk, James R., 11

racial identification, 116, 125
racial innocence, 24
racism, 14, 18, 23–24, 105–6, 130–31, 180n41
Radio Stars (magazine), 71
Randall, Karen, 91
Rappe, Virginia, 141
reality spectacles, 110–24
Reckless (Fleming, 1935), 146
Reddick, Lawrence, 23
Red Summer (1919), 6
Regester, Charlene, 108–9
Reid, Wallace, 142
Revel, Harry, 62
Rickson, Lucille, 159
right to childhood, 67
Roach, Hal, 22, 25, 27–28, 31, 148, 155
Robinson, Bill "Bojangles," 72
Rogers, Buddy, 148
Rogers, Will, 118, 119, 123, 154
Rogin, Michael, 16
Rubin, Martin, 119

Scarry, Elaine, 146–48
scene of empathy, 8
Schader, Freddie, 116–17
Schweik, Susan, 83
Screen Book (magazine), 57
Screenland, 111–12, 122, 142
Seein' Things (1924), 36, 38
segregation, 24, 31, 179n28
Selby, Charlotte, 141
self-censorship, 3, 54
Selznick, David, 160
Sennwald, Andre, 57
Shaw, Barbara, 50
silent period, 2
Silver Screen, 139, 148
Singer, Ben, 29
Skal, David, 91
slapstick, 31–39
Slide, Anthony, 4, 6, 11, 169
Slowik, Michael, 109
Smith, Angela, 85
Smith, Kate, 123
Social Security Act (1935), 69
sonic landscapes, 110–24
spiritual, 107, 112–14, 129, 134–35, 190n17
Spirituals and the Birth of a Black Entertainment Industry (Graham), 107–8
Stahl, John. See *Imitation of Life* (Stahl, 1934)
Stand Up and Cheer (MacFadden, 1934), 49–50, 52, 55, 64, 67–68, 145
Star Is Born, A (Wellman, 1937), 144
Stern, Julia A., 173
Streep, Meryl, 168, 170–74
Studio Publicity Directors Committee (AMPP), 3
Studlar, Gaylyn, 54, 63, 91
suicide: of Paul Bern, 2, 10, 12, 17, 140, 146, 157–65, 158f; the Code and, 141–48; depression and, 10, 135, 147, 157–65; introduction to, 17; speculation about, 139–40; of Thelma Todd, 17, 140, 147, 148–56

Sundown Limited (1924), 29, 44
Swanson, Gloria, 115

talkies, 2, 107–8
Taylor, William Desmond, 141
Taylor, Willie Mae, 45
Temple, George, 50
Temple, Gertrude, 49–50, 60, 67–72
Temple, Shirley: aging out, 72–76; appeal of, 55–58; cuteness of, 58–66, 61*f*, 66*f*; films as promotional vehicles, 66–72; introduction to, 16, 47–49; optimism and, 145; precocity and, 49–55
Thaggert, Miriam, 125, 126
Rose, The (Rydell, 1979), 171–72
They Shoot Horses, Don't They? (McCoy, 1935), 140, 146
Thomas, Billie, 45
Thomas, Olive, 141
Tilton, Charlene, 167, 170
Todd, Thelma, 17, 140, 146, 147, 148–56
Tompkins, Kyla Wazana, 16
Trotti, Lamar, 111, 118
Turner, Julia Jean (Lana Turner), 169

ugly laws, 83–85, 88
Ulback, Sylvia, 5–7
Unholy Three, The (Browning, 1925), 92
United Artists, 52
Unknown, The (Browning, 1927), 81–82
Us (magazine), 167

Valentino, Rudolph, 159
Variety (magazine), 112
Vidor, King, 111–12, 116

Walsh, Raoul, 53
Ware, *Jezebel* (Wyler, 1938)., 119
Warner Brothers, 1
Washington, Fredi, 125
Waterbury, Ruth, 87, 88
Wee Willie Winkie (Ford, 1937), 54
Weisenfeld, Judith, 111
Wells, Paul, 32
West, Mae, 3
West, Roland, 148, 149
Westcott, Gordon, 154
What Price Glory? (Walsh, 1926), 53
What Price Hollywood? (Cukor, 1932), 144, 157
White, Dana F., 125
White Hot: The Mysterious Murder of Thelma Todd (Wendkos, 1991), 149
white nostalgia, 17, 104, 108–9, 122*f*
Wiegman, Robyn, 43
Wojcik Pamela, 54, 69
Wong, Anna May, 18
World War I, 6

York, Cal, 141, 168
Young People (Dwan, 1940), 75–76
Youth's Companion, 88, 90–91

Zukor, Adolph, 47

GPSR Authorized Representative: Easy Access System Europe, Mustamäe tee
50, 10621 Tallinn, Estonia, gpsr.requests@easproject.com